TOTAL RUGBY

TOTAL RUGBY

Fifteen-Man Rugby for Coach and Player

Second Edition

JIM GREENWOOD

Department of Physical Education and Sports Science,
Loughborough University of Technology

Adam & Charles Black · London

796·3332/279199

For PMG

Published by A & C Black (Publishers) Ltd
35 Bedford Row, London WC1R 4JH

First edition © Lepus Books, 1978
Second edition © A & C Black, 1985

British Library Cataloguing in Publication Data
Greenwood, Jim
   Total rugby: fifteen-man rugby for coach and player.—2nd ed.
   1. Rugby football
   I. Title
   796.33'32   GV945

   ISBN 0-7136-5560-7

Printed in Great Britain by A. Wheaton & Co. Ltd., Exeter

Foreword

Play and games are socially and specially rooted in our culture. Our national philosophy has recognised, much more than most other nations, the contribution of play and games both to the balanced development of the young and to the sensible integrated lifestyle of adults. Our educationists have consistently pointed to the cognitive, social and cultural values of play and games in child development, and our psychologists and philosophers seeking a formula for a satisfying and integrated adult lifestyle recommend a balance or harmony between aspects of our life which may be described as intellectual ('homo sapiens'), work (homo laborans') and play ('homo ludeus'). The balance or harmony to be sought is not simply a matter of investing an equal amount of time to each of those aspects of life, but rather a problem of integrating the three appropriately in every human activity. This would mean, for example, that the play aspect of our lives must not only be an opportunity for spontaneous exuberant recreative activity but, if it is properly to serve its purpose, it must offer challenges to man the intellectual and man the worker.

In this book Jim Greenwood has set out, as one might expect of a man with his pedigree in rugby football, a thoroughly enlightened prospectus for the "second generation" coaches. But for me he has also produced something of equal value—a sound and sensitive philosophy for the athletic sports which is firmly based on the total needs of the athlete towards becoming an integrated, capable, stable and fulfilled person. Playing rugby football is thus revealed as an ideal environment for those suitably endowed with ability to satisfy at the same time the integrating needs of man as a thinker, as a worker and as a player. In setting out his views the author uncovers his own attitudes and behaviour as an outstanding coach and as an experienced and perceptive educator. In his own words (pp. 8—9) his purpose is "to help the player to become a complete player in so far as his physical, mental and emotional limitations allow. My job is to encourage him to enjoy and extend his abilities . . . I specifically do not want him to feel that his chief cause for self esteem is his rugby or that a bad game diminishes him as a person". He could

v

have added in support of his philosophy something I've heard him repeating often to players . . . "but you've got to *work hard* and *intelligently* if you want to be a *good player.*"

On the technical side "Total Rugby" represents a synthesis of the effective arts and sciences of coaching rugby football which Jim Greenwood has carefully evolved over years of analysing, experimenting and developing. I have had the great pleasure of observing and admiring him teaching, advising and coaching at Loughborough which has been his "laboratory" in recent years. In the process I have come to recognise and appreciate not only his impressive wisdom about the game, but his generous willingness to share with others his accumulated knowledge in order to advance the level of coaching for all. The publication of this book represents, in my opinion, a significant advance for rugby football coaching. The concepts, methods and materials that are included represent a resource that has so far not been available to coaches. In a sense rigorous coaching methods have come to be fully accepted only recently in rugby football compared with many of the other athletic sports, and as a result the application of sound principles and method may have lagged behind. The leeway would now seem to have been more than adequately made up, particularly with respect to Jim Greenwood's notions of "total rugby" which may take the understanding and interpretations of the game onto a new and exciting level. It certainly deserves the most serious attention of coaches, players and administrators.

J E KANE

Principal, West London Institute of Higher Education

Foreword

Like Jim Greenwood I'm dead against the "play-safe" approach to rugby. Let's aim to win but to win with panache, where well-judged risk-taking is an important feature of our game.

The book seeks to show how this philosophy can be turned into actions on the field of play, and with a playing background of 20 caps for Scotland, a Lions Tour to South Africa plus considerable teaching/coaching experience with school, college and English Regional sides it is not surprising that the author has harmoniously blended his experiences in a most scholarly and yet practical way.

"Total Rugby" is a book you will need to read carefully and one you will want to refer to regularly in order to understand not only "how" the skills of the game are taught but the important "cues" players should be looking for in order to make correct decisions.

It's a book well worth reading—chock full of ideas—and if it persuades even a handful of teams to change their approach and play total rugby then the author for one will, I'm sure, feel his efforts were well worthwhile.

Don RUTHERFORD

Rugby Football Union
England and British Isles

Contents

PART 1
Background To The Game

1
The Meaning of Total Rugby

TOTAL RUGBY AND PLAY-SAFE RUGBY

The rugby I'm concerned with as a coach is rugby at its most exciting—the fifteen-man handling game, in which every player is encouraged to show what he can do as attacker, defender, and supporting player, and in which the overall style of play gives him a chance to do so. This open, ebullient form of rugby is the most satisfying to players and potential players, at home or abroad, spectators, officials, and coaches. It's where the game's most memorable expression has been found in the past, and where—because of its wide appeal—its future should lie.

We need a new name for it, for play-safe coaches have found it expedient to equate "fifteen-man rugby" with reckless abandon, typified by a slavish commitment to spinning the ball wide. I believe in fifteen-man rugby, but the quality I prize most highly in a player is judgement, and one of the qualities I most deplore in a team is a slavish commitment to any single aspect of play. Total rugby is a convenient title to describe rugby that subsumes all simpler forms of the game and uses them tactically as judgement dictates, but which seeks whenever possible to play the fifteen-man handling game.

What most characterises this game is well-judged risk-taking. Much of the most immediate pleasure in games, for player and spectator alike, comes from successful risk-taking, the spice of adventure, perhaps because it affords a more complete expression of the player, or because it offers glimpses of values that go beyond the merely safe and conventional. Even in winning—that safest and most conventional measure of success—the best that the game can offer is the pleasure of winning with panache, of getting beyond the banal, the humdrum, the workaday.

To do this consistently you must be very positively committed to winning. What most clearly distinguishes total rugby is the variety and enterprise of its attacking methods, based on the all round competence of its players.

To help define this position it's useful to consider the polar alternative—play-safe rugby, which sets out to win by minimising the risk of defeat. This is based on two excellent tactical precepts— to restrict in a given position the amount of risk you're prepared to take, and to play to your strength. Both of these figure in total rugby as elements in a mix; in play-safe they tend to define and limit the aspirations of the team. As part of the mix, they bring security and confidence; in isolation, lack of adventure and lack of variety.

The critical weakness of playing minimum-risk rugby is that it gives the players little chance to exercise the full range of their talents. The critical flaw in constantly playing to the team's strength, is that it tends to perpetuate the team's weaknesses. Concentration on these elements produces, at its best, a formidable but dull efficiency always based on the power of the pack. When the basic tactics—typically, tactical kicking or taking the ball on the short side—are countered, there's often a lack of resource in alternative ways of playing the game. At its worst, possession becomes almost a liability, an embarrassment, so limited in variety is their attack. "If we can hang around their 22 long enough", you can almost hear them saying, "Peter'll kick a goal". Yet paradoxically enough, the power of their pack creates the perfect base on which to build a really enterprising team performance. What stands in the way is a lack of vision, or a lack of know-how.

The primary losers are the players. They become the victims of the play-safe syndrome: denied the preparation that would develop their talent, and the opportunity to use it, they gradually lose the techniques, the judgement, and most important of all the attitude of mind that makes enterprising rugby possible. They then become an excuse for the system—for, of course, you can't play enterprising rugby with players like that. This happens at all levels, but most blatantly at the top: some of the most prestigious teams throughout the world of rugby play this negative form of the game, teams with genuinely talented players, talents all too often allowed to atrophy. As a result everyone connected with the game suffers, and most of all the game itself.

TOTAL RUGBY AND COACHING

There was a time when the restricted form of the game was, for most teams, inevitable: coaching expertise on how to improve performance was simply not available. Teams that played something like total rugby did so through a happy coincidence of players, whose abilities and temperament made it possible. The great justification of coaching—to my mind its only justification—is to make total rugby possible for a far greater number of players. The technical knowledge now available makes it possible for any team with adequate commitment to play more enterprising, enjoyable and entertaining rugby.

The basic challenge facing the coach is obvious enough: the quality of the rugby his team can play is dictated by the thoroughness with which he has prepared individual players, and the attitudes he has encouraged in them to the playing of the game. He may not now have the players to play enterprising rugby; he could be on the way to producing them. He has to devote more time, thought, and energy to ensuring that individual players can function effectively in a greater variety of situations—the more successful he is in this, the more acceptable become the risks of employing them fully, extending the range and enterprise of team tactics.

For most established coaches this will represent a shift of emphasis. First generation coaches have tended to see their job as organisational—assembling the players available into an effective team rather than improving the quality of the individual players. They have tended also to concentrate on the pack at the expense of the backs, and on the more mechanical aspects of play rather than those involving judgement in the players. What is needed is a more systematic, more comprehensive approach to the needs of the game.

A shift of emphasis towards the individual and enterprising play would, of course, be timely. Team games are under increasing pressure from individual pursuits, and an approach that seeks to realise the individual's potential and evolve a style of play that gives him a maximum chance to show it is going much of the way to meet the challenge. Again, with educational change all around, the game will need to attract the younger player—as mini-rugby does—and keep him happy in a way that formerly was not felt to be necessary. Again, to solve the game's financial problems it's desirable that we attract not only more players but more spectators, and the slow handclap at Twickenham leaves no doubt what kind of rugby they want to see. At international level, it's becoming increasingly obvious that the winning team has to be firing on all cylinders to stand a chance of winning. From every point of view, an approach to coaching that emphasises the importance of the individual and the need for enterprising play must pay off.

Of course, the realisation of these objectives won't come overnight. Extending the range of play of the individual and the team is a gradual process. Unless you set out to do it, however, it may not come at all. There is no need to sacrifice success on the way—even if you measure success only in the most conventional way, by winning without regard to how you won. You can prepare to play enterprising rugby, and rehearse it before you put it on the pitch; you can revert to play-safe when circumstances demand it. But how much sweeter to win with flair!

THE COACH AND THE PLAYER

The critical technical question for the coach or committee man to ask is 'to what extent has being a member of our club accelerated that player's progress?'. Every player likes to feel his ability is growing, and detailed, personal help towards that improvement is perhaps the most valuable thing the club has to offer—it's at once technical aid and a guarantee of the club's interest in him.

Beyond that, every player can be helped to feel that he has a contribution to make to the preparation and development of the team. There's little scope for discussion on the practice field—you need decisive leadership to get high work-rate—but time can be made for it off the field.

And the aim of team playing policy must be to offer every player the chance to use in the match the abilities he has developed. Everybody in rugby knows how many exciting and talented players are denied the chance, game after game, to show what they can do and to build confidence in their ability to do it.

Beyond the club team, the player has his sights legitimately set on some form of representative honours. The higher the level, the greater the part that sheer talent must play in success, but at every level solid preparation by the club should be evident. The player's talent is often specialised and takes the form of one commanding talent—his strength at prop, for example; the club's contribution should be the all-round competence of his other play, the range of skills he has acquired, the attitude of mind he has developed. No representative coach has the time to coach in this sense: the club coach has to do it.

THE COMMITTEE AND TOTAL RUGBY

Committee men are, in most amateur sports, chosen less for their consciousness of technical developments than for their administrative ability and willingness to serve. (And in rugby, as in most amateur sports, the game suffers from this division of interest). They are, however, inevitably those most jealous of their club's reputation—they are the people who helped to create it. It's particularly important, therefore, that they should move beyond the "all that counts is not losing" attitude. They might take pride in the fact that their club has very much more to offer than a desperate need to win. That they have a coherent preparation policy, so that the prospective player will have a real chance of maximising his potential; that they play enterprising rugby in which every player has a part; that their talented players are given the all round competence that ensures the best chance of their talent being used at a higher level; that they often win, and that they win by playing quality rugby. If they can add to that that they offer coaching at all levels, that every team is watched, that there is a coherent, fair, selection process—that, in fact, the individual player is seen as an important club member—they will have real grounds for pride in their club and an assurance that the club is respected for the right reasons.

In one other respect the club, and especially the coach and committee, can enhance their reputation and make an important contribution to the health and attractiveness of the game. They are the people in the best position to establish and maintain high standards of conduct on the field. The referee—with the backing of Disciplinary Committees and the Union—can certainly curb the excesses of the few, but the club is in the best position to encourage a positive outlook in all its players. The reputation of the game itself has not been helped by the image of the rugger hearty, the bar-room hero from the undistinguished XV whose claim to fame is his capacity for beer and song. But the image of manliness that finds expression in deliberate intimidation and foul play is destructive of the game itself. There's little harm in attracting to the game those who enjoy simply a robust social life, but it's impossible to justify attracting those who see in it a chance for physical violence.

The committee concerned with the club's reputation can make it clear that there is no place in their team for the habitually dirty player. If we are to attract players to the game it's got to be on the basis of a robust, enjoyable, and positive activity. The atmosphere in the club itself is the best guarantee of this positive approach on the field.

It's difficult, too, to dissociate a negative approach to the style of play from a negative attitude to the game's ethics. Play-safe, nine-man rugby, by placing an emphasis on physical confrontation and often esteeming strength more highly than skill creates more situations where violence can erupt, and predisposes the team towards it. Those with a responsibility for the club's reputation might bear this in mind.

BEING A SPECTATOR

Spectators are not normally mentioned in books on rugby. "The game is for the players", with its implied and unquestioned antithesis between the interests of the player and of the spectator, is usually greeted with committed nods and applause. Spectators, however, have their place in the scheme of things, and make their contribution to the game. My most intimate friend is a spectator, and she has never even played the game.

Spectators are important because playing rugby is in part a display activity. It's important, too, that they help to create the right atmosphere for the match. We must face the probability that what soccer crowds do today rugby crowds may do in ten years' time. There are already signs of negative expressions of allegiance: not content with cheering their team, some are beginning to attack the opposition. There's a lot to be said for every club and every union emphasising that without the opposition team there wouldn't be a match, that they form part of a like-minded community and would, if they lived nearer, probably be our friends. I like our spectators to clap the opposition and cheer us.

THE COACH

The second-generation rugby coach, like his committee, can easily find a broader base for reputation than that of organising a team for play-safe rugby. The word "coach" is imbued with the notion of skill, and attention to detail, and the true concern of a coach is the skill and technical flexibility shown by his players and his team. Some coaches have derived a spurious reputation from the sheer physical prowess of the players they have available. The real question is not "how successful is that team?" but "how successful could that team be?" and the measure of the coach is how nearly the whole team approximates to that potential. This view poses a challenge to those coaches whose clubs have the best players, and offers recognition to those coaches who do sterling work in more difficult conditions.

Beyond that is the contribution the coach makes to the development of the game, and of coaching expertise. Coaches now must accept the fact that the technical development of the game is largely in their hands and part of their responsibility is to the game as well as to their club and players. This is true of the tone of the game as well as its technical content, and in both respects short-term gains—achieved e.g. by condoning violence, preaching hatred of the opposition, or encouraging minimum-risk rugby—may well prove long-term losses. Such measures are an odd basis to choose for building a reputation.

The development of coaching expertise is a challenge. There's no doubt that very, very few coaches can consider themselves well-equipped for the job even in terms of the information and methods now available. We are approaching the stage where mastering what's already available will amount to a full-time job, and may have to be undertaken at least on a regional basis by full-time staff, (a suggestion implemented almost immediately by the R.F.U.) but a grasp of the principles, use of source books, and attendance at courses will put any intelligent, committed person in a position to offer valuable help to the team.

Paradoxically enough, despite the amount of knowledge available, I don't believe that we've really got started on coaching. The next ten or fifteen years may well see radical innovations in the tactics, techniques, and coaching methods used in the game. So undeveloped are coaching techniques that every coach can expect to add something new of his own. Indeed, this is one of the rewarding aspects of coaching—that you can always develop personal insights and techniques, and take coaching a step further. Once the U.S. gets fully involved, rugby coaching may well take off.

My own aims in coaching are, no doubt, much affected by a background in teaching, and the fact that coaching and being coached are educational experiences. I want to help the player become a complete player so far as his physical, mental, and emotional limitations allow. My job is to encourage him to enjoy and extend his abilities, and take a proper pride in them. I specifically do not want him to feel that his chief cause for self-esteem is his rugby, or that a bad game diminishes him as a person—ninety-nine out of every hundred human beings have never heard of rugby, and they still get by. Nevertheless, if he chooses to play, I'd like to see him measure himself against his fellows, and be given the chance to express himself as fully as possible. To that end, the rugby we play must be total rugby.

Rugby is a tough game, but the most important toughness is the ability to be tough with yourself, to demand more of yourself than your opponent does, and that's not inconsistent with a tone in the team that's generous, positive, thoughtful, honourable.

His rugby on the field has got to provide him with something memorable, some spots of time that will live with him. The wider the range of those moments the better. They may be aesthetic or heroic, expressions of speed or power or judgement, fitness or skill, individual or group—but they've got to be memorable expressions of his youth and talent. He's got to feel the elation of winning well, with a touch of style and class, and especially of winning against the odds. He's got to recognise that he can win as an individual against his immediate opponent and against himself, even if the team loses. I'd like him to remember being magnanimous in defeat, generous in victory. I'd like him to enjoy the sense of belonging to a team, and being proud to belong to it in victory or defeat.

Some of these points I've put in the past tense, because they are a recognition of the best of what rugby has offered me, and because, like thousands of others I'm aware that given the right conditions, rugby is more than simply a diversion over a comparatively few playing years. It's up to the coach to ensure that these 'right conditions' are available to as many of his players as possible, in their interest and in that of the game.

The basic right condition is the spirit in which the game is played. In the earliest days, when referees were felt unnecessary, there was common agreement that there were things in life more important than the result of a match. Without some sense of a greater good— be it sportsmanship or the quality of the experience or the game itself—the importance of winning can grow to destructive proportions. It's up to the coach to keep some such greater good present to his players.

2
Understanding the Game

The basic pattern in the game is that of alternate *concentration and dispersal.* The laws are so designed that there's a constant clearing of the field, with a large number of players concentrated in a small area—at scrum, line-out, ruck or maul—so that there's a large amount of open space for the remaining players. The aim of this is to tilt the balance in favour of the attackers—to give them space in which to work. This is complementary to the single most characteristic law of the game—passing back—which is designed to create situations in which the player must get past his opponent in the most exciting way—by evasive running.

The space available to the attackers allows them to *stretch the opposing defence;* long passing will force each defender to defend a wider zone and give each attacker a better chance of making a break; short passing will create space on the flanks to release a speedy winger or allow a supporting overload.

The action sequence in the game is that of *stop-go* corresponding to the basic pattern of concentration-dispersion. This is of the utmost importance to the game.

a. *It makes the game possible*

Figures produced to show the amount of time the ball is actually in play (25-30 minutes) tend to suggest that there's a great waste of time—but the pauses make the game practicable: without them, the physical demands would be too great. Inducing fatigue in the opposition by prolonged pressure—e.g. physical contact, sustained ball speed—both in the short term and the long term are effective bases for attack, and a recognition of the physical limits within which the game is played.

b. *It restores order*

One aspect of the basic pattern can be seen as order-disorder: the longer the fluid phase of play continues the greater is the probability of disorder. This sets up mental and emotional pressures in the players that correspond to (and no doubt affect) physical fatigue. Restoring order—the "stop" phase—becomes more necessary as players become tired, and the laws recognise this by linking stoppages to mistakes.

c. *It creates set-pieces favouring the defence*

The basic situation at any stoppage in the game approximates to that at a set scrum (see p. 12).

The *defence line* is the line which the offside laws allow the *pressure* element of the defence to take up.

The *gain line* is the point reached by the ball before the stoppage. For either side to go forward they must get the ball across the gain line.

The *tackle line* connects the points at which respective opponents will meet—which, given an expected similarity of pace and reaction time in the opponents, will be midway between the defence line and attack line.

The *attack line* is the line along which the back division expecting to gain possession take up position. To allow the ball to be passed without undue pressure they must make space for themselves and tend, therefore, to lie in echelon. If they intend to kick, the echelon must be shallow. If they intend to do a move then individual players will probably have to alter their positions. It's highly unlikely that the most effective positioning will in fact be a straight line even for passing the ball out (see p. 187). However, the line in the diagram conveys the basic situation adequately.

The consequences of this recurrent situation are these:

i. If, as expected, team B get the ball and intend to handle they will take the ball back behind the gain line and to reach it again will have to cross the tackle line: they run the risk of losing the ground between the gain line and the tackle line. Possession is only a potential advantage.

ii. If, unexpectedly, team B get the ball quickly they ought to be able to cross the gain line before coming into contact with their opponents.

iii. Whichever team gets the ball across the gain line will have its pack running forward, which generates the most powerful impetus in attack. So far as the pack is concerned, the greatest advantage, in terms of angle of run, accrues when the ball crosses the gain line

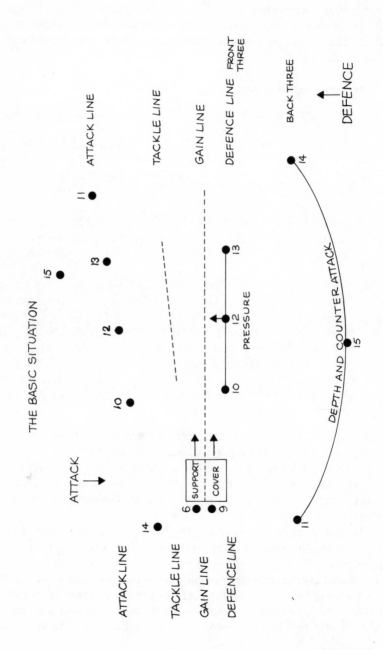

THE BASIC SITUATION

ATTACK

ATTACK LINE
TACKLE LINE
GAIN LINE
DEFENCE LINE

ATTACK LINE
TACKLE LINE
GAIN LINE
DEFENCE LINE FRONT THREE
BACK THREE

DEFENCE

SUPPORT
COVER

PRESSURE

DEPTH AND COUNTER ATTACK

close to them. The further out the strike is made the less important this advantage becomes for the same yardage of gain. It's important, therefore, that the team should be capable of attacking close to the scrum, line-out, maul, or ruck.

iv. The tackling power of each team tends, as a consequence, to be grouped in the back-row (to limit attacks close in) and in the front three (fh-ic-oc-to pressurise passing movements), with a joint aim to prevent the ball crossing the gain line against them or to minimise such gain. If they can make their tackles on the tackle line, then their team has gained ground, and their pack is moving forward. This is an important consideration in selection.

v. This concentration of defenders is one of the first elements to be considered in decision-making: the attacking team must have appropriate methods of taking them on, distracting them, or out-flanking them.

vi. Any check in the action of the game, such as those provided by the stop/go pattern, will tend to allow the defenders to regroup in the optimum defensive formation. In first-phase situations this re-grouping will be complete, and even from mauls and rucks any undue delay will result in a situation approximating to first-phase. Effective second-phase possession—a situation in which the defence has been put under pressure, the tackle ball has been kept available, and the attacking side has regrouped quickly—will lead to a much better attacking situation. Each of these elements, however, is necessary to produce an effective second-phase situation.

d. *It simplifies decision-making*

The constant occurrence of situations in which the defence positioning and tactics are predictable, and where divergences from the expected formation are significant and obvious, makes the spotting of potential weaknesses easier for the tactical decision-makers.

e. *It provides a simple basis for team tactics*

Apart from a team strategy—the overall view of how the team intends to play the game—there have to be team tactics. These are the team's response to the recurrent set-piece situations in the stop-go pattern. It is moderately certain, for example, that in every match the team will be awarded a scrum about fifteen metres from the opposing line, and fifteen metres from touch. They will know—by thought, experiment, and practice—what attacking gambits are effectively open to them and what gambits possible to them in theory are ruled out by the limitations of their players. It's then for the tactical decision-makers to select the best option against these particular opponents on this particular day on this particular ground at this particular moment in the match. Incidentally, therefore, it provides a simple basis for team coaching, unit coaching, and coaching of the individual.

ATTACKING PRINCIPLES

What emerge from these considerations are three basic imperatives:

Get possession
Go forward
Support the ball-carrier

But these imperatives, narrowly interpreted, can be a recipe for nine or ten-man rugby. Accordingly, it's useful, while appreciating their truth, to rephrase them:

Get the ball
Get it into space
Get to it first

a. *Possession*

The minimum realistic possession the team must aim for is all its own ball in the scrum, the line-out, and when your own player takes the ball into the ruck or maul situation. Whatever you get beyond that is a very desirable (see ci above) bonus. You must also be prepared to take advantage of any ball gifted to you by way of penalties and misplaced kicks of any kind.

The first priority in any team is to get possession, and the first priority in coaching the units is to ensure that you do. The critical mistake of play-safe coaches, however, is to spend a disproportionate amount of time and energy on it at the expense of preparing the team to make a varied and intelligent use of the possession when they win it.

The use they can make of it is to some extent determined by the quality of ball that's won. *Good ball* is controlled so that it arrives where it's wanted, when it's wanted, at the speed it's wanted. Ideally, it arrives under those conditions with the opposition going backward so that their defence is off balance, but that again is a bonus.

b. *Get it into space*

Possession is only a *potential advantage.* Poor quality possession, or inadequate decision-making, or poor execution—especially in the face of sensibly applied pressure from the opposition (cii above)—can make it a liability.

It becomes a real advantage when the team has the *initiative* in using it. Essentially, this means that the team has chosen how to use it, and aren't forced by their own inefficiency or the aggressiveness of their opponents into limited or involuntary actions.

Tactically, having the initiative is the key to total rugby. Any lack of understanding or uncertainties about the process of decision-making, or its attendant technical requirements will lead to some loss of the initiative, and an inability to exploit fully the abilities of the players. The coach has two jobs here: to improve decision-making and to ensure technical efficiency.

Every player must be encouraged to play intelligently since every one is required to make personal decisions—primarily about the direction of his support running in attack or defence, and about distribution when he's the ball-carrier. The *tactical decision-makers,* however, are thinking for the team as a whole. They must be thinking ahead all the time so that before the referee blows his whistle they're evaluating the situation. The sequence of decision-making is:

i. *Assessment of situation*

position in field	state of the team	guidelines
time in the match	opposing formation	situations
score	opposing strengths/	
conditions ˙	weaknesses	

ii. *Provisional decision*

The earlier a provisional decision is made, the better. The more players affected by the decision, the earlier it must be made.

iii. *Communication*

All those directly involved must be put in the picture. This always includes the back-row. It calls for a code—less to baffle the opposition than to speed communication.

iv. *Co-operation*

Every call will demand some change in positioning if it's going to have maximum effect: there's no point, e.g. in having your outside centre twenty yards back if the fly-half is going to kick. Co-operation must be effective and fast. Discipline is essential.

v. *Execution*

Up to the moment of execution, the call is provisional—it can be changed if any unexpected advantage or disadvantage occurs. No call will be successful if those involved in the action fail to act with *purpose*—they must make a positive, disciplined contribution to the action, on or off the ball.

Each team needs a *tactical decision-maker* and a deputy who takes over if the decision-maker is injured. The ideal position for the decision-maker is at fly-half. The coach simplifies his job
(1) by constantly encouraging him to get his head up and look at the situation—he has to learn to look, and to trust his reading of the situation (see p. 15);
(2) by establishing with him basic principles of attack (see immediately below);
(3) by suggesting guide-lines for decisions in the terms e.g. of areas of the field (see p. 259);
(4) by working through recurrent situations (see p. 252) with the team.

There are only four basic choices open to the tactical decision-maker, as to any ball-carrier: to run, to pass, to kick, to set up a move. It's highly important that he—or the players immediately next to him—be adept in all four. Limited decision-makers impose limitations on the whole team. This kind of limitation is critical at half-back and the coach must work to ensure that both the halves become at least competent in all four basic activities.

Decision-making implies *purpose* and whatever action he takes must be purposeful: a tentative decision-maker is a contradiction in terms. This sense of purpose must be shared by all those involved in the action—each has a job to do. Nothing must be done mechanically. This is one function of unit and team practices.

Key ideas in games are those of *variety* and *flexibility* in attack, variety so that the opposition cannot simply predict our actions, and flexibility so that when our opponents can match our basic strength or style of play we have effective alternatives. Each team needs a good "mix"—a balanced variety in its use of the ball to keep the opposition guessing and all our own players involved in the match. The coach, by establishing basic ideas, suggesting guide-lines, and working through recurrent situations, can make the player aware of the various possibilities and how they can best be deployed.

The most important guide-line that. the coach offers is in the choice of basic *striking points* and consequent *staple activities*. This is fundamental in establishing your basic style of play, and leads to coherent selection policies, and a coherent programme of team building and preparation. Within its mix, every team tends to have such a basic staple activity. It's a source of great strength provided that it's used as a matter of choice and not necessity. To select or coach simply with one purpose in mind, to leave your team dependent on one form of attack, is myopic: it may in the short term be successful; in the long term it leads to poverty of play.

The overriding tactical aim is to create a situation when the ball can be taken across the gain-line and possession retained. By choosing striking points and maximising striking power there, the coach can set up staple activities to achieve this. For the wide overlap game, which is a staple activity in fifteen-man handling rugby, for example, the most appropriate striking point is outside-centre: your aim is to get the ball to him, in space, and to attack through him, the full-back, and the winger. Once this decision is made, the coach can establish priorities in selecting and coaching, and begin to work with intelligence ar.d purpose. He knows that, whatever else they may be able to do, the scrum-half, fly-half, and inside-centre must be able and willing, when it's called for, to spin the ball to outside centre. He will begin to define what he expects from inside-centre and outside-centre, and see them as a pair. He knows what he requires of his full-back. Technically, too, he has now set himself precise problems so that he can use his time and energy—and that of his players—effectively.

An alternative striking point that every team needs to develop is that close to the set piece. The closer the strike is made to the set-piece, the more quickly you get over the gain-line, and the more quickly you get the pack moving forward. This is the most powerful source of impetus in attack, and a basic way of creating good second-phase situations. It has the added advantage of keeping the ball close to the pack, and, therefore, in the event of a breakdown, in a source defensive position.

Unhappily, as with kicking in attack, it is an art that is open to abuse: most play safe teams use some variation on this theme, without developing the means of exploiting the resultant second-phase situations, and without alternatives in the event of this staple activity being countered. It's also fair to say that most such teams fail to exploit fully the actual forward drive, by keeping it narrow rather than wide and deep—creating space in which to drive forward (see p. 54).

The basic situation can be set up by the forwards themselves, or by the backs feeding the forwards. Typical examples are the line-out peel (see p. 154), back-row moves (see p. 130), and rolling off a maul or ruck. Of these, the last has the great advantage of being performed against a potentially disorganised defence (but see p. 164).

The stocky, elusive, quick-moving figure of Sid Going typifies this form of attack. The backs may also set up moves to get the ball back in front of the forwards (see p. 199)—one thinks of the crash-ball exponents, like McRae, who by sheer committed power drive through to get in front of the back-row.

Such attacks once again must be set up on the basis of a decision, and the full chain of decision-making has to be employed. The decision-maker need not be a forward—the scrum-half can see more of the situation than any of the pack—but he customarily is. It's necessary, then, to establish a priority in the event of two calls being made—one in the pack, one in the backs. In teams that normally play total rugby, with considerable freedom and opportunity for the backs, it's acceptable to allow the forwards precedence in call; in other teams, it may be best to give the backs precedence. One result of working on situations (see p. 252) is that it helps generate a basic agreement on such points.

c. *Get to it first*

The aim of the striker is to score, and to do so with minimum delay—delay in any game is to the advantage of the defenders. The more wholeheartedly he believes this the more likely he is to complete the break, and to stretch the opposing defence. But the coach must accept that despite the best efforts of those inside him to create the chances for him, and his own best efforts to get clear, the ball-carrier will often be tackled. It's vital that *support* be there to continue the attack, or at least retain possession. For this they must get into the action area fast. Their efficiency will depend on

i. *Communication*—good decision-making allows time for communication, and organised team-play—e.g. established striking points—allows clear communication.

ii. *Personal decision-making*—thinking ahead, predicting, quick appreciation of unexpected developments—the back-row especially, but all the pack must be encouraged and helped to think on their feet (see p. 49).

iii. *Basic mobility*—in choosing his striking points, the coach may well take into account the mobility of his pack. Within limits he can select his players with a particular striking point in view, and he can obviously use his fitness training to improve the speed range of all his players. It's highly unlikely that his pack can be characterised simply as "powerful" or "mobile"—if it is he's in a difficult situation. In such a case he may well establish striking points that will impose less strain on his pack—close at hand with the powerful pack, so that they can economically bring their power to bear on their opponents, far out for the mobile pack, so that they can run their opponents around and make sure of possession before the heavy artillery arrive. Neither extreme is desirable since automatically the attacking possibilities of the team are limited, and its vulnerability in defence increased.

iv. *Support exercises*—it's comparatively easy (see p. 161) to coach intelligent support running in attack and defence, and such exercises are a basic part of team practices.

Although support is often seen as a function of the pack, every member of the team must be prepared to help. Broadly speaking, the player who passed to the player who was tackled is best placed to be first supporter (see p. 49). This must be drilled home in unit and team practices (see p. 188).

Support is the key to all team play, and speed—a product of *forethought, fitness and self-discipline*—is the key to effective support. This is as true of the centres fighting to get back in position to maintain defence or continue attack as it is of forwards arriving to set up a maul. "Get there first" is engraved on the good player's heart.

DEFENCE

There are three elements in defence: pressure, cover, and depth. These are necessary whenever the opposition have or are likely to get the ball in set play, loose play, or counter-attack.

Pressure is generated by the front three and in specific cases—e.g. defence close to a set-piece—the back-row. Its aim is to deny the opposition the initiative, to harry them into mistakes, and if possible to regain possession beyond the gain-line (see p. 212). When the opposition are consistently moving the ball wide, the front three and back-row may adopt a 'drift defence' to provide cover against overlap attacks (see p. 216).

Cover is provided by the pack as a whole with the back-row leading. It's concerned with providing safeguards to the pressure groups by creating a wide, deep, defensive pattern of cross-field running (see p. 222).

Depth is provided by the back three—the full-back and wingers. It's concerned with defence against kicks, a third line against running attack, and the generation of counter-attack.

For the pattern to work effectively, each of the groups must work as a small team giving intelligent, disciplined support to each other, and must develop a pride in their small team play. Each section must be given adequate practice and coaching in their roles.

Beyond this, it's desirable that the whole team is given adequate exercise in dealing with particular situations when the other side has the ball (see p. 250).

EVOLVING A GAME PLAN

Developing a coherent approach for a team or club is largely a matter of continuity. A coherent playing policy leads to coherent selection policy—and coherent selection policies tend to lead to continuity of personnel. Most successful teams show few changes that aren't forced by unavailability, and in the event of changes can draw upon a small number of well-prepared reserves, who know precisely their standing and what is expected of them. Building a team, and keeping it in good repair, is a continuous job, that leads on from season to season, and is characterised by forethought and early preparation.

Continuity is the key to team spirit, to a sense of the group and a loyalty to it. It fosters that sense of the other player's likely action that is the subtlest expression of team play. It also allows the conscious development of a detailed game plan. A game plan is a joint production between players and coach that seeks to establish the way that the team will handle all the situations that arise in the match in terms of time in the match, position on the field, and immediate situation. It's based on experience over a period of the possibilities in attack and defence open to the team, and a conscious selection of what seems most effective. A very simple example will make this clear: how do we handle drop-outs at the 22? Provided that everyone knows what we are going to do, we can extract maximum advantage from the situation by acting fast and efficiently. The fuller the game plan, the simpler the process of decision-making, and the more effective the execution. Continuity is the essential element to allow a game plan to go on developing. Even at representative level, the growth of regular organised squad-sessions allows the team to continue filling in the details of the plan.

3
Team Selection

Without a coherent playing policy you cannot have a coherent selection policy (or for that matter a coherent policy on team development or preparation). To put it as its most obvious: it's difficult to assess a player until you fully appreciate the role he has to play. A player who is admirable in one style of play may be incapable of playing his part in another. You need a moderately detailed *job description* to get the right man. This is not to deny that the player you finally select may be much bigger than the player you looked for, and may expand your whole consciousness of how you can use him—simply that he must have the basic qualifications called for by team tactics.

A second vital principle is that of *complementarity*. In an ideal world we might be able to turn out fifteen omni-competent footballers, each capable of meeting all the varied needs of the game. Part of our coaching programme is aimed at encouraging this all-round competence, providing a sound backing for the specific talent. In practice, however, any player offers a unique set of pluses and minuses and you are seeking in the team and in the mini—teams within the team to create an appropriate blend of these qualities. This entails maximising pluses and counterbalancing the minuses. It's extremely difficult, for example, to play total rugby without an attacking full-back; your wingers, therefore, must be selected in part because they can be depended upon to function well in deep defence. If you intend to attack wide, you need a running outside centre, and he will function best if the player inside him is a natural timer of the pass, who isn't constantly tempted to have a go himself. If you play a flanker for his attacking flair, you must look to balance him in terms of line out and maul. The mini-team in which you can least afford to use complementarity as a way of balancing strength and weakness is at half: personal limitation there, in either player, limits the variety of the whole team.

A third element is *compatibility* in character traits, personality, and attitude to the game. Team spirit may never develop if personal attitudes are too diverse. You do need a little touch of the heroic, of

22

the player who never knows when he's beaten, and who functions best when things are going badly. It's great to have a joker—but he must take everything up to and including the match seriously.

A fourth element is decision-making: you must have a *tactical decision maker* to ensure a proper use of your team preparations. The basic quality he needs is a confidence in his ability to keep reading the situation and making decisions. This ability can be improved in team practices—but the willingness to make decisions must be there. The player may or may not be your captain: captaincy involves a great deal more than this single function. It is in every way best that the fly-half function as decision maker if you hope to play total rugby.

The only foundation for consistent success in selection is *continuity*. At best it is an exercise in continuous forward planning, looking at least a season ahead. If you are not working ahead like this, you leave no time to prepare against probable contingencies. The short-term application of this is to think always in terms of a squad rather than of a team, and to have provisional selections worked out several games ahead. Nothing is so indicative of a lack of policy, incidentally, as radically different squad cover for the same key position—e.g. at half-back.

Continuity of the team nucleus is a critical example of the general principle. At any level it is a recognition of quality and of the comparative unimportance of temporary variations in form. Lack of this particular continuity probably reveals more about the selectors than about the players. It brings with it the hope of team spirit, of the development of a game plan, and the immediate benefit of shop-floor help in selection. You may not always be able to follow it, but it would be folly to deprive yourself of the advice of your players in completing a team.

Selection is an aspect of the game—like administration and refereeing—that has not, perhaps, advanced at the same speed as coaching. Too often, administrators are asked to function as technical experts. The basic qualification for a selector might well be the ability to coach the players he selects at an appropriate level. If a group of such selectors were completely committed to an overall pattern of play, and clear about the specific roles of the players, it's possible they could pick a team. It seems advantageous, however, for them to pick a squad in cooperation with the coach, and leave team selection to him. To take this to its logical conclusion, he should function as Chairman of Selectors, and appoint as selectors those whose technical judgement he respects. At Club level, there's much to be said for each team being the responsibility of a single coach/manager, and the selection committee's being composed of the team coaches under the chairmanship of the 1st XV coach.

PART 2
Practical Coaching

4
Basic
Coaching Techniques

Two questions always face the coach, in whatever activity: *what?* and *how?* The average spectator usually feels he can answer the first of these—e.g. "He isn't jumping high enough." I remember very clearly as a schoolboy scurrying down the field pursued by a monstrous opponent who threatened, if he caught me, to bury me, and being exhorted by my Headmaster: "Run faster, Greenwood." The desirability of this had already occurred to me: it was *how* to run faster that eluded me. That is precisely the technical role of the coach: *having defined the problem he has got to supply answers, and devise ways of implementing them.*

(There are times, of course, when more or less subtle forms of exhortation are of great importance to the individual and the team, and this is discussed on p. 29.)

It's convenient to think of this, initially, on two levels: the first preventive, dealing with numbers of people and a common problem, the second therapeutic, with the individual player and his particular problems. In the first case, the process runs—

1. isolate a common problem	how do we deal with an opponent who has caught the ball and turned?
2. define a basic form	we'll pivot him over backwards and put him down of the ground with the ball on our side
3. construct a practice	we'll set up a cyclic exercise in which A grubber kicks; B falls and gets up with the ball. C follows up, pivots B and puts him down; D picks up, grubber kicks; A falls ...

26

4. develop the practice

we can then add a mauling practice in which two (small) sets of forwards contest the ball on the ground. Both packs behind the grub-kicker; defenders have to go right behind (put marker on ground?) and come in (initially heads up to avoid cracked skulls); attackers drive over and secure possession.

In the second case, we are looking at the individual player in a specific action and trying to improve features of his play—a very much subtler exercise, one in which we don't, in effect, stipulate a common problem but are forced to identify an individual one, in which we aren't simply concerned with broad effects but with individual finesse; where we may be dealing with problems that arise only in a particular position, and only in the context of the real-life members of an actual unit. And yet it's utterly misleading simply to contrast the first kind of coaching with the second: they are intimately connected. Indeed, unless the first is accompanied by the same kind of regard for individual performance that characterises the second, your formal exercise may do as much harm as good. Repetition exercises are technically neutral: they'll groove faulty performances just as effectively as good ones. If the individual's performance isn't being scrutinised, therefore, the exercise must be of doubtful value. In fact, there's no such thing as mechanical, "get-it-started-and-retire-to-the-clubhouse" type coaching: you've got to be in there all the time—observing, evaluating: if you don't, it may be a waste of time and energy. People tend to confuse *coaching situations* with *coaching*. The first kind of practice described above is really a coaching situation: you get them working so that you get ample opportunity to assess what they are doing, and ample opportunity to improve it. Coaching is what you do within that situation.

OBSERVATION

The key to everything is observation—to be able to see *in detail* what happens is vital to the detailed coaching which is the great aim of the good coach. At its best, coaching is trying to make very good players even better—like a top golf coach working with professional golfers—and that calls for fine observation and refined comment.

Yet, on every course for coaches, the single greatest weakness and the weakness hardest to eradicate is the inability to see in real detail what happens. Initially, all you see is a blur of action, a confused impression that doesn't provide a basis for diagnosis or prescription. This arises partly from a lack of concentration, partly from an inadequate sense of what is (or is likely to be) significant. To bring it into focus, you need to cultivate—

1. *a clear, detailed, knowledge of what you expect to see.* Until you have a clear sense of good form in the activity, you'll find it very difficult to spot discrepancies. Not that "good form" is a dogmatically formulated creed—it's simply a useful starting point, one that you can't really do without;
2. an understanding of the *mechanical principles* involved—which may sound daunting but in practice is largely a matter of applied common sense. If you can cull analogies from other activities— athletics, for example, or other games—these often clarify problems of mechanics. The mechanical principles allow us to create a model, applicable to many parts of the game which makes it easy to shape and correct technical faults; and
3. *the ability to concentrate on one thing at a time* so that, with a line-out jumper, you can check on feet placing, weight distribution, knee flexion, arm action, and so on, *each in isolation (but with a sense of the whole).*

In running coaching courses, I've found it valuable to employ video and film facilities. With them you can literally "stop the action" and look at it in detail. But every coach has instant replay facilities in his session: he can get the player to repeat an action as often as he needs to identify the specific faults.

This last is not simply a way to improve the quality of your observation, it's a basic necessity in approaching any coaching problem. You've got to take a very, very good look before you start commenting. As you get more expert you see a lot more in the time available: just as with the expert player, you need fewer cues to help you spot what's happening, and you have more time to look at it. But if you have doubts, get him to go through again and again till you're sure. While he's repeating it you may find it useful to change your own position and see him from different angles. Give yourself every chance to see what's happening.

Coming-up with solutions

On each repetition you're forming hypotheses, and checking them out. His very variation in performance from repetition to repetition may help you in this. Quite often it won't be a single factor but a combination that's the trouble. To take a simple example: your hooker is quick, and gets to the ball, but it doesn't come back regularly. You may check the depth and consistency of the put-in, go on to examine the depth of strike, and end up altering the position of the non-striking foot and the exact line of his follow-through.

The more detailed your knowledge of acceptable form and the clearer you are on what's likely to go wrong, the quicker the process tends to be. Knowledge has to be linked to—and no doubt is in part a product of—an attitude of mind. I'm not convinced that this perceptiveness (and a related enjoyment in problem solving) is a quality common in all those interested in games, or that clubs look for it as a basic qualification in those they choose as coaches. Yet it is far more valuable than the simple playing-experience criterion so often applied—experience limited positionally and historically. Top players may make top coaches, or selectors, but if so it's because of their accidental possession of these other qualities.

WORKING WITH THE PLAYERS

The higher the level at which you're working, the more necessary it becomes to work with the player, discussing the problem with him, and the players around him, but it's desirable at every level. Joint problem-solving is simultaneously a way of creating a positive response to coaching and getting the players thinking about their game. The more positive thought that's going on the better. It isn't, of course, the only way: at different times, with different activities and different people, other approaches will pay off better in speed or energy output. But the truest voice of coaching is quiet and thoughtful. This is most obvious when you are encouraging judgement—getting players to examine the field and the opposition, and picking out the best course of action. In strength and fitness sessions, on the other hand, your voice has got to evoke staggering effort from the players, and it won't do that if you can't be heard.

COACHING AND ORGANISING

What's been said so far links coaching to the individual player, and focuses on that aspect of coaching that aims at producing fifteen players capable of playing effective, exciting, rugby. Another aspect of coaching deals with the organising of players into units and the team. The distinction between coaching and organising is real enough: I first used it when the West Midlands squad came together before we played (and beat) the All Blacks. The bulk of the players, from Coventry and Moseley, had no club coaches and I wasn't at all sure how they'd react to the idea of a coach. (In fact, they were all very keen to learn.) The first point I made was that I wasn't going to coach them, I was going to organise them. In the time we had, there was no way I could make a substantial improvement to their individual abilities. All we could do was organise so that we functioned effectively. This entailed sorting out *common policies* in terms of e.g. mauling techniques, or back row defence; *basic tactics*, when we had the ball e.g. our main striking points, or when they had the ball e.g. how we'd defend from mauls and rucks; *basic roles* for the players, e.g. that our inside-centre should be in charge of defence, or that our outside-centre should be our focal attacker. Once out on the field we were working to make these ideas effective, practising what we intended to do. This wasn't too difficult since the selections had been made with a basic game-plan in mind.

Out on the field, too, organising and coaching began to fade into each other. We had to get the ball to outside-centre with room to move and this meant working on *depth* at fly-half, *ball-speed* at inside-centre, and *width* across the front-three. But what we couldn't do—and certainly would have done had we been a club side meeting regularly—would have been e.g. to improve the length of the scrum-half's pass, or the effectiveness of the winger's defence against an overlap. This distinction is important, because it helps define the role of the club coach: in the interests of the players, he cannot simply see himself as an organiser—if *he* doesn't improve the players' abilities, no-one will. He must see organising as simply one part of being the coach. It should also focus the club committee's attention on one aspect of their responsibilities to the player: to what extent does the club help the player maximise his potential, and to what extent does it simply offer him a game?

THE COACH AND "FLAIR"

The major charge laid against coaching is that it inhibits "flair"—that it subordinates the individual to the team, and subordinates spontaneity and initiative to mechanical efficiency. This is, in fact, one result of confusing "organising" with coaching. However, the case is usually overstated because of a limited understanding of the nature of the game—and of games in general. What distinguishes the good player is *judgement*—his risk-taking (i.e. decision-making) is justified by results: he rarely makes mistakes. This implies a limitation on simple spontaneity. The good player is constantly looking to maximise the team's advantage, and this requires forethought and a continuous summing up of the situation. Behind all his play lies a sense of *purpose*, and in the best rugby the whole team is working with purpose. The purpose is often to give a single player (and often a player with flair) the maximum chance to make a break. If players don't co-operate in this disciplined way then the chances of the individual are limited.

The danger that faces the "organiser" is that he fails to prepare the individuals adequately in terms of variety of possibilities, judgement, and freedom of action. These are exactly the qualities with which the coach is most concerned.

An extension of this is the relationship between the coach and the tactical decision-makers on the pitch. You must have such team decision-makers: people whose flair in performance is that they can read the game accurately and determine the most effective way to attack or defend. It's simplistic to think of *either* the captain *or* the coach being in charge: the coach must be closer to the decision-makers than to anyone else, and an excellent measure of his coaching is the quality of their understanding. They must be free to make decisions on the pitch, and must accept that freedom responsibly. And it should never be forgotten that every player is in some degree constantly making decisions within the patterns created by the tactical decision-makers.

COACHES IN THE CLUB

"That's all very well, but what do I do when sixty assorted players turn up for my session?" Well, you certainly won't do a great deal of coaching. I don't believe it's possible to coach more than a single team effectively, and then only by careful organisation and delegation of responsibility. Once the players are accustomed to the way you work, you can handle maybe two teams, but not so well.

If you're going to coach then you must devote a fair amount of energy to increasing the number of people who can share the load. To have one coach per serious team, and one to jolly along the social players, is what the club must aim for. Fewer than that and the club is failing in its responsibility to the player—it cannot give him the help he needs, it cannot even be sure of the kind of player he is.

The first essential is to get your decision-makers assuming responsibility for their units, reflecting and confirming their position on the pitch. Briefing them properly for the practice, putting them fully in the picture so that they understand the aims and the methods, is part of their own preparation for taking charge on the pitch. The more players you can put in charge of sub-units—e.g. the front 5, the back row, the halves and inside-centre, the back three—the better. These are natural units not only for unit practice but e.g. for handling and individual skill practices.

Finding other coaches is often difficult, and compromises may be necessary that will give them the work-load they're prepared to accept. You can start with limited objectives. For example, it doesn't take long to equip an apprentice coach to master a single aspect of rugby—e.g. scrumming—and be able to do good work. From that basis he can broaden out, but almost from the start he's going to lighten your load. Again, it's not unlikely that the local schools have P.E. men or teachers who, given the chance, would come and help: I was in that position myself for years. Both specialist coaches and people from the school will need support to establish themselves with the players: don't make your invitations half-hearted. Put the players fully in the picture, and give the apprentice coach the support he needs.

TEAM TALK

The coach's job is to create steady progress for the individuals and the team. Provided they're properly prepared and structured such talks are eminently worthwhile.

We tend to talk on a Monday about the previous Saturday's game. This gives us time to assimilate what actually happened. I very rarely talk about the game until I've given myself time to sort things out, to talk to the players individually, and to hear what spectators are saying. Listen to everybody—any little point may come in useful. It's not that you give complete credence to everything you hear but you never know: even the most unlikely sources can reveal something of value. The other valuable thing about not talking immediately is that it gives you time to get back in balance. It would be a remarkably philosophic coach who didn't get involved emotionally in his team's fortunes—it's one source of energy and commitment—but it's not a good basis for decision-making. I restrict myself to the most general of good-natured remarks until I'm ready to talk to the team.

Even then, the first thing I do is to get each member of the team to talk. It's very important that each member of the team should get a chance to express what he feels and what he's noticed. He's got to feel that he's an active part of the team, and that he's got a respectable contribution to make. We start at full-back and work straight through to No. 8, with the captain contributing the last word. We discuss each point as it comes up. As each player finishes his contribution, he's asked two questions: what he learned from the game, and what he's got to work on in the coming week.

This works most effectively when the players are accustomed to it. The coach's job in this first phase is to keep the discussion positive and to act as chairman. The positive atmosphere is vital. This is a great way to get petty moans and grievances out in the open and fully ventilated. The key method in getting a positive atmosphere is to plug the notion that the people who feel worst about mistakes on the field are the people who make them, and that what they need, on the field and off, is support. One for all, and all for one is every team's motto. I've never understood the point of haranguing a player who already feels bad. What's needed is to build up a proper pride in the individuals, the units, and the team. You can do more by talking as if what you want to be true is true, than by bemoaning its absence. By telling a winger he's very quick, you can, remarkable though it sounds, make him quicker—and so on for every position. If you want a player to think, compliment him on his thinking. It may not work at once; it rarely fails in the long term: a lot of player's—or a team's—ability is conditioned by his belief in himself. That has got to be built up, and kept in proportion by the quality standards set by the coach.

Much of what you want to discuss will have come up during this first phase. In the second phase, we generally try to clarify the main issues on which decisions have to be made for the units and the team. At this stage, the coach is more evidently in charge, but if he's chaired the first phase intelligently there should be general agreement about what he puts forward. The aim is to get agreement, but the essential thing is to make sensible decisions, and the coach must take the lead in this: you cannot coach by committee.

The third phase sets out the arrangements for the week so that we all know what we're going to do and any difficulties can be ironed out.

The same principles apply when the talk is focused on the next match rather than that just past. It would be ridiculous not to use what information is available, and much of that may come from the players. But in looking forward to the next game we are less concerned with the opposition than with preparing ourselves— getting ourselves into a frame of mind in which *we welcome the opportunity to show what we can do.* This seems a much more fruitful attitude than encouraging either of the twin dangers— unreal optimism or unreal anxiety. With younger players especially these are real underminers of performance. What we need to ripen in all our players is an honest dignity of endeavour—a willingness to go out and take pride in producing our best as an expression of the self rather than a simple response to external events.

MATCH ANALYSIS

The coach (or selector) can rarely afford the luxury of being a mere spectator at matches. You give up the simple pleasure of enjoying the game, of being entertained, as soon as you accept responsibility for improving the play of the individuals, units and team. This means that you have to be on your guard against the viewing habits of the average spectator. It's worthwhile examining what these are:
1. He *ball-watches*—which immediately focuses his attention on *what* is happening rather than *why*. As a coach you have to view more widely, taking in as many of the elements concerned as possible. You must see what's happening (or what happened) *off* the ball that affected the immediate situation.

   A further result of this is that the spectator tends to see much *more of the attack than he does of the defence,* and this exaggerates his underlying preference for the excitement of attack. The coach, intent on seeing more of the game, must watch defence just as closely as he does attack. Secure defence is the only possible basis for a winning team, and it's vital that he monitors the team's defence in every match.

2. The spectator assesses performance *impressionistically*: he tends to be unduly impressed by single moments of play—in which a player does uncharacteristically well or badly. He tends also to be unaware of negative evidence: if a player isn't in view—even although he certainly ought to be—his absence isn't noted. The coach must give the player a clear notion of what he ought to be doing, and judge him in that frame of reference. Equally, if he wishes to assess a particular player he must be prepared to concentrate on him, on and off the ball, for perhaps two or three minutes at a time, at least twice in the match.

3. The spectator tends to be *blinded by his allegiance* to the team, and his judgement is clouded by his assumptions. The coach has far greater reason to be involved—it would be an altogether exceptionally well-balanced man who could give a great deal of time and energy to the team without being in a high degree affected by its performance. Nevertheless, like a good player his mind must go on working dispassionately through the hurly-burly of the game. He may find that *distancing* himself *physically*—putting himself at a remove from the action—may help, but it's more useful to distance himself *mentally*, by some objective process, such as writing notes (which presents information in a much more accessible form than talking into a recorder) or doing some kind of analysis such as is dealt with later in this chapter.

Even when he has overcome these tendencies the coach must face one fact: he can never see more than a limited amount of the game. He may change his position during the match, but he can't be in more than one position at a time—and the action may be 100m away from him. Much of what he's watching involves numbers of players at close quarters, when it's impossible to see what's happening. He can make only educated guesses at the psychological state of his players, and the reasons for it. But the radical problem is the sheer quantity of action, on and off the ball, that may be relevant to his coaching.

In view of these difficulties, the coach has got to accept that he shouldn't attempt to do too much too quickly. He must see analysis as a continuing process, in which he will concentrate on only a very few things in a given match. The key to effective analysis is accurate prediction—prediction of what elements in the team's play are most likely to require improvement. Prediction allows effective concentration so that instead of being distracted by a potential overload of information the coach can look at what counts. This can't be an exclusive concern, for the coach will register a good deal that isn't in predicted focus for him—indeed it's more than likely that the specific concern will be limited to specific phases in the play, and so in other phases he will be free to see the rest of the team.

In all analysis, as in the whole coaching process, having clearly defined expectations is an enormous help in simplifying the apparent complexities of the action. If, for example, you have a clear picture of your defensive shape, it's much easier to see what's going wrong. In this respect, rugby is a much easier game to examine than soccer: rugby can be reduced to a whole series of predictable situations much more easily than the very fluid, very open, 360° game of soccer. This applies to the individual, to the unit, and to team play. As coach you should have clear expectations in respect of each, and so be able to spot discrepancies.

At this stage you may seek to reduce your observation to figures. This is of some importance to yourself: it forces you to watch consistently, and it crystallises your observation. It's of even more value in focusing the attention of your players: they may have doubts about your subjective assessment of their play, but figures they must take more seriously.

This is already done at a fairly low level—e.g. strikes against the head, or line-out possession. It's very easy to extend it to e.g. possession from rucks or mauls where we took the ball in, or when they took the ball in; possession of the ball when one of our backs is tackled, or one of theirs. These are basically either/or situations, and, therefore, easy to check. Rather more difficult is dealing with a

BASIC ANALYSIS FORM

Ball		Pass		Run		Kick	
good	bad	good	bad	good	bad	good	bad

multiple choice—e.g. a scrum-half's use of the ball. But it's still simple enough to produce a basic analysis form (p. 36).

This is objective insofar as it establishes what proportion of the ball he received, he passed, ran with, or kicked. It's subjective in its estimate of performance quality, though the subjective element could easily be reduced by introducing definitions of "good" and "bad"—e.g. "good ball" allows the player freedom of choice, a "bad run" leads to possession being lost, and so on. In fact, the coach quickly and easily learns to assess and mark.

The use of this kind of form provides basic information for the coach—it helps him identify the area on which he must concentrate. It may, for example, reveal that even with good ball, the scrum-half's passing is bad. The objective figures will help focus the scrum-half's attention on the need to improve his pass. The coach can then take his analysis a stage further, concentrating on the passes and trying to identify e.g. a categorical weakness—passing to the right, pivot passing, or whatever. This movement from wide to fine focus is the typical progression in analysis.

I ought, perhaps, to note that very few coaches—even good coaches—do this kind of objective analysis. I do it myself occasionally *for the players*. But most coaches do employ this method of working: they may not put it on paper, but it's the way their minds work, and the way they focus their observation.

For years I made comprehensive notes, in chronological order, of the match. They were all "subjective"—the notes were my reading of the situation: that a given player was out of position, was off-balance as he placed-kicked, and so on. It was an excellent discipline, and it meant that the players were given specific advice. Looking back, it seems likely that any ability I now have in analysis, or in ideas of how it should be done, were fostered by this habit, and that perhaps other apprentice coaches could adopt it with benefit.

5
The Structured Session

In many ways, the most critical step the coach can make is to adopt a structure for his sessions. Whatéver structure he accepts will exactly mirror his aims, and the absence of such a structure can only suggest a lack of definition in his aims.

The structure should aim to give purpose, variety, progression and some degree of inclusiveness to each session. It should limit mistakes and build confidence by moving from easy to difficult, simple to complex, low pressure to high pressure, small units to larger units, more basic to more sophisticated. It should encourage the coach to give a thoughtful coverage to all aspects of the game within his immediate resources of players, time, and facilities. It should give maximum activity in the time available.

Any step towards adopting a structure, even a rudimentary one, is to be welcomed, since it implies an awareness of more elements that require attention. Naturally enough, the structure that seems best adapted to the needs of total rugby has to be fully inclusive. Nevertheless, the structure is simple, strong, and easy to use. It satisfies all the criteria of the previous paragraph.

1. *Discussion of the previous game*   – see page 32
2. *Warm up* – a. stretching   – see page 46
          b. intensivè handling   – see page 48
          c. strength exercises   – see page 62
3. *Individual techniques*   – see page 66
4. *Unit techniques*   – see page 106
5. *Team patterns*   – see page 222
6. *Fitness work*   – see page 269
7. *Clinic skills* – these are basically individual positional skills (hooking, line-out jumping, scrum-half pass, fly-half kicking and so on) that need a lot of the coach's attention. Since you cannot keep numbers of players waiting while you work extensively with one or two, you must make time for this kind of work before or after the session, or while the rest are actively engaged in exercises that demand less of your attention.)

The outline of this structured session is also the structure of the whole of this section, and details of what can be included under each heading will be found in the relevant chapters.

It's obvious that you cannot do more than a selection of exercises in any one session, and that the coach must use judgement in deciding what is to be included on a particular evening. Most good clubs have two sessions a week, each lasting for one and a half to two hours. Players giving up this time are entitled to expect that the time will be well spent. Careful preparation is, therefore, absolutely essential.

There are four requirements: *selective planning, intensity, quality,* and *coaching.*

1. *Selective planning*

Your *selection* will be guided *under each heading* by:

(a) observing what was unsatisfactory in the previous match; and
(b) having a clear idea of what will be needed for the weeks ahead, and (for the players and the club) the seasons ahead.

Your *planning* will be guided by:

(a) the structure you've adopted; and
(b) a clear, detailed idea of the team practices with which you wish to finish the technical part of the evening: you must build towards them so that their success is assured. You must finish strong.

You may very well find that you have to omit whole elements of the structure – that on a particular evening you cannot find time for a discussion of the previous match or work on individual techniques – and that you can devote only a short time to others. Nevertheless, awareness of the structure will help you over a sequence of sessions to get an appropriate balance. It would be futile to indicate how much time you devote to what – it depends precisely on your judgement of what your particular team needs at that particular time. The only element I cannot imagine leaving out is intensive handling, if only in the form of touch rugby: even if we spent all but the last fifteen minutes on discussing the game and sorting out problems, we'd have a quick handling session.

2. *Intensity*

You demand *high work rate* for your players in the match – "pass and *run*", "tackle and *run*", "jump and *run*" – and you must expect the same work-rate of the players and yourself in the practice. Of course there are times when you need a slower tempo – to solve problems, or get players thinking, or simply to give them a rest – but the emphasis in general has to be on cheerful, organised, activity. To achieve this you need:

(a) to have the programme clear, in your mind and on a piece of paper in your pocket – we don't want awkward pauses while you think of what you want to do next;

(b) to have a list of points you must personally concentrate on – preferably reduced by forethought to work with particular players in particular situations;

(c) to have players i/c each unit, each with clear (preferably written) instructions on what has to be done – this helps free you for (b);

(d) to have in staple activities – e.g. handling, or scrumming – set times, or number of repetitions for each activity;

(e) to have the spaces used clear and limited, and therefore economical and safe – and for this you'd be well advised to have say, eight ten metre square grids marked out behind the dead-ball line, and the scrum-machine in position; and

(f) to have one ball available for every four players.

These requirements are justified by the results they produce – they simplify the organisation drastically.

3. *Quality*

There is no point in practising mistakes – a sloppy practice in which players fail to concentrate on improving their performance is worse than no practice at all. If you feel they need a rest, give them a rest; if you feel they need a light-hearted games session, give them one: but don't confuse these needs with a coaching session.

As soon as you sensibly can, *set quality standards* – e.g. if the ball is dropped in a handling exercise, start that exercise again. But remember the need to move from easy to difficult: don't start with the difficult *and* high quality standards. The aim is to tune them up with steady success.

Try to *let no mistake* go *unchecked or unhelped.* You must be in there, exhorting, cajoling, but above all *explaining.*

Quality is not something that happens overnight. You have to work, perhaps for years, to attain it. And you have to work to maintain it – even to the extent of indoctrinating the coach who will eventually replace you.

4. *Coaching*

Getting quality work from the players and coaching go hand in hand. To a marked extent your enthusiasm, your commitment, your sense of standards, your energy output condition those of the players. If something goes wrong, there's a reason for it, and your job is to point it out and put it right. No exercise does good of itself – it may simply ingrain existing faults: get in there, and *coach.* If you can, introduce something *new* every session, even if it's only a variation on an existing practice. But remember that coaching is basically concerned with the hard, unglamorous work of making sure that your players do everything effectively, and that entails repetition and untiring attention to detail.

Setting up practice situations

In all aspects of coaching, we're generally moving from *technique* – establishing an effective form of action – towards *skill* – operating the technique effectively in the competitive match situation – by *conditioning* the pressures on the players acquiring the ability. This applies to establishing judgement as well as physical skills. We've already seen this process underlying the progression within our structured session – a movement, basically, from easy to difficult. There's nothing particularly demanding about it, but we've got to be aware of it all the time.

There are various elements we can control to alter the pressure on the players: the *numbers* taking part; the kind and degree of *opposition;* the required *speed* of action and repetition; the length of *time* over which we continue the exercise; and the *space* in which we are operating. We must also be very clear about the action we want them to acquire; if it's *complex* we may have to see whether it can be presented in parts that make sense, and can be mastered separately without detracting from the final effectiveness of the whole action. And, of course, we can make it easier by explaining as we go, relating the whole to the match situation, and the parts to the whole. The last requires careful rehearsal: the right words aren't always available when they're wanted, and if they're not right – exact and brief – they simply get in the way.

1. *Numbers*: the greater the numbers, the greater the potential confusion, or the less intensive the exercise for the individual player. Start small and work up.
2. *Opposition*: this is a critical factor. Initially we must recognise the need to practice both offensive and defensive techniques – that for each attacking technique there's got to be a defensive technique, and that they're equally important. But in acquiring these techniques we must – until the players reach a very satisfactory skill level – be quite clear which aspect we're working on. We must bias the practice in favour of one or the other, gradually lessening the bias as the competence increases.

   At the lowest technical level, we start with *unopposed* practice. The great bulk of the intensive handling, for example, is done unopposed so that the players can concentrate on the ball without worrying about opposition. We can then introduce *passive* opposition – e.g. standing still to provide a focal point for passing, or moving forward for the same purpose but making no attempt to interfere with the operation. You may find difficulty in getting your "opposition" to observe the conditions. We had a large, craggy, and very amiable Portuguese coach on Summer School one year who was nicknamed "Passive Defence" from his total inability to restrain his competitiveness: his good resolutions lasted till his opponent – they were working on mauling – made contact, and then it was total war. So when you can, deprive them of choice – put them in set positions, e.g. with their arms linked, so that they *can't* interfere too much. But the basic notion to get across is of a joint learning activity: they'll all get their chance. It's important that they do get to this point for there's got to be a kind of opposition in which they offer more than token resistance but a resistance *judged* so that the learners go on learning.
3. *Speed of action* is something that comes with habituation. At the start it's usually best to slow the whole thing down so that the technique is clearly and effectively carried out. This may involve e.g. carrying it out at walking pace, then trotting. *Speed of*

repetition must be controlled in the same way – starting with single attempts and working towards pressure practices once the technique has been mastered.

4. *Time* becomes important with the onset of fatigue. It's certainly true that the skill may well be used in conditions of fatigue during the match, and there's something to be said, therefore, for technical practices to match this as fitness work does. But I've found myself that technical work is best done while the players are fresh and receptive, and that exercises should finish before the interest level drops.

5. *Space* is important in designing practices, partly from the need to economise in time and energy, and partly from the need for the coach to be near enough to do coaching. If an exercise involves more movement than is necessary, intensity of repetition is lost; if players are dispersed the coach must be remote from some of them. It's desirable, therefore, to limit movement and it's recommended that this be done physically – e.g. by keeping the work between the 22 metre line and the goal-line, or by using grids. Grids – 10 to 11 metres square, marked out e.g. behind the dead-ball line – are invaluable for repetition practices. Every coach should use them.

In applying conditioning, the coach has got to use his judgement all the time. It's equally unproductive to start at too low a tempo with the gifted player, or too high a tempo with the less gifted. Nevertheless, the basics are very important: with gifted players the mistake I usually make is to expect too much, and move too fast. The other danger is for the coach to become over-pernickety and dogmatic in the conformity he demands in the form of the exercise. What he needs is to get the key-factors clear and effective form established. After all, the game is always developing and the coach's ideas should be developing with it. We should always be learning from our players, and we won't if the players are drilled into a mechanical conformity: we need to get them efficient and get them thinking. In this as in everything else, we need a co-operative venture. A coach should speak with authority based on his experience and recognition of the essentials, and his willingness to go on learning and experimenting.

PART 3
Basic Preparation

6
Stretching

One way to avoid pulling muscles is to do regular stretching exercises, and to repeat them before you do any strenuous activity. And of course if you know that you are liable to have trouble in a particular area this kind of preparation is essential. There's also the possibility of encouraging specific flexibility to meet a particular positional requirement: e.g. the hooker needs great mobility in the hips; the kicker, a long range of leg movement. This can be improved by steady work: don't rush it, or you'll do more harm than good.

The important thing in stretching is to accustom the body to the demands of the game. It does no good to impose sudden strains in your warm up – that's exactly what you are trying to avoid. So go into each exercise gently, and don't bounce. You aim to stretch to the point where you become conscious of strain. As soon as you feel it, stretch no further. Instead, concentrate your mental attention on that particular part of your body, and hold the position till your muscles adjust to it. Then gently go a little further.

The aim is to try to relax the body even as you stretch it: think loose. You cannot do this fast, or in time with other people. Get changed early, and spend ten minutes with a minimum of movement – these should be seen as static exercises. Go easy: take a little longer, and your body will work better. It will also last longer.

What exercises you use is much less important than this leisurely concentration on doing them to best effect. You may find that inhaling and exhaling slowly and deeply helps in this. You may also find that an established routine, in which you move from exercise to exercise up the body lets you slip into the right mood.

Here is a basic sequence of exercises; you can elaborate them to suit yourself.

i. *lower leg*: place your hands, hip high, against a wall, and sink your chest below your arms.
ii. *calves*: using your abdominals, pull down slowly to touch your toes.
iii. *hamstrings*: lie on your back, and bring your feet over to touch the ground beyond your head – push your heels further away.

46

iv. *groin*: sit back against a wall, and bring your feet up, sole to sole, and tucked in. Gently and steadily press down on your knees with your hands.

v. *hips*: link hands overhead, and dip steadily to either side; then describe wide circles with your hips.

vi. *shoulders*: link hands overhead, then reach back to touch either shoulder.

vii. *general*: link your fingers behind your back, and lock your arms. Then gently arch your body backwards, dropping your head, and bringing your arms up towards it. Next, bend forward, bringing your arms over and down.

7
Intensive Handling Practices

Before doing anything strenuous, explosive, or bruising, it's advisable to get the body to its best working temperature. Before working on more advanced techniques in rugby, it's essential to be handling the ball confidently. Put them together and use *intensive handling* as the major part of your warm-up to the structured session.

All of these handling exercises are also SUPPORT EXERCISES. You must hammer home at all times the vital importance of *thought* in the players off the ball: they must constantly *think* about their positioning in the movement, and *discipline* themselves to get to and remain in the best position. They must *never* run blind.

The key notion in all passing is that the hand behind the ball (the right hand if passing to the left, and vice versa) provides all the power, all the direction, and part of the control: it must stay in contact with the ball on the line of pass. The key idea in all receiving is to get the far-away hand on the path of the ball – playing down the line, so to speak – and use the other one to trap it.

Every pass must be in front of the receiver – always pass to space – and whenever possible at about hip height. It should never be a harder pass than is needed on that occasion. Check, too, that the receiver is really trying to watch the ball into his hands. You may find that in trying to run fast he tenses his arms: he's got to relax his arms, and learn to run from the hips down. You may find that as he runs he arches his back: he's got to relax his trunk and run with his head over the ball.

The classic lateral pass, swinging away over the opposite foot, is a unit skill for the backs but even they must have a varied repertoire for getting the ball away. Every player must be able to *keep the ball out of the tackle area*: he may practise passing from *above the head* and *below the knee. "Your opponent may get you – he must never get the ball."* He must also be able to *pass far* and *give and take quickly* You must hammer home the paramount need to *pass and run:* don't waste time admiring your pass – back up intelligently for the return pass. Equally you must hammer home the idea – *you are responsible for the ball until the player you passed to has disposed of*

48

it: if anything goes wrong, you are the nearest player, the one to tidy up – the receiver will certainly have over-run.

In your handling sequence, as with all practices, start easy and build up confidence before you try the difficult: success is a great motivation to keep on going. For example, move the ball left before you move it right, and keep on moving it left till the players are confident.

To get the most out of the time available use lots of balls and small groups of players – three in a group will handle twice as often as six. When you can, work in natural groups – those most likely to work together in the match.

Use a small unit of distance to aid concentration: you get far better results doing four runs of twenty-five yards rather than one of a hundred.

Set a definite unit of work: "we'll do five twenty-fives of speed passing."

Set quality standards: "If anyone drops the ball, we all start again."

Once you've said it, do it – so be careful about the standards you set.

In handling practices, the underlying need is to keep the ball spinning around. The player carrying the ball is a *target* for the opposition. Although in the match the player who gets the chance to run will run wholeheartedly, driving forward into space (or, at close-quarters, beating a man and giving a pass), the great aim in practice is to *condition the players off the ball to be up in support*. If support is always there there need never be a simple target for the opposition. Emphasise, then, speed of passing – get it and give it! – and quality of support.

A. CHECK LIST OF UNOPPOSED HANDLING PRACTICES

1. Line passing   **3s or 4s**

    (a) rhythm – move the ball easy at a trot, then faster;
    (b) length – spread wide and swing the ball;
    (c) speed – give and take as fast as possible;
    (d) all passes from above the head;
    (e) all passes from below the knee;

   (f) alternate high and low;

   (g) all passes with arms reaching out (beyond the opponent);

   (h) make up variations: e.g. 1 puts it over 2 to 3 who pushes down to 2 who puts it over 3 to 4 who pushes it down to 3 .... and so on.

2. Switch passing   2s or 3s or 4s

   (a) switch in pairs;

   (b) switch in fours;

   (c) switch in threes;

   (d) introduce dummy switches.

3. Looping   4s

   (a) loop – normal passes, left and right

   (b) loop – passes from above head, left and right

   (c) loop – passes from below knee, left and right

   (d) loop – changing direction

   (e) loop – offer and take at hip level

   (f) loop – offer and take at knee level

   (g) loop – inverted

   (h) pick up and put down

4. Bunch passing   5s or 6s

   (a) left and right

   (b) 1-5

   (c) over the top

5. Combined handling practices

Once your players are handling with pride, put together a string of passes which exercises both their ball exchange skills and their control of positioning e.g.:

   (a) 1 does a miss to 3, 2 loops to outside of 3, 2 switches with 4 . . . who feeds 3 and then 1; or

   (b) 1 does a miss to 3, 2 loops to outside of 3, 2 does dummy switch to 4 and runs out with 3, 2, and 1 running into support positions.

6. Space control practices

A further useful refinement is to call for a change of direction whenever it looks as though the movement may go into touch. If you start the players looping across the field from the corner flag, they'll drift out towards the 22. At the vital moment there must be an instantaneous change of direction while either the looping continues or is replaced by another form of passing.

NOTES ON UNOPPOSED HANDLING PRACTICES

Line passing

The basic needs are *rhythm* – so that the next man knows when to expect the pass – *length* – so that you stretch the defence, forcing them to defend more ground and thus creating gaps – and *speed* – so that your players can keep the ball alive under pressure. Keep reiterating *quality, quality, quality*. Any fool can give a *bad* pass: all our passes must be precise. *Never practise faults.* A pass that isn't in front of the receiver, even if it goes to his side, is a *bad* pass; a pass that goes even marginally high or low is a *bad* pass. Our passing must be *perfect*.

Remember that all the power and direction comes from the *hand behind the ball* – the right when passing left, the left when passing right. The longer the pass, the more you must concentrate on *staying in contact with the ball on the line of pass.* And the receiver of the long pass must discipline himself to stay that much further back – the ball will take longer to arrive. *Think, think, think.*

For *passes below knee-level* reach down with the hand behind the ball – try it one-handed. For *passes above the head,* get up in the air and direct the ball down: don't lob it. For both, *concentrate* even harder on placing the ball precisely where the receiver wants it – at hip level, in front – and at an easily-controllable place.

For *speed passing,* the passer must concentrate on giving the perfect pass, the receiver on reaching for the ball with the opposite hand and swinging it straight across in a single, fast, *controlled,* movement. *Speed* and *inaccuracy* are *mutually exclusive.*

Switches

The easy way to start switches is in *pairs*: get one player on the touch line, one on the five-yard line, switch in the middle, and go out to the lines before turning for the next switch. Making them go out is the easy way to get them *thinking*. In switches, the player receiving the ball must defer coming in as long as possible to minimise his opponent's reaction time. Remember: the ball carrier always turns *towards* the receiver, *looks* at him, and *offers* him the ball. *Never practise faults!* It's very unlikely that you will have a ball for every two players, so once they've got the fundamental form move on to switches in *fours*. Think of each four as two pairs doing switches – as each pair finishes its switch, an ordinary pass gives the ball to the other pair for their turn. Make them *think* about position: the pair waiting for the ball *must* slow down or they'll get in front of the ball. Then go on to switches in *threes*: centre man starts, runs right and switches with right-hand man, who takes it across and switches with left-hand man, who takes it across and switches with man originally in the centre, and so on. Start your players running downfield between the five and fifteen yard lines and going out to the line before coming back.

Looping

This is a great *work-rate* handling practice. It drills home the basic work-rate adage: *pass and run*. Don't loop with single men down the line: the loop used in a back division move has to be precisely set up – it doesn't fit into intensive handling. Instead, *pass and run to the end of the line* so that there is constant support on the end of the line. If they're doing it correctly, the ball-carrier should be able to move the ball *at once*: if he has to delay (and so become a target) the support is running too slowly. *Don't let it happen.* Get them looping with hip-high, reasonably short, passes to the left. Then do it to the right. Then longer passes – much harder work. Then all passes above the head – still going to the receiver hip-high in front. Then all passes below the knee. Once they're proficient, get them *thinking*. Work across the 25, changing direction of looping each time they come to a line: when a ball-carrier approaches the goal-line or the 25 his support players must keep in line to reverse the direction of passing. Then try close-contact looping: in line ahead, taking the ball and offering it, but not passing it – the receiver must *take* it and in turn offer it. Emphasise the need for the ball-carrier *not to turn* but to keep driving straight forward. Start with the ball at *hip-height,* then try it at *knee level,* and they're on their way to good mauling and rucking technique.

Inverted looping

This is a useful variation. Start with the ball-carrier on the five-yard line. He drives out towards touch and, just before he gets there, goes up in the air, twists, and passes the ball inside to the next man who repeats the action – get them to imagine they're being pushed out by the defence, and must keep the ball in play, or that they're a back-row making space by running wide and putting the ball back into the space.

Picking up the ball

Another essential looping practice is picking up the ball, running in line ahead the ball-carrier takes three or four strides and puts the ball down, next man drives past, picks up, and repeats.

Make them *think: always put the ball down away from the opposition; always control your distance and pace so that you are in position to pick up* – if you are too close or too fast you won't make it.

Bunch passing

The last category of pure passing exercises is bunch passing. They are basically for the forwards, simulating their drive forward up the pitch, but all players should do them. Hammer home the basic support notions of *width and depth* – of getting into useful and interesting support positions. Once again, all *passing* exercises are basically *support* exercises. Work to get into a position where you can really contribute – *never run blind*. Work these bunch practices in 5s, 6s or 7s. Get the players to number off – having to work in sequence is an excellent inducement to thinking ahead and work-rate. Each player calls for the ball in sequence with his number.

1. Left and right:

If the ball-carrier *received* the ball on his left, he must *give* it on his left – and the next player in numerical sequence must turn up there, calling out his number; he will receive it on his right, and must give it on his right. The supporting players are forced to *think* about their position. The effect of this passing is to keep the bunch as a whole driving straight down field but for the ball to go through what amounts to a series of switches. Hammer home *width:* we must stretch the forward defence, just as our backs stretch the back defence – we must create *space*. Hammer home *depth:* we must have *security* if the ball goes down, and *time* to select the best direction of attack.

The simplest way of introducing this essential exercise is to start with an even number of players – say six. Number them off. Assemble them on the 22, facing across the pitch, with the odd numbers on one side of the line and the even numbers on the other. Tell them that every pass must cross the line, and that each player in sequence must be shouting his own number and in position as soon as the previous player gets the ball. Once they are doing this, suggest that 3 running into position for 2's pass can run outside 1 as well as inside him – creating, in effect, a miss move; get them all to experiment with this. Then add a player. This immediately means that every player will have to switch across the line to be in position to receive alternate passes, and really gets them thinking about where they are running in support.

2. *1 – 5:*

When the ball carrier gets the ball he drives to the front. As soon as he gets there, the next player in numerical sequence calls for it, and the ball-carrier must get it to him at once. The ball receiver must be in space when he calls, so that the ball can come to him easily, and must run to present a difficult target. As soon as he hits the front, the next player calls. The sequence continues as a cycle.

3. *Over the top:*

Ball-carrier drives to front, goes up in the air, and passes to a player at back of the bunch. He in turn drives to the front, avoiding the players in front of him, and the sequence continues. Emphasise the need for the individual player to think about space, and changing direction: he must make it difficult for the defence. Players off the ball can run with arms high to make the pass harder, or with arms horizontal to encourage a driving position in the runner.

In all these bunch exercises emphasise the need for *ball speed:* as in looping, the support player must be there immediately the ball-carrier is ready to pass. The aim is to get all players thinking ahead, confident of running and handling, confident of support. If the ball is dropped, the nearest man drops on it and holds it off the ground. The rest get round behind and set up a maul.

4. Passing over the shoulder

Handling practices are an easy way of extending the players' range of skills – ways of maintaining the continuity of attack. You should be on the lookout for fresh ideas. One came my way in the second round of the Middlesex Sevens. We'd just lost Clive Woodward with a broken leg against London Scottish. The ball was going right across our line, with Alistair Harg close behind. It reached Roy Black who drew Alistair on and popped the ball back over his left shoulder: we ran straight through and scored – a score made possible by the improvised pass. But why should so potentially valuable a pass be 'improvised'? Why not make it a standard part of every player's repertoire?

You work out the mechanics – easy enough, for like every pass the hand behind the ball provides the power and the direction – and establish match needs – you evidently don't want it lobbed up in the air, so tell them 'get the hand behind the ball high, and pass in front'. Then you work on possible exercises till you get one that works. For example, get your players in fours, trotting down the 5m line. Player 1 has the ball. He swerves out to touch, and passes back over his shoulder to player 2, who's still on the line. Player 1 has moved out, taken his 'opponent' with him, and popped the ball back into the space he has created. Make sure they practise on both sides: when they've all gone down one side, get them to go back down the 5m line to where they started from.

Then get them peeling off alternately to left and right.

Then get the player who has just passed the ball to set off immediately after the new ball-carrier as a defender – he'll come from exactly the right direction to be taken out by the pass.

I've actually seen a lovely try scored by this pass being repeated four times down our right-hand touch, and, yes, we went on to win the Sevens!

B. CHECK LIST OF HANDLING EXERCISES AGAINST A CONDITIONED DEFENCE

(a) 2 v 1
(b) 3 v 2
(c) 3 v 2 switches

The exercises described in the previous section are designed to make the players confident in the basic techniques of handling. The essential move from technique to skill comes with the introduction of some opposition. What every player must aim to develop is *judgement* – his decision-making is what distinguishes the good player from the competent one. Some players, by their position – the best example is fly-half – must be excellent at this, and deal tactically with the whole team situation on the field. All, however, must acquire judgement in the immediate case of when and where to pass, where and how to support.

As in the last section, you start with the easy and seek to build confidence before you go on to the difficult. You may start with a wholly passive defence, standing still, and move through a walking to a trotting defence before exposing the attacking players to a fully active defence.

2 v 1

One of the absolutely basic situations towards which any organised team is purposfully working is the simple overlap – the 2 against 1 situation. You'll find, though, that even apparently capable players have some difficulty in dealing with it. Yet the key factors are simple:

1. To run slightly out towards the supporting player – this is essential to make the pass easy. (Precisely as in all 'throwing' events, from hitting a golf ball to putting a shot, the hips must be able to pivot: in a pass to the left, the left hip must not block the right.) The most effective – though not philosophically satisfying – advice is to "run for the defender's outside shoulder".
2. Once you have gauged the defender's position, look at your supporting player: "look early" is the best advice.
3. The pass must be made early enough for the ball-carrier to be in no danger of being caught, late enough for the defender to be

unable to catch the supporting player. This is the essential nature of *judgement* in passing or in initiating a move, and all players must be given every chance of practising it.

4. The supporting player must seek:
   - (a) to maintain a position adequately out from the ball-carrier – to "use his pass", making allowances if it's a left-handed pass;
   - (b) to maintain a position adequately behind him, in case of any slowing down as the ball-carrier prepares to pass;
   - (c) to look beyond the immediate defender for cover defence; and
   - (d) to concentrate on taking the ball

The coach must hammer home the idea that the immediate 2 v 1 is the only case where a player should draw a man before passing.

3 v 2

The coach and a player act as passive opposition to the other players working in groups of three. The aim is to make the players look at the defenders and *think*. There are three possible configurations of the two defenders:

the inside man leads – this is equivalent to a 2 v 1 situation followed by another 2 v 1 situation, and follows on naturally from the previous exercise;

both come up flat – for the ball-carrier to draw the first defender is fatal. He must delay his pass only so long as will prevent the first defender covering the third attacker. He must always allow the second attacker time to set up his 2 v 1 and put the third attacker away; *the outside man leads* – the ball-carrier must react immediately, checking his own man before swinging hard out behind the outside man and so forcing an immediate break.

These three situations are basic – they cover all the defensive configurations you are likely to meet. Working through them ensures that your players become accustomed to summing up the opposition rather than running blindly at them. All three exercises can be made progressively more difficult by the defenders moving forward – holding position relative to each other – progressively faster on each set. The defenders can go right down the pitch and the exercises then begin to develop the characteristics of a *pressure* practice, with the players having to dash back into position to set up the next repetition.

3 v 2 switches

This is really a simple development of three man switching described on p. 57 above, but the addition of even passive opposition allows the coach to refine the running of his players. The diagram shows the basic pattern of the running. The coach can concentrate on monitoring the angles of running and the timing of the pass. I normally stick out my hand as a direction marker to ensure that the ball receiver is far enough away to be safe from the tackle. You can vary the practice very simply – e.g. by transforming the second switch into a 2 v 1, or by making it into a dummy switch, with the ball-carrier accelerating away on the outside. (A moment's thought will show that in the match, the player best placed to decide whether to do switch or dummy-switch is the ball-receiver: he is looking infield and can see much more than the ball-carrier, whose attention should be on the receiver.) It's always advisable to insist that, after the switches, the ball is transferred back to the wing where it started – it's good for work-rate and positioning.

HANDLING GAMES

There are many handling games that, in some degree, relate to rugby: you'll find several in "Better Rugby", the introductory coaching book published by the R.U. But, in fact, I use only three –

1. keepball (and a variant "push-down keep-ball"),
2. benchball (as an indoor lighthearted variation), and
3. touch rugby.

Keepball

This is played between teams of two. The aim is to make as many passes as possible while you have possession. You gain possession –

    (a) when you intercept the ball;
    (b) when you get a two-handed touch on the ball-carrier;
    (c) when an opposition pass goes to ground.

It's best played in a grid. The coach emphasises such basics as moving into space in attack, picking up a man in defence, pressurising the ball-carrier, watching the potential receiver rather than the ball.

SWITCH PRACTICES

BASIC SWITCH PRACTICE
A. sets off with ball and switches with B. Both go out to the line before setting up next switch

Switch practice against passive opposition

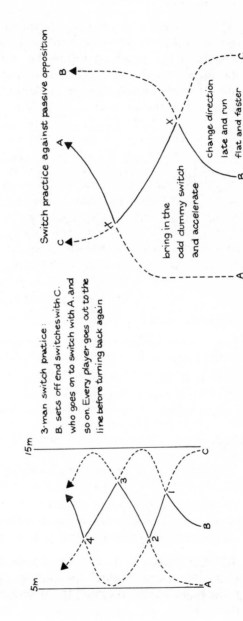

bring in the odd dummy switch and accelerate

change direction late and run flat and faster

3-man switch pratice:
B. sets off end switches with C. who goes on to switch with A. and so on. Every player goes out to the line before turning back again

A more useful variant is what I call "push-down keep-ball". This is exactly the same game except that the defender tries to catch the ball-carrier. The ball-carrier keeps possession if he can fight round and squeeze the ball down to touch the floor – the effective beginning of mauling and rucking. He is then allowed a free pass.

This is an absolutely basic game, and is, therefore, easily conditioned to suit the coach's purpose. Think of the elements you can condition:

1. kind of ball – e.g. a medicine ball
2. nature of pass – e.g. all above the head
3. number of steps by ball-carrier – e.g. none
4. method of moving – e.g. walking
5. method of losing possession – e.g. two hand touch below the knee
6. method of scoring – e.g. scoring tries
7. method of dealing with ball on ground – e.g. fall and feed
8. number of players – e.g. 3 a side.

It isn't a bad exercise for coaches to try inventing new games. It's another help with *variety*.

Benchball

Benchball is a lighthearted diversion, which we always play indoors, and which offers many of the ingredients of rugby. It's a very fluid game in which the ball-carrier can run and pass in any direction. He scores by getting behind the bench and throwing the ball to any of his team-mates standing on it. It's a game that can be easily conditioned to suit conditions and aims – e.g. by varying the division of the team between bench and play. The smaller the number in play, the tougher the game becomes.

You can use it to hammer home another basic of all games: *the need to move fast from attack into defence and vice-versa.* The moment possession changes is critical: whoever acts first can gain a real advantage. But this requires great *self-discipline.*

Touch rugby

However, touch rugby is far and away the most important (and most difficult) of these handling games. It's our staple warm-up activity and usually, by the time I arrive, there are one or two games in operation. The beauty of the game is that it offers a variety of handling experience under pressure that is real but not destructive, and it offers the best chance of developing *judgement* and *foresight*. At intervals there are waves of criticism in rugby circles about its being non-contact – as if all parts of a practice should involve contact! In every practice there must be room for contact elements and non-contact elements. The judicious balancing of these is one function of the coach.

The game is best played between teams of four or five – much larger and the individual player doesn't get an adequate amount of handling. In essence, the aim is to transform the one against one situation into a two against one. In many ways the game is closest to Sevens once possession has been secured, and it's certainly a key factor in our own success in the short game.

I use two basic conditions which bring out very different qualities in the play – single touch defence, and double touch. In both cases the defenders have to register a two-handed touch on the shorts – any less stringent condition makes it too easy for the defenders. In single touch, the defenders gain possession if they get a two-handed touch on the ball-carrier; in double touch, the attacker can go for the break, forcing it on the first touch and counting on putting a supporting player clear. If the defenders, however, get a two-handed touch on the supporting player, they gain possession. The first form of the game encourages the ball-carrier to hold the ball while support players run off him to create overlap positions; the second encourages quick appreciation by both ball-carrier and support player of a possible advantage and puts a premium on immediate action. Both incorporate basic principles of attack and defence.

These may be summarised as follows:

1. The team gaining possession must immediately *stretch* – forcing the defenders to cover more ground and creating bigger gaps for the ball-carriers to attack: the wingers must get outside their opponents.
2. Every attacking player must be *assessing* the opposing team so that the ball-carrier can *feint at strength,* and those running off the ball can then *strike at weakness* – which tends to encourage using "the short side"; a moment's reflection will show that the extra man joining a 1 against 1 situation creates a complete overlap, joining a 2 against 2 situation creates a 3 against 2 –

which in turn is better than 4 against 3 or any higher figure.

3. *The team formation* will always tend (in attack or defence) to have the fastest players out on the wings, where the easiest and most frequent overlaps will occur.

4. The defending team will adopt a *zone-defence* and it soon becomes apparent to them that all must work together, and preserve a flat-line defence. (This is equivalent to the front-three defence in the backs, and is voluntarily deprived of the essential depth in defence given in the full-size game by the back-three and covering forwards, and in Sevens by the sweeper.)

5. The defending team will soon realise the need to pressurise the opposition, forcing the ball-carrier to pass, and taking out those he can pass to.

6. The individual players come to a *proper judgement* of their own attacking ability relative to their immediate opponents.

7. All the attacking players are made to realise the importance of *ball-speed* and encouraged by the light-hearted atmosphere to improve their own speed of handling; and –

8. A vital consideration, that I've left to last – it impresses on the attacking players the importance of *space*: that simply to run at the opposition without a clear idea of how the attack is to develop is to waste that most precious commodity, space. This applies both to the ball-carrier and to the supporting players. Set it up *early*.

It's up to the coach to coach the game – his job is to help make the players aware of these considerations. In fact, beyond a certain level, this must be his *main* preoccupation. Nothing is more important for the potentially very good player than developing the kind of *forethought and judgement* I've been describing.

The variety of handling exercises and games outlined in this chapter is capable of almost indefinite extension – all the coach need do is watch matches intently and isolate any form of running or handling that seems potentially useful, then devise a form of exercise that allows frequent repetition under varying pressures. We need far more people doing this. We can never have enough different handling exercises to keep our sessions relevant and fresh through the seasons.

I never do a session that doesn't start with handling – concentrating on what seems most needed from the previous game. Sometimes

– as at the start of the season or in indoor sessions – handling is the staple of the whole session, punctuated by line running or strength work. It is a basic requirement for 15-man rugby. Indeed, *passing* and *positioning* are the most basic skills, and everyone must be proficient.

In designing the handling session, I tend to keep clear the various groups of exercise – line, loop, switch, bunch, opposed and games – and make sure that as many as I can fit in are represented. If handling is the staple activity in the session, all the players will do all the exercises; if time is limited, the backs may well concentrate in their warm-up on establishing rhythm, length, and speed in lateral passing, and the forwards on left and right.

8
Resistance Exercises

A third element in preparation for the bruising contact and muscular effort required in the game – and a longer-term adaptive programme to it – is strength work. The particular variant that works most successfully in the normal session is one that requires no special preparations or apparatus – exercises in which the individual player is pitted against his own body weight or against a player or players of the same build. It has to be interesting, demanding, and carefully monitored; it tends to be very good-humoured and popular. Essentially it involves isolating a strength needed in the game, and devising an exercise that will help develop it. Take an obvious example: building up binding strength in the pack. We want to make the required movement against resistance. One possible solution: two props lie down in their backs, head to head, arms extended sideways. A hands up; B hand down and locked on A's wrists. A tries to clap his hands over his head; B tries to stop him. Work for 30 seconds, then change over.

No area of player preparation offers an easier way of developing confidence in your own inventiveness. All you need do is set up an initial situation, and experiment in developing competition. Here are a sample dozen initial situations. Have the paired players –

1. Standing facing each other
2. Kneeling facing each other
3. Standing back to back
4. Scrumming position – on the feet
5. Scrumming position – kneeling
6. Lying on their backs – head to head
7. Lying on their backs – feet to feet
8. Lying on front – head to head
9. Lying on front – feet to feet
10. Sitting face to face
11. One standing; one in any other position
12. One kneeling; one in any other position

The other night, for example, in a short session we went through the following programme:

(a) Position 4 : each player pulling his partner down to the right
(30 sec)
each player pulling his partner down to the left
(30 sec)

(b) 5 : one player taking his partner up, the other down
(20 sec)
reverse roles (20 sec)

(c) 6 : arms sideways, wrists held: one player tries to clap his hands overhead, the other tries to stop him. Reverse roles (30 sec)

(d) 6 : same position: players move both feet to touch hands on left (5); on right (5); other player's feet overhead (10 sec)

(e) 8 : arm wrestling – right hands, left hands
(30 secs each)

(f) 1 : link fingers of both hands with opponent – push his arms back to his shoulders (30 sec)

(g) 8 : press-ups – player A sets the pace and tries to beat his partner (30 sec)
reverse roles (30 sec)

(h) 8 : breast-stroke arm action – (100 repetitions in time with partner)

(i) 7 : interlink feed – trunk curls – competition
(30 sec)

(j) 7 : player A puts feet between player B's feet – A tries to take B's feet out while B tries to push A's feet together (30 sec)
reverse roles (30 sec)

(k) 7 : feet off floor: A writes "Loughborough Colleges" with his feet; B stays with him

Some basic principles emerge from this sequence – e.g. exercising the different body areas in sequence with concentration on upper body and stomach; moving from exercise to exercise with minimum change of starting position; keeping both working simultaneously; using set times for each exercise; working with matched pairs of players; getting them to compete with each other. What it doesn't catch is my own performance – in there exhorting maximum effort, and trying to suggest the amusing side of it. (After all, I wasn't doing it!) There's no place for an extensive description of possible exercises but a few categories may help you:

1. Direct muscular confrontation – e.g. wrestling
2. Strength versus body weight – e.g. lifting partner; carrying a partner;
3. Using partner's repetition rate to spur the player working against his own weight e.g. star jumps; press-ups.

We finished the short session with a minute's complete relaxation, and a cycle of breathing: breathe out for 15 seconds; hold it for 15 seconds; breathe in for 15 seconds; hold it for 15 seconds, and repeat. The idea is to maximise lung expansion and contraction, and gradually to extend the time unit towards a (for most people) hypothetical minute. I encourage them to empty their lungs whenever they can during the game.

PART 4
Personal Skills

9
The Importance of Personal Skills

The wider the range of personal skills available to the player the fuller the part he can play in the team, and the more varied the team's tactics can be. The fundamental skill is handling and support positioning and that is why it's given so prominent a part in the structured session. In every session it's desirable to incorporate intensive handling in one form or another, but it's not possible to do the same for the whole range of personal skills. Nevertheless, over a sequence of sessions, many techniques can be developed to extend the player's range of action.

"Personal skills" covers the whole range of what the player may find useful in the match other than those abilities peculiar to specific positions – e.g. propping or line-out jumping. Even then, there's a strong case for every player's being able to perform competently such apparently specific skills as e.g. the full range of scrum-half passes. The time needed to make players at least moderately competent in these is not great, and the returns can be high. In the past only a limited number of skills were identified, and those skills were sometimes seen as specific to forwards or to backs. More precise analysis of the game, and a more open approach to the role of the players, should see a very rapid expansion of this area of coaching. The inventive coach has only to isolate an element that recurs in the game – e.g. staying on your feet, or knocking a player down – extract the key factors, and devise a coaching situation. Even more simply, he can take a skill used by a few players – e.g. the cross-kick – and make all his players moderately competent in it. You can see these approaches at work in the description above of intensive handling – that everyone should be competent in all forms of handling, and that the range of handling practices should be extended to cover as many particular cases as possible. The next stage in this may well be incorporation of the pass in which you reach beyond your opponent to get the ball away.

Broadly speaking, the staple personal skills activity in a structured session tends to be a fairly high pressure exercise designed to give a large number of repetitions in a short time. Although coaching must go on, it tends to be concentrated on a few players with specific weaknesses. A clear, well-thought-out, well-rehearsed explanation – best done, usually, by taking a couple of players through it slowly – and carefully controlled introduction of your basic exercises at the start of the season will do a lot to cut down the need for general coaching in the average session. This is especially true if in each set of four or five players – personal skills practice obeys the same basic rules as handling, small numbers and high work-rate – there is one player in charge, keeping an eye on the standard of performance.

The idea behind intensive repetition is to habituate the players to the action, and make them confident of their ability to do it. For some players that will be enough – in the next match, if the chance occurs, they'll use it. For many players, however, another stage has to be gone through, in which the coach encourages them to use it. This takes the form of the coach expressing his own confidence, as subtly as necessary, that the player can do it.

This aspect of coaching needs emphasis. Restrictive coaching – coaching that prescribes a limited role for the player – is bad coaching, and it can seriously impair a player's abilities. If a prop, to take a typical example, accepts that a prop shouldn't change pace, or swerve, he'll lose the ability to do so. But you've only to watch children running in the play-ground to see that evasive running is virtually a natural gift. It's only in the formal situation, with the bad coach's expectations in his mind, that the player develops inhibitions. The worst aspect of these inhibitions is the mental one – the player can usually be shown his ability in a physical sense, but it's harder to restore the confidence that allows positive judgement of when to use it.

One further technical difficulty ought to be noted. For every attacking skill – e.g. staying on your feet – there's an equally important defensive one – knocking the player down. Sometimes, when there is no direct competition you can coach them simultaneously, as with kicking and catching. Most of the time, however, you must concentrate on one aspect at a time. If you try to coach the early stages of setting up a maul, and simultaneously how to prevent a maul being set up you'll end with nothing but frustration. Tilt the balance in favour of one aspect at a time till you reach the point where skill levels indicate an open competition.

The grouping of skills in the rest of this section is somewhat unconventional but it is designed to make the coach and the player focus on real situations. If the coach wishes to extend the range of skills with which he can deal he's got to work from the situations that arise in the match; if the player is to gain the maximum benefit from an extension of his personal skills, he's got to see them as possible answers to problems that arise in the match. The skills have been grouped accordingly in answer to these basic questions –

1. What can I do with the ball in my hands?
2. What can I do when the ball is with an opponent?
3. What can I do when the ball is in the air?
4. What can I do when the ball is on the ground?
5. What can I do when the ball is with a team-mate?

10
The Ball in Your Hands

The earlier the player makes a provisional decision on the best use he can make of the ball the better. This is especially true of tactical decisions where you may need to communicate basic information long before you get the ball – the scrum-half, for example, needs to know whether the fly-half wants the ball running, trotting, or standing still before the ball goes in to the scrum. But even with non-tactical decisions, the earlier a provisional decision is made the better – it lets the player set things up a little better. On the other hand, the later he commits himself to decisive action the better – more possibilities are open to the player who commits himself last *but keeps the initiative.* Think of the winger who sets himself up to chip ahead, sees the full-back go up to charge down the kick, keeps the ball in his hands instead, and swerves round him. The gifted player is capable in the midst of strenuous action of thinking coolly and clearly, and looking around him: get your head up, your eyes open, your brain working. Think ahead, but be ready to adapt. Stay loose, physically and emotionally; stay sharp, mentally.

All of that is easier to write about than to do. So far as coaching is concerned, it's a matter of talking to players, persuading them that they can do it, encouraging them to try, expecting it of them. It's a matter, before matches, of creating a proper positive outlook, in which the players don't freeze up with nerves, but see the match as a great chance to show what they can do, serious but confident. And it's a matter, in the succession of coaching sessions, of providing them with a wider repertoire of skills.

A. PASSING

Handling has already been covered in some detail. Before the ball reaches him, the player has got to be thinking about the support available to him, close to and wide. At that moment there's less pressure on him, and thinking is easier. In a well organised team he'll know what to expect, where his support is likely to be. If he's a good player, he'll be thinking more widely – considering the possibility, for example, of a chip to the winger. Broadly speaking, though, he'll be looking to continue the particular movement by keeping the ball alive and in our possession through handling. Again, in a well-organised team, only those support players who are better positioned will be calling for the ball – shouting the ball-carrier's name.

The wider the range of his handling skills, the more likely it is that the ball-carrier will be able to get the ball away effectively, i.e. in a way that promotes the attack. Attacks sometimes fail not because the pass hasn't reached the support player but simply because it has made him check.

B. EVASION

I preach to my players that you can always beat one man. Effective forward handling, for example, often means that you get past a man and give a pass. Neither of these statements is absolutely true, but they are a working basis for attacking play. What's important is not that the players should persistently try to beat a man, but that they should all feel capable of beating a man, and confident of the coach's support when they do so try – if it was really on!

The key idea in evasion is "run for daylight". The ability to run into an opponent and keep the ball available is very valuable, but is a second-best: too many things can go wrong at the moment of impact. The first aim, therefore, is:

i Run into space

Before the ball reaches you, before the pass has to be made, try, if you can, to get into space. This is a fundamental notion of all team games. Get your head up, look for space. It may be the outside-centre swinging outside his opponent into the gap as the inside-centre prepares to pass, or the winger coming in for the switch as the touchline gets near, or the forward cutting back behind the ball-carrier so that when the ball reaches him he can run forward. Setting it up early so that you can run forward into daylight is the first principle of evasion, but – especially in switches – delay the decisive movement as long as you safely can.

ii Change of pace

For the individual as for the unit or the team a vital element in deception is changing pace. The three-quarter line that moves comparatively slowly so that the full-back can come in at speed, the team that controls the tempo so that it can briefly work faster than the opposition expects, both are using a change of pace to deceive the opposition. It appears in all the evasive tactics of the individual player – in the swerve, and the side-step, as well as on its own.

In theory change of pace is available to every player. Even if he is not particularly fast, he can run slower than his top speed, and set his opponent up to intercept at that speed, then accelerate past him. In practice, he seldom has a single opponent to beat, and if he slows down he will be caught by the cover defence. The players for whom a simple change of pace works best are those with a high cruising speed, and the ability to accelerate sharply from that.

iii Swerving

Swerving is the natural evasive action of the bigger man who lacks the strength-weight ratio that allows the sudden check and acceleration required for the side-step. It conserves the available energy rather than absorbing it and having to create more. Fundamentally, it conserves space on the outside – by checking the opponent – and maintains the direction of run, from inside out. It's much easier as a rule for the average player to beat his man and the cover by swerving than by side-stepping.

It's a mistake to present swerving as a piece of expertise that involves a complicated sequence of foot, leg, and body movements. It's far better presented as an intuitive answer to a problem, and then improved by judicious comment.

The thing to do, then, is to set the problem and condition it in such a way that the player can gain in confidence. The simplest way is to split the players into groups of five, four of whom kneel in line about five metres apart, midway between the touchline and the 5 m line. The fifth player, without the ball, then has to swing alternately outside and inside these players.

Broadly speaking, the further apart the kneeling players are the easier the movement is, but it must be difficult enough to call for genuine changes of direction. The runner must stay between the lines.

With this basic set up we can provide graded opposition.

1. the defenders kneel and try to trip the runner;
2. the defenders kneel but can fall sideways and try to trip the runner;

3. the defenders crouch but can fall sideways and try to trip the
   runner;
4. the defenders crouch but can dive and try to tackle the runner.

Fundamentally, what the runner is doing is moving round an arc of
a circle whose radius is a little wider than the defender's range of
action. It is pointed out to him that he needn't worry about his upper
body – all he has to do is keep his feet, and later his hips out of range
of the defender. Almost unconsciously he'll change pace, accelerating as he swings round the defender. Sooner or later a defender will
get to him and then the coach must drive him on through the tackle –
he must keep fighting his way forward, must keep running. By the
time he gets past the fourth stage, he can be given the ball. He'll find
it easier to swerve if he has it under an arm, and if he finds himself
isolated in the game that's where he should put it – wingers may do
it, for example, if the ball reaches them crossfield, or if they're quite
confident they can beat their man and then the cover, or if they have
a very powerful hand-off, or brush-off. Normally, however, putting
it under one arm, even if it is the outside one, makes it very difficult
to keep the ball available for support. Get them when they can to
keep the ball in two hands.

As they become more confident you can suggest that they check
the opponent – either by moving the ball to the inside as they begin
to swing out, or by turning the shoulders, outside shoulder to the
front, so that it looks as if they're going for the inside.

This quantity practice is simply to create in players a confidence
that they can make defenders miss them, and for most players,
meeting their opponents at close quarters, that's all that's necessary.
For the backs, however, who are likely to get the ball in space and
find themselves running against a solitary defender setting them up
for a tackle, a little more guidance is helpful.

The first thing that the swerver must do on getting past the first
line of defenders is to preserve the space outside him. Unless you
have a great deal of space and a lot of speed it's futile simply trying to
run away from the full-back. It's good to take him slightly out,
making him believe that you intend to outrun him, because it makes
your subsequent feint to go inside – the merest check – that much
more credible, but you must preserve space on the outside. You
must straighten up.

By going out and taking him with you, you also create a good
immediate situation. It's most likely that the full-back will try to

force you outside by positioning himself so that you can't come inside. This can be to your advantage as soon as you check him: you want to start your swerve at least on the line of his outside shoulder, so that all the movement is outside him. If you start on his inside shoulder, much of the movement is wasted – you aren't getting much further away from him.

If you are clear of the cover defence, it's useful to slow down slightly so that your change of pace can be decisive. On the other hand, make sure that you still have the energy to accelerate, and that the ground will allow it.

The next stage is for the player to incorporate the swerve in a short sequence that he can practise alone – e.g. pick-up, cruise slightly out, check and swerve, chip the ball ahead...and repeat.

The player can then go into a one against one situation against a defender conditioned to two-handed touch. The defender is given a limited length of the game line to defend, and the ball-carrier is placed on the 22. The defender must stand on the line of or inside the ball-carrier. The ball carrier has to start moving out. He gets five points if he can come back inside, and one if he goes outside – so that the defender is very keen not to let him in, and the practice has a greater chance of success.

iv. Side-step

The difficulty of doing a side-step varies with the speed at which you are moving: the spectacular high-speed side-step demands a very high strength-weight ratio, not unlike that of a good triple jumper; the close quarters variety, at a much slower speed, is possible for most people.

The most important point to grasp is that it's the movement – and, precisely, the lack of balance – of your opponent that makes it effective. The easiest way to think of it is as a step inside a player committed to taking you on the outside. He is coming across, straining to get there; you check, to let his momentum take him further across; you drive – off your outside foot – in behind him, and try to accelerate clear of the cover. Even if you can't accelerate away, your wrong-footing your opponent may create the time for support to reach you: it doesn't need to be spectacular to make it valuable.

Once the situation is there, you've got to register it: get your head up, and look. Without this your timing may be bad; at close quarters it will probably be instinctive. You check by letting your outside leg absorb your weight. You step inside by driving off it. It's this combination of absorbing and driving that demands the strength. You can reduce the demands by spreading the check and drive over two outside-leg strides: check, hop, drive. This, however, means you start further away and give him a little longer to react.

Setting up a practice for side-stepping has two phases: unopposed habituation to the movement, and conditioned opposed to help the timing. Get the player trotting down the touch line, and every third or fourth outside foot stride, check and drive across towards the 5 m line, where he repeats the process off the other foot. Get two players doing this, one a couple of metres behind the other. The player behind can then watch the player in front and use him as a conditioned opponent – timing his side-steps to force a change of direction on him. You can then go on to a variation of the final swerve practice – but reverse the scoring so that the defender loses five points if the attacker goes outside and one if he comes inside.

This treatment of swerve and side-step is effective, but a little too clinical. One of the problems is precisely to avoid inhibiting the players by suggesting that you are dealing with "techniques" rather than innate abilities. You can redress this by playing pursuit games in a restricted area: children's games like "tag" will reveal evasive qualities that your players may have forgotten in the "serious" world of rugby. This is another indictment of bad coaching.

C. COUNTERACTION

"Run for daylight" is the great imperative, but there are times when contact is inevitable, and support isn't at hand. This often happens close to the opposing line, when the ability to break the tackle is of maximum importance. It's then that practice in the hand-off, brush-off, and hip-swing pays off. Get the ball under the outside arm for a start.

i. The hand-off

There are basically two forms of this, depending on the size of the ball-carrier. If he is big he can aim to knock his opponent back; if he is light he aims to push himself off the tackler. For both he needs a good target – the base of the neck where it meets the shoulder is much more effective than the head – and he needs to look at it very intently. Don't just see an opponent – see the target area. The critical difference in the action is that the light player seeks to lock his elbow before contact and run round the outside. In both, it's advisable to keep the thumb close to the index finger.

The hand-off is most effective when the tackler has misjudged his tackle, coming in too high or rather too low.

ii. The brush-off

When the tackler takes off rather too far away, so that his body-weight is not going to be effective, he finds himself reduced to grasping with outstretched hands. The attempt can then often be brushed aside by a more powerful arm action which knocks his extended arms off course. Look for his hands and drive them aside.

iii. The hip-swing

The powerful player can sometimes break a tackle by lowering his hips and swinging them into the tackle. This has two effects on the tackler: he finds himself hitting a very much more solid target than he expects, and he hits it before he expected to. Again the key idea is to watch him: the later you lower and swing, the more he will be committed to his false reading of the situation.

At the moment of impact the ball-carrier must be completely committed to continuing his leg action: he must keep running; he cannot trust the hip-swing to be totally effective of itself.

D. KICKING

It's essential both in attack and defence that your key decision makers be accomplished kickers, and that all your players should attain some competence in kicking as a means of keeping the ball going forward or shifting the axis of attack.

i. The punt

The punt in attack is best seen as a set-piece kick. It is properly a tactical weapon, to be used with judgement and by choice. In the great kickers it's a leisurely activity from good possession and a long pass. I use the following sequence as a basis for long spinning kicks.

1. Stand the players in pairs, one on the touch line, one on the 5 m line. The kicker holds the ball, one hand on each end, at right

angles to the long axis of his foot. With his knee high and his toe down, he lets the ball drop high on his ankle and roll down his foot. This roll is the safest way of creating spin. As it rolls down his foot he pushes it, caresses it almost, into his partner's hands. Repeat this till the ball is spinning accurately. Get the players to check their performance – is the ball going down high enough on the foot? is it going down on top of the foot and not to one side? is the lower leg swinging straight towards the catcher? is the knee high and the toe down? has the kicker got his eye on the ball?

2. Repeat the exercise over 5 metres and emphasise the need to judge strength as well as direction. Get them now to start with feet together and take a single step before kicking.

3. Now alter the angle of the ball across the foot. The long axis of the ball stays parallel to the ground but is now at 45° to the long axis of the foot, with the inside point forward. Continue with the exercise.

Once you get to this stage you will find that most of your players are doing fairly adequate punts. They must be in balance, and a check on this – very useful when you come to the non-dominant leg – is that after the kick, the kicking foot comes back alongside the non-kicking foot. You'll find that some players try to make the ball spin by cutting across it – this can work admirably, but it's much less certain than the method outlined.

Gradually encourage your players to open up the angle of the hips to the direction of kick. The ball will always tend to swing left from the right foot, right from the left foot, so get the left hip slightly forward for the right foot kick and vice versa. The distance that the ball is allowed to drop is a matter of compromise. The further it is allowed to drop the greater the length of kick, but the greater the chance that the ball will not land accurately high on the foot. Encourage them to trust in timing rather than kicking *at* the ball: the knee remains flexed till the ball leaves the foot. Get them to think of the golf-club flexing as it swings through and its astonishingly long contact with the ball.

For specialist kickers – e.g. the fly-half and full-back – it's essential that the ball goes precisely where it's intended. A game that drills this home is played using a goal-line as a guide. One player is in the field of play, inside the 5 m line about 2 metres from the goal-line; the other diagonally opposite him in the in-goal area. Each gets one point for punting across the goal-line in the near side of the posts, two for between the posts, and three for punting across the line beyond the posts. He loses five points if he fails to punt across the line. The results will almost always come as a surprise to the kickers. Concentration is essential.

The top-spin on a ball kicked as described ensures that it will tend to roll on rather than bounce up. This is a much better bet for the attacker: if it bounces, it may bounce into an attacker's hands but the odds are long against it; far better to keep it rolling forward to be played with the feet, or seized in an attacking fall.

The fly-half has got to practise the basic attacking kicks – to the box, high up the middle, and out to the open wing usually from a midfield position. He should also work on the ball that clears the centres and drops short of the full-back: if he can place this accurately on the full-back's weaker side and vary its strength, it's a potent form of attack. For all of these it's best to work in small units first – in this case, of course, fly-half with scrum-half, each time with the code call for a pass standing still – and then as a unit practice with the support players moving up in balance onto the ball. Finally, of course, it will be incorporated in team practices. Punting is far too important a weapon to be left to chance.

ii. Coaching the goal-kicker

When the goal-kicker hits a bad patch, the coach must be able to help him. This is the kind of sequence he might adopt:

Take him out with several balls and another player to catch and return them. Get him to kick from the try-line at a single post. This offers several advantages. Initially, it relaxes the player: he has been set an impossible task – no one can expect him to hit the post, and if he does it's a big bonus. The try-line itself is very useful to the coach. It enables him to check up quickly on the direction of follow through, and the precise placing of the feet after the kick.

No matter what style of kicking is used, the follow through has to be accurate – straight towards the post. The kicker will find the try-line useful as a precise guide; when he goes out in front of the posts, he can scratch his own guideline, straight through the ball, or in line with the non-kicking foot. The next critical factor is balance. For consistency, the kicker must be in balance throughout the contact, follow-through, and return of the kicking foot to the ground precisely beside the non-kicking foot. (The coach can test the truth of this last point by getting a right-footed player to punt right-footed and then left-footed, checking in each case where the kicking foot ends up. As soon as the player consciously tries to get his left foot back beside his right foot, his accuracy improves.) With round-the-corner kickers, especially, this has to be carefully monitored – some drop the inside-shoulder as they move into the kick, some continue on the outward path, and both of these lead to lack of balance which can be clearly seen in the foot placing.

Contact with the ball should be on the line of the big toe. Toe kickers should aim to hit the ball not with the toe of their boot but with the up-turned point of their big toe. Instep kickers should aim to make contact with the length of the big toe. The aim in both cases is to stay in contact with the ball within the limits set by the need to stay in balance – don't kick *at* the ball, swing through it.

Round-the-corner kickers, especially, may find a tendency to rotate on the non-kicking foot. This is usually associated with their failing to follow through straight down the line. They can compensate by moving up on to the toes of the non-kicking foot. This, and the straightening of the non-kicking knee, contribute to the single feature that all consistent kickers share: the hips rising at the moment of contact.

The placing of the non-kicking foot is less critical than is often made out. It's got to be about as far from the kicking foot at the moment of impact as it is when the player is standing normally. The coach should check that it's fairly consistent, and can work at what placing relative to the ball is best for the kicker in question.

Power in kicking is related to the length of arc of the knee of the kicking leg. The natural kicker has a long arc that reduces the need for lower-leg speed or speed of approach. It's this consideration that makes it difficult to "make" kickers: if the player hasn't got it, he'll never develop consistent power. If you have to make a kicker, pick a runner with solid legs: all the same mechanical principles are involved.

Through the moment of impact, the upper body must be approximately vertical as seen from the front or from the side. Once again, there's an acceptable range of attitude. What is important is a measure of relaxation, associated with lack of emotional tension. Some kickers find that a conscious effort to slow the breathing will help them relax physically and emotionally and concentrate mentally. Most adopt a ritual that acts in the same way. Most of the mistakes that a good kicker makes will be attributable to a loss of concentration resultant on physical tension, and expressed, as in golf, by not focussing on the ball, snatching, and pushing the head up. He's got to stay loose, take his time, trust in the swing.

A comparatively slow approach is best in that it maintains the relaxation, and gives a far better chance of staying in balance through the moment of contact. The kicker may be able to generate more power by lengthening or speeding up his run, but he'll pay for it in consistency. In the interests of his own technique and morale, and for the good of the team, he shouldn't be expected to go for kicks that aren't within his normal range, and that range should be known to his captain. So, too, of course should be his preference for right or left side of the field.

The importance of concentration is reflected by the fact that in the coaching situation outlined the kicker may well hit the post. This can be sharpened by finishing with a set number of kicks – say, half-a-dozen – at the single post. Indeterminate kicking often leads to diminished concentration on each separate kick. When you take him out in front, start with the easiest kick: aim to build confidence on success. What he needs is to see the ball sailing between the posts. Belief that that's where it's going is basic to success.

iii. The drop-kick

Your scrum-half, fly-half, inside centre, and full-back must all be encouraged to see accurate drop-kicking as a basic requirement. The team must have its drop-out drill at 22 m and half-way firmly established, and for this accuracy and length are essential. But inadequate attention is paid to the drop-kick as a simple, effective way of scoring points precisely in that area of the field where defence is at its most committed. From set-pieces and indirect penalties especially, where possession is probable, it can be, with practice, relied on to score points.

The basic conditions are precisely those outlined for goal-kicking:

1. Balance – you must be comfortably in balance to be consistent. Don't try to force it – find your effective range, and wait for the chance. Practise with the player most likely to pass to you: make sure he knows precisely what you want so that you're in balance when the ball reaches you. After each kick check where your kicking foot ends up.

2. Contact – push your toe down to lengthen the lever and maximise contact. Try meeting the ball along the line of your big toe. Swing through rather than kick at the ball.
3. Follow-through – to the target, allowing for wind-drift. To allow an easy follow-through you should open your hips, clockwise for a right foot, anti-clockwise for a left foot kick.
4. Placing the ball – give yourself room. As in place-kicking, the last stride is long to let your hips lift into the kick. It also allows a slight backward lean of the upper body, which makes a full follow-through easier. So, a longer left foot stride, and the ball placed near its toe. Make sure it is placed a normal distance to the right: if you put it too far to the right, it will disturb your balance.
5. Control the ball – so that it bounces slightly back onto your foot. It is vital that you watch the ball onto your foot, that you place it – "drop" is too vague a word – precisely where it is wanted, tilted slightly backward.

In your practice, you can follow precisely the same pattern described under place-kicking to establish good form. You must then move to the situations where you are going to use the kick to establish your accurate range. Don't play at it: it repays serious application.

iv. Kicking in loose play

There is a whole category of kicks which are not tactical, but improvised answers to immediate difficulties or opportunities. Typical of these are the chip ahead, the cross-kick, the defensive kick over the shoulder, and the grubber. The kick over the shoulder is essential for scrum-halves, and highly desirable for the back three; the others should be available to the whole team. The kick over the shoulder is also an example of the specific needs of the scrum-half, many of whose kicks must be made in uncomfortable but predictable situations – e.g. from the base of the scrum or from indifferent possession at a line-out. In coaching these kicks, I haven't come across any great difficulties: the important things for the coach are the need to recognise that they can and should be coached, and a reasonably experimental approach to coaching methods.

The chief technical point about all of these kicks other than the grubber is the need to offer the maximum target area on the ball.

This is simply done by holding the long axis of the ball at right-angles to the long axis of the foot. These kicks are easier too if the kicker thinks of keeping his knee high, so that he can place the ball fairly accurately. His foot position controls the actual flight of the ball, and he should be encouraged to experiment in keeping his toes down or pulling them up.

The critical point in the grubber is less the technique – toe down, knee forward, pushing the ball forward – than the need to use it only when you are actually in the gap, and the chance of its being intercepted virtually nil.

Most of these kicks can be practised using simple drills – e.g. cyclic exercises (grubber, fall, feed, grubber...), grid games (grubber between partners; opponents try to fall), handling exercises (handle the ball to the right in 4s, chip back to the left). What is needed is usually practice rather than coaching – though comment must go on.

Positional kicks may need coaching. For the kick over the shoulder you might, for example, start facing the scrum-half, throw the ball over his head so that he can turn and catch it easily, and get him immediately to kick back into touch over his left shoulder. You can then build up pressure by throwing and following up progressively faster. The next step is to help him kick straight back by rolling backwards and kicking as he rolls. Give him support initially by hanging on to his collar and lowering him fairly slowly. Do this in front of the goal posts so that he has a definite target (and, of course, give someone else catching practice at the same time).

In the same way, you can encourage the scrum-half to practise kicking almost as he picks the ball up, and getting his knee and toe coming up sharply to get immediate height. Or get the centre to practise bouncing the ball accurately into touch, as he may need to if there's a check in handling. The message for the coach is always the same: look in detail, isolate the element that's likely to recur, make sure the players concerned are given a chance and help to improve.

E. CONTACT WITH OPPONENTS

Rugby is a contact sport, and every player must be equipped to deal effectively with the physical challenge of an opponent when he has the ball in his hands. Ideally, in attack, he will have immediate support and need never become a target (see p. 49), but the ideal state is seldom sustained. He must therefore learn to stay on his feet and keep the ball available.

Staying on your feet

The first thing to realise is that each second you can stay on your feet lets your support get three or four yards closer: staying on your feet for two or three seconds is all it needs for support to be fairly sure of arriving.

The second is that to stay on your feet you've got to set your opponent problems: you've got to be just as vigorous and determined in your action as he is in his.

The vital key to staying on your feet is to be in balance. The best way to be in balance is to try whenever you make contact to lift your opponent up. If you simply run into him with your shoulder you will certainly be off balance, and probably on the way down. Hit with your shoulder but drive up into him: you'll find that your feet go automatically into the right position, and that your knees bend, getting your centre of gravity low. If you are running fast you may find it pays to check just before impact, for otherwise your impetus may take you down. This, provided he's alone, may not be a bad thing, but, if he has support around him and you aren't sure of your support, it pays to stay on your feet.

Once you hit and pick, your main concern is to keep the ball available. You'll never do this consistently if on impact you squeeze the ball to your bosom: keep it in two hands. Fight your way round with strong jagged movements, getting your head and shoulders inside your wheelbase, and look for your support; get the ball initially back and down – about knee level; bang it into your supporter's chest, but if a maul is on, don't let go. You'll know if a maul is on by what the supporter does. If it is on, force your head and shoulders back and up into your opponent. If it isn't, you've done a screen pass, and your supporter is on his way.

If you fail to prevent your opponent getting his hands on the ball, don't engage in horizontal contest: squeeze the ball down. If you don't break the wrestling match, the odds are the ball will get stuck, and the impetus of attack will break down. It will help in squeezing the ball down if you get your arm in a strong position – e.g. more than 90° at the elbow. To achieve this, first bend your knees to get lower, then force your head and back up and away from the ball. As soon as your arms feel strong, drive the ball down. If you can't do it, then try to get your feet out of the way and sit down.

The importance of knowing how to cope in this situation must be brought home to everyone. It's the prelude to rucking and mauling, and too often is reserved for the forwards. In fact, the backs are just as likely to be the initial ball-carriers as are the forwards. It may not always be fair but it's a useful coaching dictum that the man who takes the ball into the tackle/maul area is responsible for getting it back. That's why, in the late '60s, I devised the phrase "keep the ball available" as the imperative for the ball-carrier.

The initial practice for this is simplicity itself: get the players in 2s, give one the ball, and get him to shield it from his opponent with his body. He's got to keep it available – free to give to his supporter. At this stage, encourage the opponent to go for the ball, not the man.

Bring in a third player to support the ball-carrier. If the ball-carrier can stay on his feet, the supporter goes in, the ball-carrier bangs the ball into him – but doesn't let go – and the supporter "jacks him up". He gets his shoulders under the ball-carrier's chest, with his hips away from the ball-carrier's hips, so that they form a wedge, and pushes him up and forward. This is the start of effective mauling. If the ball-carrier goes down before the supporter reaches him, he must still try to keep the ball available. In the split second as he goes down he must make up his mind whether he can land on his back and present the ball to his supporter, or whether he must release it onto the ground. The supporter, in either case, has to dive in, getting his shoulder over the ball, and his hands on it. Once the idea is established, bring in a fourth player to compete with the supporter for the final possession.

Mauling

Just as everyone must practise keeping the ball available, everyone must take part in mauling practice. This provides the intensive repetition needed to habituate the player to the action.

In my first draft of this section I outlined ten different exercises to build up skill in mauling. They've had to go, and I'm going to outline one. It's the one which at the moment we use as a staple pressure practice.

Split the players into three sets of five. Two sets stand, facing each other, some 15 m apart, with one player slightly in advance of the other four. The third five then shuttle back and forth, mauling the ball back as they hit the ends.

This is a very effective high work-rate set-up, and provides plenty of opportunity for coaching. Initially, you may wish to condition what the end fives can do: start with only as much opposition as the maulers can handle, and gradually relax the conditions. Again, the distance apart of the ends is important: start fairly wide, so that you can hammer home the great imperative – you must arrive together.

With the five who are running, you can once again control their running speed to make it easy. I tend to trot alongside them, and talk as we go.

The great point initially is that by the time they hit, the supporter should have his hands on the ball and be ready to jack up. This means that ball-carrier and supporter must between them – usually by slowing down and speeding up respectively – arrange to arrive simultaneously. Once the five have all got the idea, you can usually arrange a few passes on the way.

If the first two get their wedge set up properly, with the ball in four hands, the odds are that it will come back cleanly no matter what the rest do: they will have isolated the ball from the opposition. The job of the rest is to isolate the wedge-men from the opposition, driving to and if possible a little beyond them. Naturally, you want them to think as they arrive so that they don't all drive in on one side of the maul.

The tighter they drive the better. If you place the two ends just in front of lines, you'll be able to demonstrate how effective the drive is in the maul. Drive together, and get hold of a shirt. Those on the outside use the outside arm to tidy up.

In this practice you only have five mauling. These split into the wedge-men, two driving beyond them, and a fifth player who goes in for the ball ready to feed it to the scrum-half. In the practice, though, he simply turns and sets off for the other end, and the practice continues. It's advisable in the practice as in the match for him to give a shout as he peels off the maul.

One great advantage of the reduced numbers in this high-work-rate exercise is that it makes very clear to the third and fourth players – those isolating the wedgemen – that they must think about positioning: it's very evident if they don't go in one on each side.

You will find a simple introductory mauling exercise on p. 102, and a more advanced one among the photographs.

11
The Ball on the Ground

As in every other phase of the game, the player faced with the ball on the ground has to exercise judgement and make decisions. If the coach can simplify this by giving some guidelines it'll speed up the player's actions and effectiveness.

1. THE PLAYER IN ATTACK

(a) if you've got time, and the ball isn't rolling away from you or wet, pick it up.
(b) if there's only one opponent and the ball's rolling away from you or wet, get your foot to it, then dribble.
(c) if there are several opponents close, no matter what the ball's doing, make an attacking fall.

2. THE PLAYER IN DEFENCE

(a) if you've got time, and the ball isn't rolling away from you or wet, pick it up.
(b) if you've any doubt whatsoever fall on it and get up fast.
(c) if you're isolated from support and near touch, push it into touch with your foot.

As with all guidelines, the moment the player starts making finer, more fruitful, personal judgements, is the moment where coaching justifies itself.

Dealing with the ball on the ground is a critical phase of play – typically it sustains attack after the tackle, and is a corner-stone of defence. Every player must be adept at it.

a. Picking the ball up

It's best to suggest that this is what the player does only if conditions are favourable. "If you've got time..." covers two aspects: the 50/50 situation, with an opponent, and the difficulty of controlling personal speed in supporting the ball-carrier. Simpler solutions are preferable wherever there is doubt.

You must set the mechanics of picking up in a context. The player tackled puts down the ball on the side away from the tackler – which allows the support player to predict a good line of approach. The support player (see p. 54) has to govern distance and speed. It's an absolutely typical support situation, and work on picking-up in the form of a cyclic game is valuable as a basic exercise in support play.

The mechanics of the pick-up are simple. Set it up so that the ball is on your better side – i.e. for most people on their right. Judge your approach so that you put your right foot beside the ball. This gives you greater flexibility in case the ball is bobbing about. Eyes on the ball; mind thinking ahead. The right hand makes contact first, and scoops the ball a few inches into the left hand. Hands relaxed; fingers slightly spread.

It's dead simple but needs unceasing practice. Set up cyclic games:

1. *pick-up...put down*

   four players, numbered. 1 trots out, puts ball down, 2 picks up and so on in sequence. Gradually build up speed.

2. *pick-up...pass...put down...turn and pressurise...*

   the exercise goes on but now with a conditioned resistance. After putting the ball down the player turns to offer opposition. The new ball-carrier can drive in as for a screen pass, or get the ball away before contact. The ball can go to either supporter, who in turn puts the ball down and turns.

3. *pick-up/put down shuttle relay*

   Use four marks a, b, c, d and two balls, one on a, one on c. Each runner picks up the ball and puts it down on next mark. Start with two players at the a end, one at the d end. Insist on accurate put-down.

   These exercises are, of course, only coaching situations: the coach must attend to the actual coaching.

b. The attacking fall

At close quarters, especially if you are outnumbered, or there are opponents ahead of you, the first aim is to secure possession, and the quickest way to do that is by a controlled dive onto the ball. Imagine you're a soccer goalkeeper – dive with both eyes open, and both hands reaching for the ball, pulling it under your shoulder.

Once you've got it you can either roll onto your back and hold it up for a supporting player, or squeeze it back towards your own players, or if you're lucky, get a pass away. If you do pass, pop the ball up gently rather than throw it back.

A cyclic exercise to give intensive repetition of the action is described on p. 104.

c. Defending falls

There are two basic forms of defensive fall. One deals with the situation when the defender is going forward to meet a dribbler; the other, when the ball has been pushed behind him and he has to go back for it. Both call for intelligent anticipation to get into the right position. In the first case, the defender must position himself to force the dribbler to one side – as in tackling; in the second, he's got to judge the path of the ball, and arrive in balance.

1. You aim to dive on the ball and roll between the ball and the dribbler so that your shoulders and back hit his lower leg. Pull the ball in, and curl round it so that your head is tucked in with your chin on your chest.
2. You do a soccer sliding tackle onto the ball, and land with the upper body curled round it and the upper hand pulling it into the body. You land on the outside of your lower thigh, with the lower leg flexed out of the way, and the upper leg pushed out in front. The impetus of your slide, and the fulcrum of the upper foot should help you immediately back onto your feet. This is a much more active fall then (1) above.

Intensive practices for those falls:
1. use the dribble v. falling practice on p. 90.
2. a cyclic exercise – falling and turning him over

See p. 99 for the way of dealing with a player backing into you. Put your players in threes. No. 1 puts in a short controlled grubber kick; no. 2 falls, bounces, backs into 3 who is following up; no. 3 turns him over...and the cycle continues. This is illustrated in the photographs.

d. Dribbling

Ideally we want to get the ball in our hands, but dribbling has its place. The key idea in dribbling is to *push* the ball as far as you need: don't kick it.

Dribbling is a one-footed exercise: two footed dribbling is far too slow – it allows the cover to get across. You dribble with the outside and inside of your better foot. Treat the ball gently so that it stays close; lean over it; use your arms for balance and not speed. Keep the ball dribbling ankle relaxed.

I've never improved on the two basic exercises described in "Improve your Rugby" (Penguin) –

1. mark a spot on the ground, and take the ball round it using the outside of your foot. Curve your toe around the ball, and guide it. Start slowly and gradually find the speed that you can work at. Let your body lean into the centre.
2. using the inside of your foot and keeping it in contact with the ball as continuously as you can, drag the ball sideways and slightly forward across the pitch.

The player must keep his eye on the ball. The best time to beat opponents is when they are in mid-air for the fall. Practise moving the ball sideways as in (b), and then bringing it sharply back as in (a) at the moment you glimpse them falling.

An excellent intensive practice has four players in the grid. One has the ball at his feet and tries to keep possession as long as he can; the other three are all trying to fall on the ball, gain possession, start dribbling.

Dribbling affords another good situation for encouraging intelligent support patterns – giving width and depth to the movement, and immediately responding to changes in the ball's position. Think in terms of a 3-4-1 pack with the ball at the hooker's feet. As soon as the ball player loses control he accelerates ahead and rejoins at No. 8; the remaining players alter position to maintain the 3-4-1 pattern.

There are situations and conditions that dictate *kicking* the ball on the ground. A full-back near touch, isolated from support, with opponents bearing down on him may have to kick the ball into touch – but "kick" does not mean a wild "fly-hack": it requires precisely the same concentration as a place kick. Again, if the pitch is very heavy you may have to kick the ball forward – but again you *judge* it. Whenever the ball is near touch, for example, you either want it in touch or you don't, and you must concentrate on your objective. When you're following up a kick that takes the ball near touch, you must run to get between touch and the ball, and play the ball back inside.

12
The Ball in the Air

The primary concern here is the ball in the air after a kick. Taking a pass is covered under handling, and line-out catching under line-out.

DEFENCE

Catching practices are basic – being able to defend effectively, and being able to counter-attack, depend upon certainty in catching. Throwing the ball up and watching it with your hands is a simple way of building basic confidence. In pairs it's best to start throwing and as confidence grows, throw higher and higher. Every kicking practice is also a catching practice, but won't be until the kicking is moderately accurate.

The mechanics of catching are simple enough:

1. move to the predicted landing area;
2. if it's coming to you, call for it – if more than one player calls, the player furthest back should take it;
3. assess what your opponents are doing early – as you move into position: once you lock onto the ball that will take all your attention;
4. get your lower body set for what you expect to do – it may be as different as running or taking a tackle – but keep the upper body and arms relaxed: you may find that breathing out helps you relax;
5. get your hands out and up to welcome the ball – this brings your elbows together, so that the ball doesn't slide through;
6. keep your head and chest up as long as you can;
7. pull the ball in to your chest. Some rotation of the upper body in the direction of your goal-line takes the way off the ball, sets you up to take a tackle, and lessens the risk of a knock-on.

In the catching practice it's well worth while getting the players, feet solidly on the ground, to call for a mark: make all your players aware of the possibility, and go through the procedure with them. This will reveal difficulties, such as kicking to touch from midfield.

A player who can catch the ball in his hands, without pulling it into the body, is able to move it much more rapidly, but this is a secondary consideration if the player is in a genuinely defensive position.

Once the catching is efficient, the coach must turn his and the players' attention to the need to support the catcher. He should never have to catch alone – the other players must give him support in defence and for counter-attack (see p. 221). As in all support, width and depth are the key ideas – and here especially depth.

Once these basic abilities are established, the range of catching situations can be extended. In practice it seems adequate if one deals with one further catch – where the ball goes over the catcher's head. This is particularly important for the scrum-half and for the back three – the full-back and wingers. Stand facing the player about five metres apart on the five metre line, and lob it over his head so that the ensuing catch will be easy. Once he's doing this confidently – observing the rules for an ordinary catch cited above – get him to catch and kick over his shoulder to touch (see p. 83). Once he's doing this confidently, lob further and follow up the lob to try to touch him before he kicks. A natural extension of this is to encourage the player to experiment with beating his opponent by a dummy turn followed by a pivot the other way. Broadly speaking this means a dummy turn towards touch – holding the ball wide on that side – and pivoting out to give a better angle for the kick or start counter-attack. It's much safer for the right-footed kicker to try this on the left touch, so that he ends up with a dominant-foot kick.

A sensible general kicking and support exercise puts two pairs of players A and B, C and D in opposition. A kicks to C as accurately as he can; D runs off C into position for an easy pass, collects the ball, and kicks for B, who feeds A...and so on. You can then add a fifth player, E, to the A/B group. When A kicks, he can then follow up his kick and pressurise the catcher – and the game goes on. This will allow the catcher to try dummying a single opponent approaching at speed.

ATTACK

In a 50/50 catching situation between an attacker on the move and a defender at a halt, it's much easier for the attacker to go up and take the ball early. This can be practised at kick-offs, but is true anywhere on the field. The attacker must always keep the possibility in mind as his first choice of action. More often, however, he will find a situation developing in which the defender will be able to catch the ball. If he's moderately sure of making an effective tackle, that is his second choice of action. If he isn't sure, he should adjust his line of running and his speed, to limit the catcher's range of action. In general he should encourage the kicker to turn towards touch so limiting the possibility of counter-attack, and the range of the touch kick.

Many attacking kicks are angled across the pitch, and the supporter's first aim then is to get between the ball and touch. If he cannot be sure of catching the ball, he must make every effort to keep the ball in play with his feet – concentrate on the ball and *push* it inside. All wingers must practise this.

Just as with the defensive catcher, the attacking catcher following up the kick needs support. Support practices for the forwards are described on p. 161. The team as a whole must follow up kicks maintaining their basic defensive formation – pressure, cover, and depth. The whole team can fit into the forward practice – start in position and follow up as a team.

The specific case of kick-off catching and support is dealt with on p. 272.

13
The Ball in the Opponents' Hands

The defensive skills are every bit as important to the complete player as the attacking skills, and his attitude in using them must be just as positive. To become "defensive", for the player as for the team, is to hesitate and lose the initiative. The aim of the coach in dealing with situations when the opponents have the ball is to make the player see them as the basis for another form of attack: when we've got the ball, we attack their line; when they've got the ball, we attack them. And this attack needs the same forethought, the same decisiveness, the same skill in execution as attacking the line.

1. TACKLING

The classic tackles are those that tend to be performed by the back row, the front three backs, and to a lesser extent the back three. They take place in the open, and they tend to form part of a defensive plan. The aim of the plan is to limit the possibilities open to the attackers so that their attacks become predictable and defensive roles become easier to fulfil. These plans are described later on p. 212.

Planning can go only so far, and every player in the team may be faced with the need to tackle. Even on the personal level, though, the first aim of the tackler is to set things up so that the ball-carrier's options are limited. What the tackler is always trying to do is to create a situation where the ball-carrier is forced to go in one direction, and preferably forced to run on the outside of the tackler. This allows the tackler's impetus to go into the tackle, and may force the ball-carrier to run further than the tackler. Ideally, too, the ball-carrier is channeled between the tackler and the touch-line, or another defender, or a scrum or maul. This imposes a further limitation on his movement.

The other aspect of planning a tackle is timing. Ideally the tackle is made simultaneously with the arrival of the ball: the less time the ball-carrier has to set himself up the better. In loose play, especially, the most effective tackles are made by defenders who have predicted who's getting the ball next, and made sure by intelligent running that he stands no chance of using possession. This is particularly important on the fringes of scrums, line-outs, and mauls or rucks where dangerous situations will develop immediately the ball gets in front of the opposing pack. The easiest time to stop these attacks is before the first ball-carrier gets moving: as soon as he appears he's got to be knocked down.

In general open play, therefore, it's generally true that intelligent anticipation makes for easy tackles. This is linked with a key idea in all aspects of the game: to start fast but arrive in balance. Starting fast means two things: a quicker assessment of the situation than the average player, and quick acceleration. You must get into the tackle area fast, but when you get there you must be in balance. A potential tackler running flat out is too easily beaten.

This in turn is linked to personal safety: only a fool tries to damage an opponent at the risk of damaging himself. The easy, effective, tackle is a better bet than the spectacular one. Tackling can be a very effective way of sapping an opponent's morale, and a great way of turning defence into attack. There is certainly a place for the crash tackle – but don't try it unless conditions are absolutely right.

The second factor in safety is that you always aim to hit with the shoulder, and hit something with more give in it than your shoulder – just above the knees, or the solar plexus, are good examples.

The third factor is to keep your eyes open so that you can put your head where it is not going to be hit – generally, behind the ball-carrier's thigh. Create as wide an angle as you can between hitting shoulder and neck. I've seen American players using the head as a battering ram – as if they still had helmets resting safely on shoulder pads – but I wouldn't recommend it.

The first aim of every tackle is to put the ball-carrier on the deck; the second is to get possession of the ball, or at least prevent him from playing it. Whenever possible, the tackler should try to do both – but never at the risk of not putting the man down. If the ball-carrier can stay on his feet he sets up fresh attacking possibilities. In the act of putting him down, however, the tackler can make sure he doesn't roll to keep the ball off the ground – try to put him face down on the pitch – and as soon as he's safely down make a real effort to get hold of the ball. The only time you try to roll him is when he's about to cross your goal line.

The great majority of tackles in the open tend to be from the side and behind; comparatively few are from the front.

Side and rear tackles

The aim in side and rear tackles is to have the shoulder hit just above the knees and buckle them. This is accompanied by a powerful sweeping action of the hitting shoulder arm operating just below the knees, pulling the knees together and pulling them into the tackler's chest. If the arm is slightly extended before the tackle it brings the hitting shoulder into a more powerful position. The other arm wraps round to bind the tackle. In all such tackles you must allow for the ball-carrier's moving away from you – aim beyond him, and in the rear tackle aim high to come down in the tackle area.

You avoid most difficulties if you accelerate into the tackle, putting the ball-carrier's timing out. The acceleration should give you the initiative.

Front tackle

This tends to occur when your opponent is channelled on to you, or believes he can run over you. The key idea is to stay upright as long as you can before you commit yourself to the tackle.

There are two basic forms of the tackle, one aimed at the solar plexus, the other at the knees. In the first you wait for him to come to you and just before the impact drop your weight onto your front foot, drop your shoulders fractionally lower, move your head out to the side, and let him run onto your shoulder. As he does so, you swing that arm round him and channel him onto your shoulder. This is astonishingly effective: it stops him dead, and you may not even feel the impact.

In the second form you delay action till the last moment and then go into a full knee bend. You let him run onto your shoulder, wrap your arms round his knees, and let yourself roll backwards.

Tackling practice is vital but must be carefully conditioned. Make sure that the players are properly warmed up with handling and strength work. You may find that early in the season time spent on basic practices are valuable.

a. Introduction – in grids

Have the ball-carrier walk just inside a grid-line. The tackler crouches and drives into him with the object of knocking him over the line. Gradually move the ball-carrier further into the grid so that the tackler has to develop more power. Keep coaching the salient points.

Repeat for the second version of the front tackle, and go through the motions of the first version so that the tackler knows what to do.

b. Habituation

Put the tackler in the grid and have say four other players trotting across the diagonals so that he alternately has tackles on the right and on the left. Most players will tend to be stronger on the right shoulder. Encourage a powerful arm action on the left. Vary the pace – start at a slow tackling tempo and build up, and very gradually encourage a little more running speed.

c. Pressure

The basic form of pressure practice puts the tackler in the grid with the four ball-carriers trotting back and forward on fixed lines across the grid. The aim then is to see how many tackles the player can make in a fixed period – e.g. 30 or 45 seconds. The grid prevents the ball-carriers from moving over-fast, and the continuous presentation of bodies to be tackled affords tackles from a wide variety of angles. The need to notch up just one more tackle than anyone else is excellent for increasing work-rate.

2. KNOCK DOWN

Very frequently the player is in a close contact position where classic tackling is impossible: he needs practice in knocking a *static* opponent down. This is precisely the kind of practice that is rarely done.

The most effective form approximates to a shoulder charge at the upper body with the leg on that side hooking the back of the knees. It's most effective if the shoulder charge is slightly up to lessen the ball-carrier's contact with the ground.

Start this in pairs and introduce two further competitive players to dive in for the ball as soon as it appears. It's obviously best to work the players in groups of comparable weight. Emphasise the need for the supporter to get down to the ball – don't stand up and grope around, get your shoulder over it, and dig it out.

3. TURN OVER

Quite frequently, the player is faced with an opponent backing into him. The aim then is to put a leg behind him and turn him over so that he lands on the ground between the ball and his own players. Grab the far shoulder and rotate him hard over your leg, and down onto the ground.

Introduction

In pairs. Player 1 does a short grubber kick. Player 2 executes a sliding fall (see p. 89), rocks onto his feet, and drives back into Player 1. Player 1 turns him over. Introduce a third player to snap up or dive onto the loose ball.

4. TURNING THE MAN

If the ball-carrier is static, turning him over may be difficult. One alternative is to turn him to face your team-mates. The key to this is to lift him off the ground, and swing him round using a wide grip – e.g. one hip and the opposite shoulder – to increase leverage. An effective refinement is to get your arms round his neck to the far shoulder – this gives good leverage and prevents him from tucking down round the ball. The lift comes from your knees – so get them bent – and your back – use it to keep him upright.

Introduction

Ball-carrier stands, braced, on far side of grid facing out. Turner and supporter trot across. Turner turns him, and supporter takes the ball. At this stage condition the ball-carrier to release the ball easily. Supporter trots back to far line as ball-carrier, and previous ball-carrier becomes the turner.

Taking the ball

The weakness of turning the man is that it tends to lead to a prolonged wrestle for the ball and a delay that reduces the value of possession. If you're going to use it, you must devise a technique for getting possession quickly, and give your players practice in applying it. If the ball-carrier can wrap himself round the ball, there's no way within the spirit of the game to take it from him quickly. It's essential that the turner should keep him upright. Even then, if he keeps his elbows in, it's difficult to get enough purchase on his arms to dislodge the ball. The aim is to get a shoulder into his chest above the ball, push down on and behind the ball, and try to pull one of his hands off the ball. A reverse push is quite effective – push the ball up hard so that he is forced to push down, and then quickly push down.

I can't say I'm happy with any of this: it's better to get him down on the ground so that he has to release the ball.

You can develop the previous practice so that an extra support player comes in and two of them with defined roles – e.g. removing a hand, removing an arm, pushing up, preparing to push down – take the ball.

Pressure

For a pressure practice with two sets of forwards in contention, see p. 105.

5. ISOLATING THE BALL

When the tackler is much lighter than the static opponent, he may be able to capitalise on speed by swinging round him so that he gets between the ball and the ball-carrier's supporters. This is perfectly legitimate provided he's the first to make contact. This sets up a stalemate situation which the ball-carrier may well try to resolve by pushing the ball down – and if the tackler is alert he may be able to kick it back on his side.

14
Cyclic Exercises

Cyclic exercises provide a high work rate situation based on looping and hammering home the basic notion – "do it…and run". They can be applied to many of the basic techniques of the game and offer intensive repetition under easily controlled pressure. They are advantageous in that several techniques can be put into a sequence, and that some degree of opposition can be built in. They are also a good basis for light-hearted relay races. And for the inventive coach they offer an adaptable form that can be developed easily and effectively.

The idea is most easily understood from an example, in this case the first that occurred to me.

Number four players 1-2-3-4. 1 has the ball and sets off at a trot from the goal-line towards the 22 with the rest following. 2 tackles him, and 1 makes the ball available on the ground. 3 picks up and passes to 4. 1 tackles 4…and the cycle continues.

The pressure can be increased (a) by cutting out the pass, or (b) by decreasing the numbers taking part. You may well find that starting with five players makes for an easier introduction.

It's important that the exercise is seen as a coaching situation, and that accordingly it's introduced at a tempo that encourages learning. You may find a tendency for the ball-carrier to run too fast: he needs to take three or four fast strides to get in front of the other players, but then he must slow down.

As in most repetition exercises for the basic skills, you are dealing with antithetic pairs: in broad terms, attack and defence. The players are simultaneously practising carrying on an attack and checking it, being tackled and tackling.

In using such exercises, you need to clarify in your own mind the elements involved so that your coaching is thorough. In all cyclic exercises involving movement down the pitch, the basic elements are:

1. Judgement of position and pace

There is no point in a player's rushing blindly in support. He has to arrive in balance. This means judging what's going to happen and running accordingly. Cyclic exercises are an easy introduction to this. The coach has to emphasise this – and initially he'll find ample opportunity.

2. Keeping the ball available

Unless the player has quite exceptionally large hands, carrying the ball in one hand is an excellent way of losing possession. As soon as the player comes into contact with an opponent, he will tend to pull the ball into his body, and after that the advantage of being in possession is as good as lost. Keeping the ball available is a matter of control, and the easy way to do it is to keep the ball in two hands.

3. High work-rate

To keep the cycle going every player has to "do it and run": if he doesn't, he won't be in position to continue the cycle. After the tackle, the coach is shouting "get up, get up" to both the players. Every exercise, however, produces a fresh set of techniques for the coach to comment on and improve.

So far as this particular exercise is concerned we can check on these elements as well:

i. *The tackle*

When the player is moving away from you you must aim higher. Check that the tackler is winding his arms round, pulling his opponent's knees together, getting his shoulder in, and keeping his head out of the way.

ii. *Being tackled*

Stay loose, and concentrate on the ball: that's the important thing. Try to put the ball down on the side away from the tackler – if it goes down near him he'll try to kill it. If you can't judge that, put it down on the side away from the last set-piece – and this can be stipulated by the coach. The ball must not run forward, and must not get covered (unless in the match, you are behind the gain line).

iii. *Picking-up*

To be sure of picking-up you must be thinking ahead so that

you're in the right place moving at the right speed. If you get right behind the ball, you're in trouble. See p. 88 for a description of the technique. It's a great help if you know where the ball is likely to go down (see ii above).

iv. *Support position for the pass*

Here again, to be fully effective, the player must be thinking ahead. Never run blind: get into a useful, interesting position, and let the ball carrier know where you are. Call his name – the opposition may be calling as well!

v. *The pass*

The pass has got to be good – see p. 51. Aim to get it away quickly, and give yourself practice in different kinds of pass as the chance arises.

vi. *Work-rate*

The coach will start this off at a gentle tempo, to establish the form and make his coaching points, but at the back of his mind is the fast tempo that will establish work-rate. He'll move towards that as seems appropriate for these particular players, and he'll cut down the length (in time, or space) of the exercise as the tempo increases. All of these cyclic exercises have the potential to be exhausting.

Once the basic form has been established, it's easy to *develop* this practice. The obvious development is that the ball-carrier on being tackled fights to roll and feed his support player, either in the air or off the ground. The most likely fault here is that they throw the ball back: if it's accurate, fine, but if it goes astray precious yards are lost, and the movement may break down. It's a better bet to pop the ball up in the path of the supporting player.

Again, it's a useful practice for the ball-carrier to roll and simply hold the ball up for the supporting player to take.

Each time you alter the practice you will find a need to make conditions. For example, if the ball is being popped up, the whole exercise will go faster, and you may have to add an extra player or limit the running speed still more. Again, if the pop-up is to be successful, the ball-carrier must fight his way round to see his support. The obvious corollary of this is that the tackler must always try to prevent it – but don't point this out till the players have had plenty of experience of rolling and popping.

This first practice is a basic practice for continuity of attack. A similar one which we use a lot deals with the ball on the ground in the open. It's essential that we get possession, and picking the ball up is much slower than diving on it. The attacking dive to gain possession is at least as important but much less practised than the ball in defence. Again in 4s, the players trot down the pitch. No. 1 does a short controlled grubber kick, chases it – in balance, dives onto it, rolls, and either holds it up or pops it for the supporting player, no. 2, who repeats the exercise. This is illustrated in the sequence of photographs.

Once again, this is a coaching situation and the coach should get clear the elements involved: the kick, the dive, the support, the feed. This time, though, the ball is less under control – even the best grubber can bounce badly. The coach must, therefore, encourage a *wider support pattern,* and point out that anyone may be called upon to fall, and that consequently anyone may have to act as supporter.

The techniques involved in cyclic exercises need not be done unopposed. In any of them you can very simply create at least a token opposition. The easiest way of achieving this is for the ball-carrier to drive to the front, put the ball down, carry on for several strides, and turn to act as opponent. You can condition the degree of opposition he offers by controlling the number of strides he takes after putting the ball down, and what he's allowed to do in contact. Once again you balance the need to learn attack and defence in such a way as to encourage the aspect you're immediately concerned with.

A simple mauling practice will illustrate this. Use five players initially. No. 1 trots ahead and puts the ball on the ground before turning to offer opposition. no. 2 picks up, drives in and up and rolls to offer the ball, no. 3 goes in and jacks him up, no. 4 completes the wedge, and no. 5 takes the ball. He trots ahead...and the cycle recommences. (For details of mauling method see p. 85–86). The previous forms of the exercise have all started with the whole group trotting together down the pitch. You can devise useful cycles from other starts.

a. Split players into teams of four, about five yards apart. 1 stands on goal-line, 2 ten yards infield, 3 ten yards beyond 2, and 4 ten yards beyond 3. This form allows practice of all the scrum half passes, little cross-kicks, grubber kicks, punts. As soon as 1 has made his pass he dashes ten yards beyond 4, ready to receive 4's pass, and the cycle recommences.

b. Shuttle relay allows intense activity without using much space: all the players stay close to the coach. Simple examples will make clear how this form can be used:

*Turning and taking:*1 has caught the ball and turned
                              2 runs in and turns him
                              3 takes ball and runs back ten yards
                              1 runs after him and turns him...

*Picking up the ball:*1 and 2 at one end, 3 at the other
                              1 runs out, picks ball up, puts it down
                              3 runs out, picks ball up, puts it down
                              2...

Mauling: two groups of four players facing each other, ten yards apart. Third group with ball shuttle between them mauling (or rucking) each time they hit.

These forms in particular are useful for work indoors, though even the first form can easily be adapted to it.

The cyclic principle can be applied on a bigger scale just as simply. Take, for example, the forwards working on cover patterns against the back three. The forwards follow up the kick from fly-half, catch the fielder and maul the ball back. The fly-half kicks...and the cycle continues.

Here is a sample list of cyclic exercises. You will see that the form is easily adaptable to meet the need for intensive repetition. Remember, though, the need to control the tempo, and to use it as a coaching situation.

a. 1 pick up put down turn
   2   pick up   pass
   3   take pass   put down   turn

b. 1 pick up put down turn
   2   pick up   drive in and up   offer ball
   3   jack up
   4   complete the wedge
   5 take the ball...put it down...turn...

c. 1   pick up   put down   turn   front tackle
   2   pick up   roll and feed
   3   take ball   put down turn...

d. 1   grubber kick   fall   offer
   2   take   grubber   fall   offer
   3   take...

e. 1   trot with ball   get tackled   put ball on ground
   2
   3   pick up   trot   get tackled...

f. 1   trot with ball   get tackled   roll and feed
   2   tackle
   3   take and trot   get tackled...

g. 1 trot with ball   get tackled   roll ball back
   2   tackle
   3   pick up and trot   get tackled...

h. 1   grubber   defensive fall   bounce back into tackle
   2   turn him over
   3   dive in and dig it out
   4   take   grubber...

PART 5
Unit Techniques
— The Forwards

15
Scrummaging

The easiest way to play attacking rugby is to dominate the tight scrums. Physically, tactically, and in terms of morale, the opposition are put under heavy pressure and your team are given an equivalent boost. It affects the whole team performance. The opposing halves cannot commit themselves to attack, lose confidence in decision-making, may find themselves getting ball of such poor quality that it's an embarrassment. Your own backs have the perfect platform to mount concerted attacks. Moreover, since the team taking the ball into the maul or ruck have the edge in getting it back, you have the promise of effective second-phase play.

Tactically, and this is a point little appreciated, the chance of a break's being decisive is greater at a scrum then at a line-out, where the opposing defence has greater depth and longer to cover.

Coaching effective scrummaging is easy: it's a limited, clearly defined, mechanical exercise. With powerful forwards, even a mediocre coach can produce a winning team. Unhappily, all too often that's where the team's aspirations are allowed to stop: a marvellous platform for inventive, exhilarating rugby is used to set up dull play-safe exercises. Time, energy, and thought *must* be devoted to winning the ball – the pack must work on its scrummaging at virtually every practice session – but equally hard work must be devoted to the way you intend to use it.

The importance of scrumming is reflected in selection: in all other positions, you can weigh strengths against weaknesses, but a prop who is not first and foremost an effective scrummager is nothing. You hope to get a bonus in terms of loose play – only an idiot would plump on principle for a prop you *don't* see in the loose – but the basic criterion is his performance in the tight. This is a compound of temperament, strength, and shape – controlled competitiveness, natural upper-body strength developed by power-lifting, and short levers. All the power generated by your pack is transmitted to the opposition through their spines, and they are in an intensely competitive situation with their opponents. If they are inadequate, it will cripple the efforts of the rest.

Scrummaging is the best defined expression of the pack's solidarity, and for a critical moment of drive every player in your pack must be dedicated to it. Before and after there has to be thought, communication, and prediction, but in the moment of the drive there has to be complete mental and physical commitment. At that moment, you must have four locks, with both flankers committing themselves to that rôle. A moment's thought will show that the flankers' shove, since it is nearer to the opposition and therefore less absorbed in body structures, is more effective than that of the no. 8. They are also less physically constricted than the locks. They make, in fact, a critical contribution in developing the pack's power. Selection should have an eye to this, as one element to be considered, and coaches must drum it home.

The emphasis in coaching, once the technicalities have been established must be on *concentration*. Scrumming is the kind of power event, where, for most people, deep resources are never tapped. If you put an olympic class athlete in an unaccustomed position – e.g. putting the shot standing with both feet on a line at right angles to the putt – you can improve performance not once but several times simply by calling on the athlete to draw deeper on these resources. The same thing is true of a pack.

Probably once a session and certainly once a week the pack must have a concentrated scrumming session. This must be done, whenever possible, against an opposing pack. A scrum-machine is essential equipment for technical work – for getting all the detail right – and can be loaded to provide the resistance required for stiff work-outs (early in the season we push ours up hills) but it can never supply the confrontation quality of scrumming against opposition.

Such a confrontation must be carefully conditioned. It must be conditioned in terms of numbers of repetitions, defined purposes, and resistance, and it must give the other pack some measure of success.

It must also be conditioned carefully in terms of immediate action after the ball has left the scrummage. It's desirable that each scrummage should lead to a further action by the forwards – drilling home the essential work-rate maxim: do it and *run*. This may be in terms of back-row runs and support, scrum-half break and maul, or simply running to specific points as part of a support pattern, each followed by sprinting back to the scrumming point and getting down first. But there's a limit to how many of these a pack can do

SCRUMMAGING   the basics

1 The pushing position - imagine a little man pushing against a wall

 A.

if he pushes with his left leg?
can he push with his right leg?
where is his weight going?

 B.

if he pushed with both legs, where
would the energy go?

so he should be trying to get into a position like this :—

 C.

check hips below shoulders
chin forward to straighten back
90° between trunk and thighs; 90° between
thighs and lower leg - knees near the deck.

2 Stability — seeing him from behind

a narrow base is
unstable

a wide base is stable - get your
feet comfortably far apart -
think wide and low.

3 Power - all the drive comes from your legs

acute angles give a long
drive but slow to get started

obtuse angles give a fast
drive but not very far

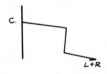

experiment to find the most effective
compromise for you - at the moment of
drive drop your knees a little lower: you
can cope with the more acute angle because
it's dynamic.

4 Traction

You need as much foot-ground contact as possible at the moment of drive:
experiment to find a comfortable position - e.g. toes out - that improves it.

5. Transferring the power - all the drive is transmitted along your spine

If you shove on 1 A above, you'll push his hips up; if you shove on 1 B, you'll simply
bend his back more - his spine and your spine have got to be flat; your backs have got
to be like a table top.

if you are at the back and you shove low on his leg,
all you'll do is drive his leg forward - then you'll slide
and he'll go up.

So you must shove as nearly as possible on the line of his spine :—

and he must make sure that the knee of the leg you're
shoving on is behind his hips: if he's the loose head
prop and he doesn't do this, he'll get popped out.

(cont.)

6 Getting low — the lower you get, the more effective your drive will be.

Keep your hips below your shoulders and get the whole of your trunk lower by getting your feet further back and your knees nearer the ground. Your hooker can still strike if he has worked a hip flexibility or is lying across. On an 8-man shove you get very low indeed, and go for more acute angles.

If a prop is in trouble the best thing he can do is get his hips lower.

7 The Drive — feel the power !

At the moment of drive, drop your knees a little lower, pick your head up and drive forward and up off both legs. Your opponents will brace for the drive, but tend to relax immediately after: get in position immediately for the second drive.

8 Locking — stay where you are !

On your own ball it's often best to settle for not going backward: lock your knees and lock the scrum.

a

start as low as your hooker will allow and more extended - obtuse angles; get your feet wide.

b

drive into a locked position — hips slightly lower, legs braced. Let your skeleton and ligaments take the strain.

9 Crabbing — don't let them get set

As soon as the scrum goes down, get your weight on your right foot, bring your left foot in slightly, shift your right foot to the right, — and so on: the whole scrum shifts to the right, making it hard for them to set up an 8 man drive or wheel.

10 Front row

As their opponents see them the front-row's shoulders look like this :-

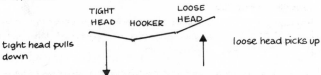

TIGHT HEAD   HOOKER   LOOSE HEAD

tight head pulls down

loose head picks up

But excessive picking-up or taking down will prevent your pack's power being transmitted directly to the opposition — stay horizontal on the 8 man shove. It's occasionally useful to cooperate with your opponent — if he wants to go up, go up like a rocket !

and retain their composure: you cannot work effectively in terms both of very high work-rate and thoughtful concentration. Mixing the two does not create a good learning situation. Essentially, pressure practices should be kept separate from the coaching of good form. Indeed, I'd prefer always to coach technique using a scrum-machine.

BASIC TECHNIQUE

The basic driving position to which so far as possible all members of the pack approximate is shown on page 108. The essential points are:

1. Shoulders slightly above the hips – "getting down low" means getting the hips down low, and the shoulders come down low as a consequence.
2. Spine not merely flat, but depressed in the middle.
3. Thighs approximately vertical. It's obvious that the more acute the angle of the knee the greater the potential range of the drive, but the more strength is required to initiate it. Any given player will be strong over a given range of movement – cossack dancers are strong over an extended range, but you have only to go into the full-flexed position to release that a drive from that position is very much slower and more difficult than a drive from a half-squat. Players tend to assume the position in which they feel most capable of a snap drive. On the other hand, the smaller their degree of flexion the smaller the range of drive. For a six-foot player, a flexion of 90° at the knee produces a potential forward movement of about a foot, which allows for a snap drive, and the necessary continuation shove. That is more than enough for all practical purposes, and may well be seen as a maximum.
4. If points 1 and 3 are observed, the knees will be quite close to the ground.
5. The feet should be in effective contact with the ground. It doesn't seem particularly important how this contact is attained. The weakest position is with the feet pointing straight forward with the heels off the ground: the flexion of the ankle is a potential weak point – far weaker than the flexion of knee or hip. This is remedied by shoving more off the sides of the feet, inner or outer. What is essential is that the players feel comfortable and strong.

6. In general, every player in the scrum other than the hooker should seek a wide base. The scrum must be stable, and having the feet close is a source of instability.
7. The actual foot placing is most important in the front row, and for the left-hand flanker on his own put-in. The front row placings are shown in the photograph section. The flanker must have his right foot in position to prevent the ball shooting out of channel one. For the rest of the pack the really important thing is that they should feel comfortable and powerful. If you adopt the "on your marks" position advocated below, with all four in the second row kneeling on the inside knee, you'll find that they automatically move into satisfactory positions.
8. Shoulder height in the front row determines how low the pack can get. From every point of view, the lower the pack gets the better – provided the hooker is capable of striking. It's better to work with your hooker on hip mobility, and on lying "along the tunnel" (i.e. pushing his head to the right on his own ball so that his body is inclined to the right and his legs are in a flatter striking position) than to settle for a high position. Against the head, it's better to get even lower than usual. What this comes to is that the props get closer and closer to the basic driving position, with their feet further back and wider, their hips correspondingly lower, and their upper bodies close to horizontal. This has two advantages: it restricts the opposing hooker's strike, and may even prevent it, and it ensures a more powerful and effective drive. It's worth pointing out that most scrum-machines are set too high to allow effective low scrumming practice.
9. The only people whose stance need differ in any large degree from the norm are the loose-head prop and the hooker. The loose-head prop has to counter the downward pressure of the opposing tight-head and allow his hooker a clear view of the ball. To do this he has to keep his feet further forward and his body rather more upright. For effective use of the available strength a stocky figure with comparatively short levers is the best shape for a loose-head prop. For no-one is weight training more important than for the loose-head. The hooker's main concern, if he is to strike for the ball, is to go down in a position that creates space for himself. In general, this means getting his hips in front of those of the props, staying fairly upright, with knees bent, before he goes down.

SEVEN-MAN, EIGHT-MAN, AND LOCKED SCRUMS

There are three distinct organisations of the pack. The seven-man scrum is the normal scrum, with the hooker hooking and the rest driving; in the eight-man, everyone concentrates on the drive (and everyone has to modify from the seven-man position); in the locked position, the side putting the ball in commits itself to not going backward rather than trying to go forward. Each is based on a different appreciation of the situation.

The seven-man shove assumes that the opposing hooker will strike, and that our seven can push as effectively as the opposing seven.

The eight-man shove assumes that the odds are very much in favour of the opposing hooker's getting the strike on his own put-in, that the best bet is to minimise the value of that strike, and that our eight-man can outpush the opposing seven.

The locked scrum assumes that the opponents' eight-man shove will be more powerful than our own seven-man shove, and that the bent knees which are a potential source of power going forward are a source of weakness as soon as the pack moves backward. We, therefore, seek to replace muscle-power by skeletal/ligamental strength, and adopt a position in which so far as possible the body and legs are in a straight line.

General procedure in scrumming

There are three distinct phases in scrumming – corresponding to "on your marks"..."set"..."go" in track athletics. The first is concerned with getting the pack into optimum position for engaging with the opposition; the second, with taking the initiative at the moment of engaging; the third, with a co-ordinated snap drive.

Seven-man scrum: front row "on their marks"

Before the scrum goes down, it must be organised. The moment of going down, of engaging the opposition is critical in taking the initiative. It's impossible to do this unless the entire pack can move immediately and as one man into the drive.

It's vital that the front-row should not move its feet as it goes down. All three must therefore have their feet in the desired "set" position before they go down, and must be the right distance from their opponents: too far away and they will lurch forward and force every other member of the pack to shuffle forward; too near and they will be forced to engage without adequate drive. The suggested set up is seen in the section of photographs. Both props have a stance comfortably wide, to give stability and to get the hips adequately low without having the feet uncomfortably far back. The hooker virtually sits on the loose-head's right thigh. The props' inside feet are close together.

The binding in the front-row must be absolutely solid. Binding over on the left and under on the right gives the advantage of an easier strike – it allows the hooker's right side to sink and right hip to move nearer the ball. However, it is a much more vulnerable binding. The best binding is over on both sides. The hooker's shoulders must completely overlap the shoulders of his props. He binds on their shirts as far round as he can get. The tight-head prop binds on the waist-band of the hooker's shorts; the loose-head on the shirt of the hooker as far round as he can reach at arm-pit level. (If the loose-head binds on the waist-band, he tends to inhibit the hooker's strike with the right leg.) The prop nearer to the ball binds first, and the other binds over his arm: the more important bind is always that nearer to the put-in side.

The hooker is the focal point: he must judge the right distance from the opposing front-row. He must also give the word of command for the pack to go down – loud enough for all the pack to hear it and aggressively enough to spark their drive. Before he does do this he must be able to count four heads – a flanker, two locks, and a flanker, all in position, all ready to drive.

To gain the initiative, the pack must hit the opposing pack with their full weight. The front-row must be driven forward by their four immediate supporters. Practising on the scrum-machine, I tell the complete second row that they must try to hit the machine with their heads, and so propel the front-row into the machine. The front-row must *dip and pick* – dropping their shoulders below the level of the scrum-machine, then driving up into it – picking it up. In effect, this puts them in a lower position than their opponents. In addition to dipping and picking, it's desirable that the front-row should also drive up to the right, moving the opposition further from the ball, and getting the hooker into a position where it's easier to lie along the tunnel. Some teams intensify this movement by forming up with the loose-head a little further from the opponents than the tight-head so that he and the hooker can engage with more power. I feel that this is valuable only if it does not cause too great a shifting of the prop's feet as he goes down.

It's essential that the inside thighs of both props should not be inclined forward once they are engaged with the opposition. If their knees are in front of their hips, the locks will begin to slide down, and the props may be forced into the air – get "popped-out".

Simultaneously with dipping and picking, the props must bind with their opponents. There are two basic positions for the outside arm of the loose-head prop. He tries either to swing his arms in an upper-cut action up and over the back of his opponent, to bind as far round on his shirt as possible, or he punches straight forward to grasp the waist-band of his opponent's shorts turning his elbow so that it is on top. Both are aimed at creating a cantilever so that the opponent provides purchase to counter his own effort to keep the loose-head down. In each case, the loose-head's skull is tight in to his opponent's sternum. If he is under heavy pressure he can shift his head to the left, out from under his opponent's chest: this lessens the leverage upon him, but strains the binding of the front-row. If his opponent bores in – i.e. tries to drive his head between the loose-head prop and the hooker – the loose-head should make every effort to bind even tighter before going down, should drop his inside shoulder lower than his outer, and (using the second binding position suggested above) try to pull his opponent's hips out, so exaggerating and weakening his opponent's position.

The tight-head prop is in a comparatively strong position and can afford to adopt a mental attitude much more aggressive than that of the loose-head. He has two aims: to bring pressure to bear upon the opposing hooker and his binding with his loose-head prop, and to keep his opponent down. His aim in achieving the first is to get his head close to the opposing hooker's chest as he goes down; in the second, he binds with his opponent's shirt quite close to his shoulders (where the leverage is greatest), pulling down and preventing him from moving his head out. Some tight-head props find they can exert more weight and power on their opponents by moving their outside leg far forward and pulling their opponent down onto the thigh.

Both props will find some advantage in making sure that the outside shoulder is higher than the inside shoulder when they engage with the opposition. This gives them improved leverage to exert or resist pressure.

The hooker with the put-in is in a favourable position for pressuring his opponent – applying pressure with his head – if his front-row have engaged with adequate aggression.

Despite well-intentioned changes in the laws, what I've described is the normal activity of the front-row, but it's all too often engaged in without adequate thought. The overall aim of the pack is often sacrificed to the personal aim of the prop. A moment's thought will show that the tight-head prop, for example, who succeeds in taking his opponent low may be negating his pack's superior shove – directing it down into the ground rather than straight into the opposing pack. Equally, a loose-head prop who can stay on his feet while allowing his shoulders to be taken low may be able to absorb or redirect much of the opposition shove. Whenever a pack has a decided advantage in driving power – through weight, or strength, or greater efficiency – it's to their advantage to have the props concentrate not on displacing their opponents but on transmitting the drive, and augmenting it. Quite frequently, props are so intent on single combat in the vertical they omit the need to drive in the horizontal.

A gambit which we have used quite successfully in the front row is that of reversing roles. This is particularly effective with the tight-head. Normally, his opponent is straining to lift him up and he is resisting powerfully. If occasionally he reverses his drive and drives up into his opponent he gains an immediate surprise advantage, and a longer-term doubt in his opponent's mind. In the same way, one occasionally sees a loose-head prop under heavy strain reverse his drive, leaving the referee to decide who is responsible for the inevitable collapse.

All chins in the front-row are customarily thrust forward, to straighten the back and bring head pressure onto the opponents. It's worth pointing out, however, that the hooker striking for the ball may gain an advantage by allowing his head to hang down and so gain a better view of the ball than his occluded opponent. This is less easy than it sounds: we are very unaccustomed to relaxing our neck muscles, and it's got to be a conscious effort.

Front-row before the put-in: 8-man shove

The eight-man shove calls for changed tactics by everyone in the pack. The critical changes in the front-row concern the position of hooker and the distance from the opposition at which they get set. The hooker is now concerned wholly with binding and driving once the pack is down. His hips are in line – or as close to it as his back-length allows – with those of the props. His feet must be far enough back to let him drive forward, but so placed as not to complicate life for the locks: it's easier if the front-row legs don't overlap. All shoulders should be virtually parallel to the ground. Most important, however, is the need to get lower than usual. This is particularly so, of course, for the loose-head, who no longer seeks to pick his opponent up. It means that the hooker must line up a little further away from the opposition so that on engaging all the feet in the front-row are further back, and the hips lower. For the eight-man shove to be fully effective, the props must concentrate on transmitting the drive rather than moving opponents up and down. If anything, both props and hooker should be seeking to drive parallel to the ground for the first few inches, and then slightly up to prevent a collapse.

Second-row before the put-in: 7-man shove – with the hooker hooking

The factor conditioning the forces in the second-row when the hooker is hooking is the need to allow room for him to strike. Basically, all the force generated by the second-row must be channeled away from the hooker and through the props. Accordingly the left lock pushes only with his left shoulder, and the right lock with his right. I've come across the occasional hooker who finds it advantageous to have the right lock push him towards the ball on his own put-in – it's worth experimenting with.

The forces generated by the locks must be counter-balanced by the flankers pushing in – forcing the props inwards. The flanker on the left at any given scrum must find a compromise that allows him to be effective in pushing in and giving his scrum-half some protection yet allows him to have his right foot ready to control the channeling of the ball. The flanker on the right has less need to drive in – the tight-head prop needs less support – and more need to drive forward, since the wheeling tendency of the scrum is towards him. In the tight, both flankers must think of themselves primarily as locks on the outside of the scrum.

Binding the second-row to the front-row is a matter of what works and what the players find comfortable. I don't like any form of binding that encumbers the props since it reduces their efficiency. Binding on the inside leg has the added disadvantage of allowing the lock's shoulders to slide down. Accordingly, I feel that the best forms of binding are either between the legs and up to grasp the waist-band, or on the outside of the hips, pulling the prop onto the outside shoulder. Points to look for on the first are that the lock's elbow is thrust far forward – which brings the shoulder into a strong pushing position – and that the grip on the waist-band is more effective if it's across in front of the lock's shoulder,

Whichever binding system is used, the locks must always transmit their power along the line of the prop's spine, and the nearer their shoulder to the prop's spine the better. To push lower down on the thigh is simply to expose the prop to the indignity of being popped out of the scrum.

In the seven-man scrum it is less important that the locks bind tightly with each other at shoulder level than that they should be tight at the hips. Accordingly they should try binding on each other's waist-band. This helps reduce pressure on the hooker.

The flankers should find it fairly easy to push along the line of the prop's spine, especially if the locks are binding under rather than round. There's a theoretical advantage in their binding very tight with the lock, but in practice, to carry out this other job, most flankers find it more convenient to bind fairly loosely with the back of the lock's shirt, and depend on their inward drive to hold the prop in.

Given that the referee is moderately strict in having the scrum take place on the point where he awarded it, and that the opposing scrum isn't hanging back, there's everything to be said for all four players in the second row getting into position with the inside knee on the ground. This automatically gets the hips well below the shoulders and helps all four drive the front row forward without getting high. Practice on the machine will allow you to establish where the feet should be in the set position to get the thighs into an appropriate position for the drive (see above).

The normal placing of the lock's head is against the inside thigh of the prop, and provided the hooker stays fairly upright this is convenient. If he moves over – lying along the tunnel – for the strike, however, it becomes increasingly difficult for the lock to find a place for his head. In the last two seasons we've experimented with the left hand lock binding on the outside of the prop's hips, with the prop sitting astride his neck. This allows the lock to drive from directly behind the prop, and has proved effective – our present loose-head prefers it. It also allows the hooker to adopt the very desirable "sitting on the loose-head's thigh" position. The forces operating on the tight-head make this positioning impossible on the other side of the scrum.

Second-row before the put-in: 8-man shove

With the changed role of the hooker, the locks are now free to shove on him as well as on the props: this allows them to direct their drive straight down the pitch. It also enables them to bind tight at shoulder level as opposed to binding on the waist-band. The flankers no longer have to counterbalance an outward drive – they, too, can direct their drive straight down the pitch, and bind more effectively with the locks. In all other respects the second-row act as they did for the seven-man shove.

At the put-in

So far we've looked at what happens before and at the moment when the packs go down: the "to your marks", and "get set" positions. The aim of both is to take the initiative at first engagement, and to get into effective shape for the subsequent drive – the "go". This has to be concerted: there has to be concentration in unifying the pack, and then a trigger to fire it. The *concentration* is vital – I used to chant to the Scottish pack at every scrum "bend your knees, straighten your back, squeeze". There's (in practice as well as theory) never a time when you can't concentrate a little harder on welding yourselves into a more cohesive unit, and a little harder on developing power. The coach has got to make the player completely aware of this, driving it home at every practice scrum.

The actual *drive* is initiated by a slight dropping of the hips – this gives a slight increase of angle at the knee, which can be accommodated because the sequence is dynamic, and ensures that hips are below the shoulders. This leads straight into a violent drive forward and upward, by everyone (including, at that moment, the tight-head prop).

The *trigger* has to be either visual or audible. On your own put-in, there's everything to be said for a visual signal. The old "Coming in now!" has real difficulties: the scrum-half finds it difficult to co-ordinate the put-in with the words; half the scrum find it difficult to hear; and the rhythm is equally effective for the opposition. (We do occasionally use a variation of "coming in now" at sevens – with the ball coming in on a predetermined syllable which changes from scrum to scrum.)

Communication between scrum-half and pack has to be two-way. The first element is that the hooker must tell the scrum-half that he's ready for the ball to be put in. He can signal this by a movement of a finger – and most referees now accept that this is permissible. This signal may also function as a "put-in now" signal, with the scrum-half putting the ball in "simultaneously" with his perception of the signal. In this case, the scrum-half can deliver the ball down and in in one movement from the knees – giving the opposing hooker a minimum view of the ball. The rest of the pack co-ordinate their drive from the movement of the hooker's foot – everyone must be looking for it, and make sure that they can see it.

A second system can also come into operation with the scrum-half's reception of the "ready" signal. He then holds the ball at ankle level, and provides a visual signal for the whole scrum that the ball is about to come in. These signals should come from his left side – easier for his own pack to see, and harder for the opposition. We've used two main ones: the left foot moving in to the right foot as the ball is about to come in, and the left thumb being left off the ball and coming down to touch it as the signal. Referees tend to object that in the first case the ball is not being delivered down the mid-line of the tunnel. The second is easy and simple to use. The rest of the pack drive on the thumb movement, or on the movement of the hooker's foot.

For the eight-man shove the time to strike is when the opposition are at their weakest – immediately the hooker has struck. At that moment the hooker is off balance, the props are concerned with sustaining his weight, and with their binding, others are thinking about channelling the ball. So: everybody watches the opposing hooker's feet, and drives as he strikes. It may help if the right flanker talks to his scrum while the opposing scrum-half is preparing to put the ball in.

Any system that delays the put-in will be to the advantage of the stronger pack for the delay allows them to grind away at the lighter opposition. It also allows them to get properly set for the drive. One

THE MECHANICS OF THE SCRUM

1. 7-man scrum with hooker hooking

All the power goes through the props, and the basic unit looks like this:—

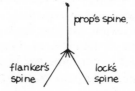

prop sits on flanker's right shoulder and lock's left shoulder
lock drives forward and out; flanker forward and in.

prop's spine is the line of resultant force – so the lock and flank
will probably <u>not</u> push at the same angle.

Put two of these units together, and you get the basic shape

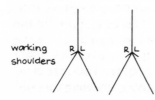

The right unit tends to have the prop angled
in slightly, the lock pushing straighter

The hole in the middle is free for the hooker

The left prop drives forward and up; the right prop
forward, in, and slightly down.

Add the No.8. who shoves rather harder with the right shoulder till the ball comes back,
and you get the 7 man scrum. This can be a driving scrum or a locking scrum.

2. 8-man scrum — everybody driving

All the power goes through the entire front row, and the basic unit looks like this:—

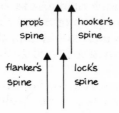

Put two of these units together, and you get the basic shape:—

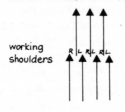

Everyone is driving straight; everyone is lower.
The props desist from vertical mayhem.

When you want to wheel, everyone thinks "left shoulder"
and channels all his power through it. But make a great
effort to go forward on the right before you start.

3. Wheeling

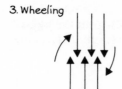

The couple on the front row means that
there's always a tendency to wheel
clockwise in the scrum.

of the disturbing features of play in the last few seasons has been the effectiveness of the drive in the eight-man shove and the consequent difficulty of setting up enterprising rugby from bad possession. One way of dealing with this is reduce the delay in getting the ball into the scrum and out again. It can be seen clearly in sevens: we practise by putting the ball in and hooking at the moment of engagement. This minimises the advantages of a side committed to wheeling us. The same thing can be done with a full-scale pack. The pack stays up until the scrum-half is ready to put the ball in, and the hooker strikes immediately the packs have engaged.

Again, the eight-man drive is effective in proportion with the length of time the ball is in the pack: the faster it's out, the less point there is in the big drive. This means more work on the scrum-half/hooker tie-up; more work on the precise line of draw-back by the hooker; and more use of the wide no. 1 channel. This may create problems for the scrum-half, but the alternative is problems not only for him but for the whole pack.

The third organisational system in the scrum – the locked scrum – is a direct attempt to limit the effectiveness of the eight-man shove. It calls for two basic changes:- that the pack and especially its right side should get as low as possible, and that their initial engaging drive takes them into the locked position (see p. 111). The locking on the right provides greater resistance to the wheel, and locking on the left means that we don't actually contribute to it. We've found that adopting the locked position for all our own put-ins is technically effective, and energy-saving, but can lead over a period to too defensive an attitude.

(The suggestions above are designed to limit the effects of being wheeled but every team must be equipped with methods of dealing with the situation in which the scrum has been wheeled – e.g. moves that will take the ball to the left, or give it to the scrum-half in space: see p. 130.)

Channelling the ball

There are in practice only two ways by which the ball can emerge from the scrum: between the left hand flanker and the left hand lock – Channel 1, and on the right of the no. 8 – Channel 2. Channel 1, as has been outlined above, has the great asset of speed: it, therefore, minimises the time for which the pack has to face the opposition.

When the pack is under pressure you may have to use it. It has, however, one major flaw: it delivers the ball, under limited control, at a place where the scrum-half may easily be pressured by his opposite number. It's fair to say that even limited control ought to be used – that if the left flanker can check it, take the speed off it, make the opposing scrum-half hesitate, he'll be making life easier for his scrum-half.

The other channel leaves the ball longer in the scrum, but delivers the ball where both the no. 8 and the scrum-half can use it. To get the ball quickly to the right of the no. 8 is not easy. It demands a carefully angled strike by the hooker, careful attention by the left flanker, a willingness to keep on working by the hooker, and intelligence by the no. 8. The locks don't come into it: if they move their feet, the whole pack will start moving backward. The flanker can correct the angle if the ball is coming back down channel 1, and push it over to the right. If the ball gets stuck in the middle of the scrum, however, the person best placed to help is the hooker. All too often, the hooker loses concentration once he's struck for the ball: he ought to be looking for the ball, and be preparing to push it on its way. The no. 8 can sometimes help in this but ideally all he needs to do is move his body over to the left to give the scrum-half maximum protection.

The movement of the ball through the pack ought not to be easily predictable by the opposition. Holding the ball, and moves directly from the right must be part of the team's repertoire. The key idea in holding the ball is that it should always continue moving relative to the opposition: i.e. it is best used when the pack is capable of going forward, e.g. on a secondary shove, or when the opposing scrum-half is coming round fast. There is no point in holding the ball if the situation is static. Perhaps the most effective method of taking the ball forward in the back-row is after a half-wheel. The half-wheel (i.e. about 45°) will tend to detach one or two of the opposing back-row who must guard against a break to their right. This allows a more effective forward movement.

WHEELING THE SCRUM

All wheels tend to be clockwise as seen from above. One still hears the odd coach who talks in terms of a wheel to the blind side. So far as I can see this works only when the blind side happens to be on the left of the scrum. It's convenient to distinguish the eight-man wheel to disrupt the other side's possession from the seven-man wheel in which the side in possession seeks to outflank the opposition, by taking the ball out to the left in their back-row.

The eight-man wheel must seek to start by moving forward. This calls for a great effort at tight-head to overcome the immediate wheeling tendency against him. However, a wheel without this initial forward movement is never so effective – it's worth the effort. After the forward drive comes the wheel. The aim is to exaggerate the natural swing in the scrum. The simplest way of doing this is for every forward to think "left shoulder" and channel all his drive through it. Once the wheel has started it tends to progress fast. All too often its momentum causes a loss of control: you sometimes see a wheel so complete that the two packs exchange starting positions. This is potentially even more dangerous for the pack that initiated the wheel than for those who have been wheeled. The maximum necessary wheel is of about 90°. This simultaneously opens up the opposing back-row and probably the ball to our scrum-half and right flanker (who ought always to detach himself once the wheel has started and move right to cover any back-row move), and restricts the pass to his right by the opposing scrum-half. As you approach 90° the chance of your left flanker being in a potentially off-side position increases, and he ought to be made aware of this. Beyond that you are approaching the point where more of their forwards are nearer your goal-line than most of your forwards – and that's a very dodgy situation. Your scrum-half and right flanker ought to be very aware of the potential danger and ready to nip it in the bud. The image is accurate in as much as the best time to stop any attack is at the moment it starts. This means that both must be ready to drive in as soon as the ball emerges.

We've already looked at possible methods of dealing with the straight eight-man shove – by getting lower, locking, using channel 1 – and these are the most effective ways of stopping the wheel. One further point is that the maximum wheeling impulse is transmitted through their open-head prop, and that our tight-head may be able to deflect part of this either down, as he normally does, or by a reversal of roles – up.

There's no doubt that a most effective way of stopping the wheel is to collapse the scrum, but it would be extremely irresponsible of any coach to suggest this: when the scrum collapses, people can get hurt.

HOOKING

One of the interesting things about the clinic skills – i.e. those skills (or more basically, techniques) which are peculiar to certain players at particular moments in the game – is the reluctance of coaches to examine them in detail. They are seen as esoteric almost inscrutable activities. Yet there isn't one, on the technical level, that cannot be reduced to a mechanical solution to a mechanical problem within limits set by the laws and the behaviour of the opponents. In practice, therefore, we can set up an ideal model to which the player approximates within the limits set by the referee and his opponent. Hooking is a precise example of this procedure.

The immediate need is to get to the ball first. This requires speed and reach. The second is to propel it through the scrum at a pace and in a direction required. Speed comes from using short levers – it's evidently quicker to strike with a kicking motion from the knee followed by a draw back than in a sweep from the hip. But this is a short range movement. We can extend it by allowing the support leg to bend, and perhaps by pressing forward off the support foot. We can increase the speed by making sure that the striking foot is not taking any weight, and the range by moving both feet towards the ball. If we can lower his opposite side slightly – i.e. his right side on our ball – that too will facilitate the strike. He will inevitably be striking rather across the line, which increases the difficulty of timing: we can reduce this difficulty by arranging that this whole lower leg comes across more nearly parallel to the ground. To do this he will need to incline his head and shoulders further to the right, on his put-in, and his feet to the left – lie more along the tunnel. Correspondingly, against the head he'll need to lean to the left and get his hips and feet further to the right. By applying these ideas we can get speed and reach.

Once we introduce the notion of control and direction we can begin to modify the basic action. All experience shows that a right foot strike on your own put-in gives far more directional control. Accordingly, it's far better to coach a right foot strike provided that, using it, the hooker is getting to the ball first. On the other hand, the left leg is nearer the put-in point and is fractionally longer in reach. It's highly desirable, therefore, that in addition to the right foot strike your hooker should be capable, against good opposition, of striking effectively with the left leg. To be effective, near foot striking has got to incorporate a powerful retracting movement to get the ball back, and the only movement available is that of the heel pulling back towards the thigh. To be able to use this movement, the hooker has to turn his toes and his hips slightly away from the put-in point, and lower his hips. This is the basic position for all strikes against the head as well as for near foot striking on your own put-in.

Once you have organised the basic mechanics of the strike, you can begin to insist on tactics and detail. The most common mistake by hookers is to strike too shallow and quick improvement can be made by encouraging them to strike deeper than seems necessary. Working with hookers I find it useful to demand an exaggerated action – not just in depth, but in speed and reach. I use a coin (being a Scot, it's usually a penny) and start with a fairly easy challenge: I drop it from a height that makes it comparatively easy to hit before it touches the ground, and at a point that doesn't demand much reach or depth. Gradually, then, we begin to move the dropping point lower, further away, and deeper. All the time, I'm talking about relaxing the striking leg, taking all weight off it, and getting the hooker to imagine the speed of the rattlesnake. As I move further away, the hooker will start to move his feet further over, let his hips sink, and he'll make false starts. This is good: in a very competitive situation, the hooker who doesn't occasionally get his foot up isn't really hooking. It's exactly analogous to the flanker who's never off-side or the sprinter who never beats the gun.

Once the basic action and feelings are established we can begin on the scrum-half/hooker tie up. This is critical and there's never a week that we don't work on it. The first point to be decided is the inclination of the long axis of the ball to the mid-line of the tunnel. (The long axis must, of course, be parallel to the ground though I've known wily scrum-halves who fed the ball left hand down, bouncing the ball towards their hooker.) Unless the hooker is much more comfortable with a 90° or 180° presentation, there's everything to be said for 45°, with the front point aimed towards the hooker – unless the opposing hooker gets right beyond the ball any contact he makes with it will be in our favour. The second point is to determine how far into the tunnel the scrum-half should aim to pitch it. This is a matter for the hooker to decide in the light of experience. If it's too far in, the opposing hooker should have less trouble in reaching it; nevertheless most scrum-halves don't put it adequately far in. It's useful to give the scrum-half in practices something to aim at – a mark on the ground under the prop's shoulder line, at the intersection with the right side of his neck, is a good starting point. This is a help to the scrum-half, and it gives the coach an essential check on what is happening: very few scrum-halves can pitch the ball on a given point. It's helpful if he gets into the habit of looking precisely at the point where he wants it to pitch, and he must work on the length till he's accurate.

The flick straight of the lower leg and the draw-back are as nearly continuous as possible. One of the commonest faults of hookers is that the draw-back is virtually non-directional. You'll often find that the striking foot comes back against the non-striking foot. This results in shallow strikes with the ball hitting the non-striking foot. The follow-through of the striking foot must be straight to the no. 8. I stand behind the prop – for a practice like this you work only with the front row against a scrum machine – and show the hooker my hands along an arc from the middle of the tunnel to a line behind his support foot: he has to put the ball into my hands.

This is a very concentrated practice, and it's futile to keep them down for long. After two or three strikes we get them up and have a word or two, with the scrum-half, hooker, and props all contributing.

Striking against the head is a matter of depth, length, and strength. I put the ball on the ground rather further away and deeper than is likely in a match, and simulate the put-in by putting my hand on top of it. By keeping my hand on top of it, it's possible to increase the pressure against which the hooker has to draw the ball back. We can then move the ball to encourage greater depth and length of strike. This kind of practice so closely resembles that of the hooker situation in the match that the hooker will tend almost unconsciously to develop modifications that make him resemble top-class hookers.

The basic reason for the emphasis on depth of strike against the head is that by striking deep, across behind his opponent's leg, the hooker may do enough to let his tight-head prop get a foot to the ball. If the ball can be checked, the tight-head prop has a real advantage over the opposing loose-head: he can set himself up with his left foot wide and his hips dropping in against his hooker so that his right foot is free to strike.

Given a player of adequate strength and reactions, with an aggressive and competitive temperament, you can make highly satisfactory hookers. We frequently have to do this for our team, and very frequently for our seven.

Hooking, in fact, is never simply a matter of form: there's got to be a concentration of will and effort by the entire front-row to ensure our getting a little more than our fair share of the ball. They work together: it's a truism that a hooker is no better than his props. If they can put pressure on the opposing hooker, and on the opposing binding, life is that much easier for the hooker. And behind them the four men in the second-row must concentrate in just the same way.

16
Back Row at the Scrummage
Attack and Defence ·

One fundamental aim of moves in the backs is to set up a handling attack in the forwards. If you can get your pack moving forwards in space with the opposing pack forced to chase them you have created one of the strongest possible attacking situations – the heavy overload. For this you need to involve as many of your pack as possible, to have created in them a keen appreciation of width and depth, and to have brought their handling to a high level. To ensure success they must also be adept at moving from the handling situation to the maul or ruck.

The forwards, however, must be capable of initiating their own attacks. As in defence, you must have encouraged the scrum-half to see himself as being in some phases of the game a member of the back-row, and the front five to see themselves as an extension of the back-row. The basic reason for the break-down of "back-row moves" is that they don't get adequate support or adequately quick support. The pack must strike as a pack, just as, in defence, they hunt as a pack. When you practise back-row attacks, therefore, you must bring the rest of the pack into them; you must move to the whole pack situation as soon as the back-row action has been established.

Unlike attacks by the three-quarters, moves by the forwards must be worked out in principle rather than in detail. It's even more important, therefore, since they are working initially in fairly restrictive situations to emphasise the need for individual effort, to encourage them to beat or at least wrong-foot an opponent, and to get them supporting intelligently. There's even less hope of their "going through the motions" of a move and succeeding, than there is with the backs.

ATTACK FROM THE SCRUMMAGE

Relieving pressure from the opposing drive and wheel

With the increased use of 8-man drives, getting the ball is

sometimes an embarrassment. The scrum is wheeled and the scrum-half finds himself with problems. The back-row can relieve the pressure in two ways:

(a) *By the no. 8 feeding the ball back to the scrum-half* who stands a couple of yards behind the scrum. The left flanker and the right flanker give the no. 8 as much protection as they can. The no. 8 gets his feet closer to the scrum and his left foot under his body so that his knees are bent and he's reasonably stable. As his head emerges for the scrum, he picks up the ball, and turns clock-wise to feed the scrum-half.

(b) *By developing an attack to the left.* Normally back-row moves have gone to the right – away from the opposing scrum-half on your own put-in. The development of the wheel, however, has made it not only necessary but desirable that the back row should be able to break left, able that's to say, not only to relieve pressure from the wheel but to turn it to your advantage. Those with long memories – and especially Scotsmen with long memories – will remember the days when the pack in possession actively tried to create a wheel with the object of outflanking the bulk of the opposing pack – moving them round to a position where they could contribute less effectively to defence, where they were no longer able easily to get between the ball and their line. The theory is identical for any back-row break with the wheel; the difference lies in playing the ball on the ground, or in the hands.

> *The ball on the ground.* The ball must be checked at the feet of the left lock. The wheeling action of the scrum allows him to get his head up with the ball at his feet. He will immediately be challenged by the opposing scrum-half, and his immediate response is to push the ball left to the no. 8, the scrum-half, and the right flanker coming round. The ball goes left into space before going forward. It's vital that each player fights to keep the ball under close control and that as soon as possible the rest of the pack take up a support pattern.
>
> Dribbling is in danger of becoming a lost art. Yet it is one more weapon at the disposal of the complete player, and there are times when it can prove invaluable – for dribbling exercises see p. 90.

Handling. This is essentially a use of the same movement with
the ball in the hands. The ball comes back to the no. 8, who
holds it at his feet – better, at his knees. He needs to get his left
foot far forward under his centre of gravity to let him pick up
the ball in balance. He turns clockwise to feed the right
flanker. Meanwhile the right flanker drops out and back
setting up the angle of his run. Every foot he can get back
helps him run onto the ball with power. As soon as the no. 8's
head emerges from the scrum the scrum-half (who has been
giving him what protection he can) gets out to the left to
support the right flanker's drive. If the right flanker hasn't got
deep enough, the timing of his run is difficult. He must wait
till he sees the ball in the no. 8's hands. As with all back-row
breaks he's got to do the running, and the rest of the pack
must be in support positions immediately.

Attack from a heel against the head

Provided the actual heel is fast and accurate, taking the ball
against the head is potentially the best possible situation for
attacking from the base of the scrum. Given the fast heel, the scrum-
half or no. 8 ought always to go for the break.

The initial movement is away from the opposing scrum-half – to
the left. Any wheel on the scrum is then to the attackers' advantage,
since it will tend to take the opposing back-row to the attackers'
right, and will make it easier for the no. 8 to get his head up and
move forward. The quick heel should also preserve some of the
depth in the opposing three-quarters, allowing a freer development
of the attack.

The basic forms of the attack will differ according to whether the
scrum-half or the no. 8 initiates it. For speed in getting the ball into
space the scrum-half has every advantage – he doesn't have to
control the ball, get into balance, get his head up, pick up the ball,
and disentangle himself from the scrum. His best line of running,
provided he's moderately quick, is flat – across the face of the fly-
half and inside-centre, to whom he can offer dummy switches – and
forward to link with his outside-centre.

The no. 8 cannot hope to move with such pace. His best bet is to
go forward, take on or take out any defender near the scrum and
feed the scrum-half and right flanker on the outside. The left flanker
will probably not be in a position to help directly, but he can cover

behind. Once again, the whole pack must try to give width and depth in support. The move is complete only when the entire pack are driving forward.

Attack when the opposing pack are moving back

Generally speaking, the front-five make back-row attack possible. If the front-five are under pressure, back-row breaks become less and less profitable or even possible. The best that can then be expected is a feed from the no. 8 to create space for the scrum-half.

Attack is possible from a stationary scrum, but the opposing back-row ought in that situation to be at least as well placed to defend as the side in possession to attack. It then becomes a question of personal superiority and commitment.

Provided the scrum hasn't been wheeled, there's more space to initiate the attack on the right – away from the opposing scrum-half. On the other hand, an attack to the left will have the merit of surprise.

(a) *The dummy break.* The simplest forms of advantage derive from a dummy break, and this can set up a penalty chance close to the opposing line. The dummy can be created by the scrum-half running flat with his body turned away from the opposing flanker, or by a flanker dropping out as a dummy fly-half – dropping out deep, watching the ball, and setting himself up as for a crash ball. The essence of either move is speed – once the opposing back-row see where the ball is, the dummy is impossible.

(b) *The feint break.* Where there's a short blind-side on the right, a feint back-row attack can be very effective. What's wanted is to pull the opposing back-row, and if possible the fly-half and full-back, across to the blind. The chances of actually scoring on a limited blind-side are small – it can be too easily filled with defenders. The feint attack is made with the intention of pulling defenders into that area, but making absolutely sure that possession is preserved – it's a drive with the ball snapped back before the risk of losing it becomes high. The scrum-half stays back, immediately behind the ball, ready to attack on the other side of the scrum with the fly-half close on his outside.

(c) *The standard breaks.* There are two basic forms of the standard break, and two basic intentions. The ball is either taken forward close to the scrum, with support coming on the outside, or it is taken wide to force the opposing back-row wide and played back to support on the inside. The basic intentions are to get the pack driving forward, or to involve the opposing fly-half so that the second-phase attack is against a depleted defence.

The attack is launched almost always to the right, away from the nearest defender – the opposing scrum-half. The basic difficulty is in accelerating from a static position, and this is exaggerated if, fashionably, you field a long no. 8. On your own ball especially, it pays to have a compact no. 8, able to hold the ball at his feet close to the scrum, in better balance to feed the ball in the event of a wheel, and faster into his stride if he attacks personally.

The flanker on the right is handicapped in his efforts to contribute to the attack on the right. He is usually required to work hard in the tight against the wheel, and consequently he has to wait till the ball is in front of him before he can come out. Even when he does, it's very difficult for him to join the movement with any pace. Basically, therefore, we have to think in terms of an initial thrust by no. 8, scrum-half, and left flanker, with the right flanker acting as cover or a static pivot.

The left flanker and scrum-half between them must offer some protection–channelling the ball, and guarding the no. 8s left side as he gathers. As soon as he's on the move, however, he needs support – preferably before he makes contact, since no matter how powerful he is he cannot hope to be as accurate in distribution after he is in contact. The obvious person to provide this is the scrum-half, who should be able to run into the pass with more pace than the no. 8 has generated. The left flanker can also be expected to be moving fast and function as a striker in support of the scrum-half. The actual running line adopted by all three, and their lateral spacing is a matter of judgement and will depend on what the defenders have chosen to do. The vital thing is that support for the ball-carrier should be immediately available, and that the bulk of the pack are there to carry on the drive or set up the tackle ball.

The most economical way of setting up a practice situation is to set up a scrum with both sides locked and feed a ball to both sides – who then both attack to their right or to their left. This creates a virtually unopposed practice. Once the basic form of the attack is established, ask for variety in passing and running lines and gradually get the whole pack to handle, and once they're doing that lead up to a maul or ruck. Then you can go back to using one ball and setting up one team as attackers, one as defenders. You can condition this so that the defenders think first of position – e.g. make it only two-handed touch. If the packs are not evenly matched you can keep both packs in the locked position and get them to wheel as you direct.

The temptation is for the odd player to try too much – emphasise that it's basically a support exercise, and that the usual support priorities apply – speed into position, use of width and depth, variety of passing, variety of running.

Each session should end with at least a few runs in earnest: it's pointless leaving the players with the feeling that if they just go through the moves they'll be successful.

The secondary drive

An excellent device for getting the pack moving forward is the secondary drive. On your own put-in, there's every advantage in locking against the initial drive – but it precludes the pack's moving forward. Once their initial drive has been absorbed, and the ball is safely at the no. 8's feet, a concerted effort can start the pack moving forward. We use the no. 8 to call "ready, ready, ready . . . *now*", and the whole pack puts everything into a drive. Near the opposing line this has led to some beautifully controlled push-over tries.

IMMEDIATE DEFENCE AT THE SCRUMMAGE

Defence by the pack as a whole is dealt with on p. 224. It's worthwhile, though, emphasising here the need for complete clarity about the immediate actions of the scrum-half and back-row when the ball is lost in the tight. It's vital to prevent the opposition getting the ball over the gain line close to the scrum, and highly desirable that the ball never gets in front of the opposing back-row close to the scrum. Attacks in that area must be snuffed out at once – and that calls for clear thinking, immediate action, and speed over the first few yards. In this area it's imperative that defence be aggressive – that you go to meet them and knock them down before they get started. You won't go far wrong if you imagine that the off-side line

BACK ROW IN DEFENCE

1. Close to the scrum - immediate aims : a pincer, two on each side

2. As soon as the attack becomes clear : an overlapping defence

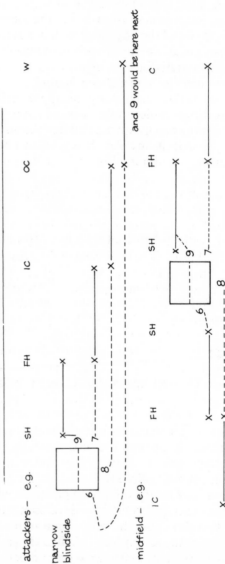

These diagrams are notional - the basic duties if the attack developed in that direction. As soon as you see -

e.g. in the midfield diagram - that the ball is going left, 7 sets out cross-field as 6 did in the first diagram,

and the opponents may not be the players expected - but never mind - "check I cover 2" all the way out.

Read the commandments - see text.

is your goal-line: you mustn't get off-side, but you must tackle as far ahead of it as possible.

Your actions, however, must be the result of a decision. Simply to go forward when the ball is already on its way to fly-half is futile – it cuts down your effectiveness in cover. For the same reason, a flanker never goes right round the opposing pack in pursuit of the ball – he comes back behind his own pack and concentrates on getting across between the ball and his line. Try always to avoid being out-flanked, so that you're chasing the ball from behind.

Once the ball has been struck by the opposing hooker, the back-row are faced with a choice: do they continue to shove, or do they use the time that the ball is moving through the opposing pack to get into advantageous positions? As a broad guide-line they continue to shove if the pack is committed to an 8-man shove, and break if it isn't.

On the 8-man shove, the flanker on the right must be prepared for the first signs of the likely wheel: as soon as the wheel starts he must get into a position to cover a possible break to his right by the opposition. He will have this scrum-half in front of him taking the first opponent – his job is to take the second. He must, therefore, get three or four yards wide of the scrum and prepare to take out the first ball-carrier who gets into the clear. If the ball goes to fly-half, those three or four yards will help him in the basic fh-ic responsibility. If it goes to e.g. their right-hand flanker, his spacing will let him see immediately and move forward quickly.

On the 7 man shove, the back-row stay down only if the opposing pack are holding and driving forward. It's very important, therefore, that the back-row should keep their eye on the ball, and be ready to react quickly, especially near their own line. That their opponents merely hold the ball is not important – except that it makes life easier; it's their forward movement that calls for the back-row to stay down.

If the opponents are not moving forward, or tend to get the ball into space quickly, the back-row should use the time that the ball is in the opposing pack to get into useful positions, wide of the scrum, where they can react quickly to any developments. For two of the back-row – the flanker on the side opposite the put-in, and that honorary member, the scrum-half – their action is fairly automatic. The scrum-half pressurises his opposite number and aims to take out the first attacker on his side. The flanker on the opposite side moves out three or four yards ready to take out the first ball-carrier or move out on the second.

The actions of the other two will depend to a great extent on where the scrum is taking place and their estimate of where the attack is likely to take place. Their normal distribution from a *mid-field scrum* is aimed at getting two defenders on each side of the scrum – the near flanker with the scrum-half; the no. 8 with the far-side flanker. If, however, there's a *blind-side,* these two players may recognise that a single defender can cope with an attack there, and one go across to reinforce the open-side and get into better covering position.

For the mid-field situation, you'd expect to see both flankers three or four yards from the scrum, and the no. 8 five or six yards out. They drive forward *if and only if* there are signs of an attack aimed at that area; if the ball is going wide, the great aim is to get into the cover pattern.

Two situations create real problems for the back-row in defence (and open up excellent possibilities for the back-row in attack): the heel against the head, and our pack going backwards. The second is too important to be left to chance remedies. If the opposing pack can get the ball and still move forward you have no option but to use an eight-man shove. Losing the ball on your own put-in calls for immediate action by the back-row, and more especially the right flanker and no. 8. They must cover the probable attack close to the scrum on their right. Once again this means the flanker getting three or four yards wide to take the first ball-carrier and the no. 8 getting wide outside him to take the second.

The back-row is one of the most important mini-teams with the team. Each member must be capable of sustained concentration and be a habitual reader of the game. Each must be confident of support from the rest. They must talk to each other, off and on the field. The coach can aid this by getting the defensive plan clear to them and working through defensive situations. Get two back-rows, and two sets of halves, and set them up as for a scrum. The coach stands in the middle of the "scrum", feeds the ball, and arranges for "wheels". The attackers run through attacking possibilities using the back-row and halves, and the defenders go through their response – using two-handed touch instead of tackling. The coach ensures that it works realistically, legally, and intelligently. The next stage will derive from full-out scrummaging practice – each scrum that's suitable ending with a back-row break and calling for back-row defence. It's obviously important that any player likely to come into the team in the back-row must know the complete plans in attack and defence and these practices are a step towards ensuing it.

17
Line-Out

The line-out has long been a problem area for the law-makers, and this is reflected in the difficulties encountered by the players, the referees, and the coaches. The basic objectives of line-out are to bring the ball back into play, to clear the field for subsequent attack, and to involve a different set of skills for the players. The legislators recognise the second objective by limiting the length of the line and the approach of the backs; they would improve it by confining all the forwards, whether or not they are involved in the line-out, to the 15 yard area. Their main difficulty lies in reconciling the third and the first: their efforts to create a straight jumping competition have led to difficulties in obtaining good ball. If they focused simply on the' need to get good ball, encouraged all positive attempts to do so – e.g. lifting, double banking, blocking – and penalised all negative, spoiling, play, the situation would be easier for all concerned. As a polar alternative, they might simply give the non-offending side a tap penalty on the 15 yard line, with forwards on both sides confined to the 15 yard area – a substantial inducement to keeping the ball in play.

Getting good ball is the prime concern of the coach. Fundamentally, this means giving the ball to the scrum-half when, where, and at the pace he wants it, and creating enough time for him to use it effectively.

So far as the fly-half is concerned, it's to his advantage, if he wishes to set up a handling movement, to be relieved of pressure from the back of the line-out. For a given length of scrum-half pass, the fly-half and the line outside him will derive more advantage if the ball is thrown long than if it is thrown short (see p. 141). This has to be balanced against the difficulty of throwing accurately over a longer distance when weather conditions are less than ideal, and the need to guarantee protection for the scrum-half.

1. THE THROW

It's impossible to organise an effective line-out if the throw is

LINE-OUT TARGETS

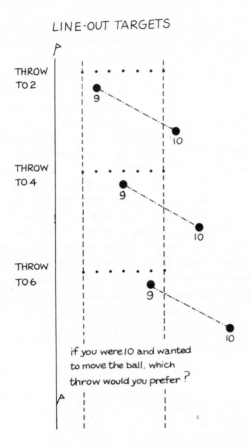

if you were 10 and wanted
to move the ball, which
throw would you prefer ?

inaccurate. There's obviously a range of acceptable tolerance, but the coach must be coaching for pin-point accuracy.

This is twice as difficult if you employ two throwers – a substantial argument for employing a forward as thrower-in. He will also get twice as much practice each match, and his being a forward will simplify the organisation of practices. Conventional non-thinking prescribes the hooker for this job, possibly on the grounds that it gives him a slightly better chance of avoiding injury, possibly because hookers in the past may have been slightly less large than the rest of the pack. In fact, throwing accurately is in part a talent, and other things being equal the coach should be looking for the most talented thrower.

The only way to give the thrower some feed-back on the accuracy of his throws is to give him in practice a fixed mark to throw at. If your jumpers do a sargent jump beside a wall and mark the spot with chalk, the thrower can retreat the requisite distances – 5 metres plus 1 metre for every place back in the line – and he can then set about learning to throw accurately. You could, presumably, do this outside but the basic work is best done indoors.

As with place-kickers, *concentration* is paramount: both have as much time as they wish beforehand, but only one attempt. The coach may take the thrower through quantity practice initially, but he's got to end up with a limited number of throws that are accurate. And, of course, the practice must end actually throwing to the jumpers – unopposed – and getting feed-back from them.

The style of throw is obviously less important than the results obtained. Once he has settled on a style, the thrower will probably stay with it, but it's not a bad thing at first to get him to experiment with the different possibilities. There's no reason to suppose that what's fashionable is necessarily the best for this particular player. The basic styles are these:

i   *Two handed throws*
   (a) lob from below the waist: this style of throw has a range of disadvantages – e.g. the jumper doesn't see it early; it lacks variety of trajectory – but it is very straight, and is useful for throws over the top of a short line.
   (b) soccer throw-in style: this is completely unfashionable but looks as if it could be easily and quickly developed.

ii *One handed throws*
   (a) New Zealand bowling action: this allows all the necessary variations, and presents a fairly easy ball to catch.
   (b) Push action: the ball is balanced on the throwing hand, long axis at right angles to the hand, in contact at the base of the fingers, with the middle finger up the seam – a very good, accurate, method of throwing.
   (c) Orthodox spin: the ball is held near the end, with finger tips along a seam to help create the spin – very accurate once it has been mastered but easier if the thrower has large hands and the ball is dry.

Coaching the thrower

As in all coaching, let the player throw at the mark and have a good look at what he's doing. With a right-handed thrower you expect a certain amount of swing from right to left but this will be intensified if the left shoulder droops. Suggest a slight lean back from the hips, head up, and following through down the line. The lower body and legs are there to provide a balanced base; to make longer throws easy the left leg should be in front with the left foot slightly to the left: this allows a transfer of weight, and lets the hips move forward square to the line of throw. The single most critical factor, however, is the follow through of the throwing hand down the line.

There are two basic trajectories: flat, and lobbed. The flat throw is basically for the front of the line. The lobbed throw aids the high jumper – it allows him to go up and meet it. For every position, the thrower should be able to adjust to the throw in front of the jumper, and the lob that comes down just behind him – so providing every jumper with alternatives against his opponent.

The timed throws – in which the jumper initiates the sequence – means that the thrower must practise throwing without a take back: his arms must be ready cocked for him to fire the ball at the jumper in mid-air.

In throwing to the jumper, he must be absolutely clear about the line-out signals, and concentrate on that point in the air through which he intends to throw the ball.

Once he has thrown he must be immediately ready to take part in the game again – basically, to get into the middle of the five yard area and be ready to close it up against attacks around the front. He can be used as an attacking player if from a short throw the ball is pushed back down to him.

On the opposition throw, he should position himself to get a clear run at the opposing scrum-half or the loose ball from a throw to the front. From a long throw he should check that the opposition are not bringing the ball back blind before he sets off on normal covering. This is particularly important near his own try-line.

2. JUMPING

The key notion for every jumper is *control.* In many ways it's better to have no ball than bad ball. However he deals with the ball – catching, throwing from the top of the jump, deflecting with the inner hand or the outer hand or both hands – his success is to be judged less on the fact that he got to the ball than that he delivered it straight to the scrum-half.

He won't get to the ball unless he watches it. "Keep your eyes on the ball" is a dead cliché: he's got to see the stitches on it. More than that, he's got to feel "That's my ball", and that nothing is going to stop him getting to it. Concentration is the name of the game.

He makes contact with his hand. The key idea here is that he plays down the line rather than hooking – that he makes contact with the palm of his hand at right angles to the throw rather than parallel to it. Real control begins when he looks for the ball and stops it, looks for the scrum-half and gives it. The sequence is, of course, continuous and extremely rapid – but it's the consciousness of the scrum-half's waiting hands and the need to pilot the ball there that makes for accuracy. Get the scrum-half to show the jumper his hands.

The hand that makes contact – and even if he has such remarkable ability that he *can* catch it, one hand will make contact first – has got to be relaxed, but in a strong position. Strength comes from the ability to keep the arm slightly bent – a straight arm is a weak arm, easily displaced. The aim in jumping, therefore, is not to get the hand high, but to get the *active shoulder* high, so that the hand is high but strong. Concentrate on that shoulder.

Power in the jump – the ability to resist body contact or pushing hands – comes from getting the body mass moving in as well as up. This happens either by getting the shoulders in on the line of throw, or by getting the hips in. The first of these is most effectively achieved by jumping with the outer arm going for the ball, tilting the shoulders powerfully in, and keeping them so far as possible at right-angles to the line of throw. If you allow the head to drop in this intensifies the movement. This jump also, of course, allows the use of the right arm at throws from your right touch-line.

Spring is basically a matter of leg strength. You can experiment with different foot placings, rolling onto the jumping foot, taking off both feet, altering the angle at your knees. (The advantages to be gained from arm action are ruled out by the need to reserve them for dealing with the ball.) When you come down to it though, it's strength – and strength can be improved. You don't even need weights: get under a basket ball backboard, and do 40 jumps to hit it – and do it twice a week throughout the season. If you can get hold of a diver's belt and load it to the point where you can just touch the board, and do 4 sets of 10 jumps with a recovery period between, that will accelerate your progress. Link that to half-squats (see p. 283). Your jumping will improve very rapidly.

Every jumper must have at least two *variations* to his jump. The basic variations are to go up in front of your opponent to meet the ball earlier than he does, and to vary that with a feint go forward and an actual jump up behind him to take the ball lobbed over the top. To get the footwork right start with your feet side by side.

A third variation is desirable for the jumper at 2. If your opponent at the front of the line has a height advantage you may have to rely on a two-handed drive, forward and up, for the ball thrown hard and flat – a very vigorous action that calls not for wild abandon but extreme concentration – especially on getting your hands across the line of throw. If the front man in the opposing line doesn't get his arms up to prevent this it's probably because he reckons his team get the advantage from your lack of control. A timed jump is a far better bet. Work out with your thrower your strongest position going forward and up for the ball. You then work out with him the timing that allows you to jump – getting up before your opponent who is waiting for the throw – and the thrower to whip the ball into you in that strongest position. Once you've done this, your opponent is forced to react to any forward motion and becomes vulnerable to the lob you take behind your starting point.

At the back of the line even more care is needed in dealing with the ball, since if it isn't controlled your opponents can get to it easily. A further complication is that the ball is a long time in the air and the opponent jumping against you has equal opportunity to react to its flight. The throw, too, will be less accurate than those to the front and middle of the line. As is typical of back-row situations, you must rely to a great extent on your own instinct. As deputed jumper you must commit yourself to the ball: all the general principles already stated apply to you. You've got to work on your jumping as carefully as the locks. If you have any problems, push the ball forward towards the middle of the line-out where there's maximum cover for it. For the peel your aim is to get your hand to the ball, stop it, and let it drop on your side of the line – don't pull it down, let it drop. This gives the first ball-carrier the maximum chance of catching it. Try to make sure it drops where your line still offers protection – in front of you – so that the ball-carrier can concentrate on catching it without distraction from the opposition.

It's customary to station your jumpers at 2, 4, and one from the end of the line. Two offers minimum chance of interference by the opposition – a jumper at one will always be suspected of taking the ball before it reaches the five yard line; four gives excellent protection for the scrum-half; one from the end allows your jumper to concentrate on the jump, confident that the man behind him will cover any mistakes. Most jumpers will wish to specialize in a single position. Broadly speaking, the jumper with more spring will do best at 4; the jumper with more aggression at 2. However, it's desirable that they should be able to switch positions – simply to keep the opposition guessing, or to take one of your jumpers out of a situation where he is being unduly pressured. An effective variation is occasionally to put all three together, all jumping for the ball – this creates a power block when the opposition are making contact a little early, and lessens the need for absolute accuracy when conditions make it difficult to throw with precision. Having a fourth unsuspected jumper makes this even more effective. If, for example, you have one other forward capable of getting up and catching you can use the grouping of the three jumpers at the end of the line to distract attention from the short ball to him at the front of the line. If an opposition jumper stays at the front, then you throw to the back.

It is, of course, highly desirable that at least occasionally you should be able to catch the ball cleanly and hold it. Every book on coaching describes what you do after you've caught it – landing, back to the opposition, with the ball held out in front of you, not too low, knees bent to make you more stable, head tucked in to save it from being torn off. And, of course, it's all sound stuff – if you can catch the ball cleanly and hold it. In normal match conditions, however, the odds against it are long. The only hope is to go up one handed – the inside hand – check the ball and deflect it to your other hand, or to deceive your opponent into jumping back when you are going forward or vice versa. You cannot expect to jump as high two-handed as you can one-handed. It's futile to concentrate on it in practice at the expense of increasing your ability to get to the ball one-handed and guide it to your scrum-half.

The other possibility which creates something analogous to the catching situation is to steer the ball not to your scrum-half but to another forward in the line. This is useful at all times but especially if the ball is wet. It allows you to use a one-handed jump, but keeps the ball under better control. The usual target-man is the player immediately in front of the jumper, and the ideal way of getting the ball to him is to stop it and give it the gentlest directional push that the situation allows: make it easy for him. He makes it easy for the jumper by stepping across, with his back to the opposition, legs partly flexed for strength, eyes on the ball, showing you his hands and arms. For him it's less like taking a pass than catching from a kick. Deflecting the ball to a player behind you in the line is another possibility but it calls for an inordinate sensitivity of touch – if it works, fine, but the odds are against it. It's better to concentrate on the easier alternative.

A refinement on the push-down system is to use the jumpers themselves as target-men. No. 2 deflects to no. 4; no. 4 pushes the ball forward to 2; no. 6 pushes the ball forward to no. 4. This has the added advantage that it preserves the basic rôles of the players: the jumpers keep their heads up, and the blockers continue to concentrate on blocking.

It is occasionally possible for the jumper to give the ball direct to someone not in the line – but he's got to expect it. The jumper at 2 may well find it possible to push the throw straight back to the thrower, and near the opposing line this is well worth trying. Provided your own thrower expects it, it's much more effective on their throw – push the ball into the five yard area, straight towards touch, and let him run onto it while their thrower is still contemplating his throw.

Coaching the jumper

To improve the jumper's performance the coach must:
1. set quality standards;
2. encourage him to improve his leg strength;
3. comment on his technique;
4. create feed-back situations for him.

The most important quality standard is that of the ball provided for the scrum-half. Until the jumper accepts that as the main criterion of success, with everything else simply a means to it, he isn't going to make real progress.

Building strength is the only way to make a radical improvement in jumping capacity. The coach's job is to provide guidance on how to acquire the strength and constant encouragement to work on it. He cannot, of course, afford to spend much time on e.g. supervising weight-training himself.

The most effective form of training for jumping is repetitions of depth jumping. This involves the jumper dropping from a raised surface – eg a chair – and immediately springing to touch a target with his hand. It's demanding, especially when weights are added, and should be started only when fully warmed up, by adult players: it is not recommended for younger players. Pairs of players can work on sets of 10,12,15 jumps, and rest alternately. The most effective form of weight is a diver's belt strapped round the waist with 10,20,30 pound weights added as power improves.

Commenting on technique is the same in jumping as in every other aspect of the game. Watch systematically what he does. Is he concentrating? is he really intent on taking his ball? is his hand in the right position? is his arm strong? is his shoulder high? is he getting his weight in? does he need to experiment with foot position? bend at knee? is he effective in going forward for the ball? going back for the ball? and so on. You should have a clear idea of what you expect to see: check any divergence – but take your time, his idea may be better than yours.

Feed-back situations give the jumper concrete proof of his performance level. The most obvious one is his delivery of the ball to the scrum-half – insist that he looks for him and pilots the ball. At this stage, it's best to reduce distractions – let him jump unopposed, and let him use his better hand.

To test that he's jumping *forward and in* place another player astride the line of throw, two or three feet in front of the jumper, facing away from him. If the jumper is going up properly he'll take the ball over the player's head and hit him fairly hard and fairly high. The player is encouraged to take the thump and deny that any contact took place. I haven't found it valuable to modify this for the *backward* jump. What's more important there is timing – the move forward, the suggestion of a throw and then the move back and up to take the lob.

I rarely have a straight competition between jumpers. I prefer when the lines come together to condition one side to getting through and let the other gain confidence in their jumping and blocking. When I do bring them together in a straight competition it's usually to make a point – to establish physically the truth of what I've been saying.

I'm working on improved forms of take-off for the jumper, and hope to publish some ideas shortly.

3. BLOCKING

Giving specific roles to players in the line-out depends to a great extent on being sure of the thrower's accuracy and the jumper's ability. If you cannot be sure of them, it's impossible to organise effectively.

The ball is basically the responsibility of the jumpers: if the throw is to 2, 4 concentrates on the ball but gets in position to block; if to 4, 6 does the same. The other forwards have two responsibilities – to ensure that the jumper has a clear jump, and to ensure that the scrum-half has the time to deal with the ball, and freedom to concentrate on it.

I tell them that there are two imperatives for everyone in the line other than the jumper:

move toward the jumper, and	'Compress' and
move toward the mid-line of the line-out	'Pressure'

If you get your players to concentrate on these simple ideas, and get your scrum-leader to hammer home the two words, you'll immediately get a far more effective form of line-out.

Naturally, these objectives are acceptable only within the referee's discretion: to the extent that he permits them, we employ them.

1. Protecting the jumper

The need to protect the jumper from contact would be lessened if all coaches and referees concentrated on positive aspects of play and discouraged the negative. As it is, however, the players immediately next to the jumper and more especially behind the jumper must work to give him protection. One way of maximising this is to alter the normal order in the line so that the blind-side flanker moves to one, and the props to three and five – just behind the main jumpers. You then have a specialist forward on the potential blind-side, and moreover one who – if he stops there for their throw – may be very effective in intercepting the opponents' throw to two. Since interference with our jumpers is less on their throw-in, he could, of course, revert to his normal position on their throw, and be available for normal defensive duties.

The basic need for the immediate blockers is to get between the opposition and our jumpers. Whichever form of blocking is used, this means stepping towards the mid-line and slightly in behind the jumper. There are two basic forms of this:

Method A

The blockers before the throw are facing the mid-line, hands or knees, feet fairly close. They take their timing from the jumper's feet: as they leave the ground the blockers begin to move. They step forward into scrummaging position on the foot nearer the jumper, interposing their shoulders horizontally between the jumper and the opponents. As they step forward, their near arms go in behind the jumper to lock with the other blocker – preferably getting hold of a shirt.

Their starting position conceals where the ball is to be thrown, timing is easy, and they end up in a position equally good for initiating or resisting a drive.

Method B

From the same starting position, the blockers pivot on the foot nearer the jumper and step across with the other foot coming down near the mid-line and behind the jumper. This presents their backs to the opposition, and since they are standing more upright they offer protection higher up on the jumper. Once again, as they step forward, their arms go in behind the jumper to lock with the other blocker's shirt. They take their timing either from the jumper's feet or from the ball.

They end up in a position that gives good protection, and makes it easy for the front blocker to adapt to catching the ball pushed down to him by the jumper.

In both cases, the binding is on the other blocker and not on the jumper. This cuts down the risk of interfering with his jump and eases the referee's mind about illegal lifting.

Each method has its attractions. The first method offers the chance of a drive and if anything goes wrong the players are in a good position to go through the opposing line after the ball. It also puts the players in a position that referees seem happy about. The second allows the blocker to keep the heads up and get a better view of the ball – e.g. for the push down. You can, of course, have the front blocker using method two, and the rear blocker using one as a compromise.

The timing of their move is subject to the referee's supervision: if he says they're moving too early, they must slow it down. On the other hand, it's much easier and quicker to destroy than to create: if they don't move fast, the opposition can get in. This is one fairly obvious case in which the referee might concentrate on supporting the positive.

Since a majority of the jumps tend to be forward, the blocker behind has a rather harder job – his step across and towards the jumper must allow for the jumper's movement away from him: each blocker should start with his feet fairly close together. The coach must ensure that they don't make contact with the jumper early and impede his jump or control of the ball.

2. Protecting the scrum-half

While the immediate blockers are protecting the jumper, the major concern of the rest of those in the line-out is to protect the scrum-half.

Failing a catch or a push-down to a supporting forward, which can lead to a normal maul situation with those on the outside tidying up, and the ball fed back when the scrum-half calls for it, the basic aim is to create a wall. This wall is designed to prevent the opposition following the ball in precisely the same way that a scrum, a maul, or a ruck is a more-or-less organised attempt to stop the opposition following the ball.

The first stage in forming the wall is that everyone stays in the line but moves towards the jumper with the aim of eliminating holes. Once again, this is broadly speaking harder for those behind the jumper than in front. It's got to be done quickly and that calls for concentration. You replace the open-mouthed gazing in the air by an organised movement towards the point to which the ball is thrown. You *compress towards the ball* so that you form a short, tight, line.

If you are using a player to tidy up – because, despite your efforts, the throwing and catching is not efficient, or because bad conditions, or destructive play by the opposition make it necessary – he gets out of the line at once. He should be as near the end of the line as possible to minimise the need for movement by the rest . He and he alone should go. I believe that the integrity of the line is first priority and that given the wall's protection the scrum-half should deal with the ball. I tend, however, to accept the players' judgement on this.

The players in the wall so far as possible are facing their opponents. Those at the ends have a special responsibility – shared by the thrower-in – to ensure that nobody comes round off-side, and you can't do that facing your scrum-half.

The wall is sealed by binding and the best binding is on the shirts of the players in front of you and behind you: get hold of a shirt.

All the above is simply a codification of practice. Like all the rest of the game, you approach as close to the positive mechanical idea as the referee allows.

4. SIGNALS

Signals imply decisions and decision-making in the line-out is just as much a matter of judgement as in any other aspect of the game. Someone must be thinking ahead, looking for the greatest advantage, weighing the possibilities, and making decisions. Sometimes these are simplified by the quality of your jumpers; too often, however, absence of forethought leads to stereotyped, mechanical, calls. The coach must select as decision-maker an intelligent player capable of concentrating and keeping the team's repertoire of throws clear in his mind. In most ways, the ideal position for him is at scrum-half: he, after all, has to deal with the bulk of the ball provided, he can see what's going on more clearly than anyone in the line, and he can communicate easily with the line and the thrower. He's also usually one of the earliest players to approach the position of the line-out, and is well placed, therefore, to call variations in the length of the line before it forms.

Whatever signals you use must be difficult for your opponents to break, and easy for your players to follow. They fall into two categories – visible and audible – and it's customary to provide as much distraction in the shape of irrelevant "noise" as possible. Visual signals may be given by anyone that the whole line can see – normally, but not necessarily, the scrum-half or thrower. Common instances are the skin to skin, skin to cloth, no contact set of signals, and foot positioning by the scrum-half; ball on chest, one hand on ball, two hands on ball by the thrower. Audible signals can be given by anyone with an adequately loud mouth – and varieties of them are legion. Words beginning with curved letters: *orange;* straight letters: *tangerine;* blended letters: *peach,* form an elegant one.

The signals most difficult to crack, however, are those based on arbitrary groupings known to your team but not the opposition. This first occurred to me when coaching a regional team, drawn almost wholly from two clubs, against a touring team. We used the names of players in one club's 1st XV to denote the short throw, in the other's to denote the middle, and anything else for the end. This can easily be applied to the club situation: take any two moderately large, discrete groups known to the players and not known by the opponents and you're away. You use your signals, of course, in every line-out practice.

Your thrower-in is best placed to function as code-cracker on their throw – he can set himself up as an expert on codes, but he'll probably learn more from watching for the unconscious preparation of jumpers about to jump, than watching or listening to the thrower-in.

5. SCRUM-HALF POSITIONING

Most scrum-halves stand about six feet back from the line-out. When there's doubt it's probably better to stand a little deeper – it's easier to come forward, than turn and come back.

They usually stand roughly opposite the third man in the line – concealing where the ball is going, but in easy touch with the main jumpers. There's something to be said, however, for their starting at the front of the line-out and moving along it just behind the ball. This puts them in a position where it's easy for the jumper to switch attention to them as soon as the ball is in hand, and where they're virtually set up for a straight or dive pass. For a pivot pass they're best positioned slightly behind the jumper and turned to face him. For kicking, too, they're better off standing still. But the essential thing is that they must be ready to deal with what happens as it happens: in balance, on a narrow base.

They must be prepared to play an active part in defence. It may be possible to share this, in bad conditions, with designated forwards – e.g. the thrower-in at the front, or one of the back-row further back – but scrum-halves who refuse, for example, to go down on the ball are a real weakness in defence.

6. THEIR THROW-IN

Too often line-out practices concentrate on the team's throw, often to the exclusion of practising methods against the opposition throw. Certainly our own throw should get greatest emphasis – we must be looking to take our own ball – but the opposition will throw in just about as often as we do, and we need to take some of theirs.

On their throw they will tend to be defensive minded – concerned with protecting their jumper and scrum-half – rather than actively concerned with breaking through our line. We can afford, therefore, to commit ourselves to attack. If we do get the ball, our scrum-half will have a little time to deal with it while the opposition adjust to the situation.

Our jumpers will jump against theirs. They may find that moving one in front of their jumpers is effective, especially if the opponent hasn't worked on the ball dropping just behind him. At the front of the line, our player can stand with his hands up or actually jump for the ball, seeking to push it down to our thrower-in. The jumper at the back of the line should be ready to get up and push the ball back towards the middle of his own line. At the tail of the line-out, two at least of the players should be thinking in terms of cover – one checking that their scrum-half has passed, and going out across the front of fly-half, the other going for fly-half and then inside-centre. The opposition are more likely to pass then kick until the two three-quarter lines are fairly close. If the ball goes loose near the end of the line, however, their job comes back to that of all the forwards not otherwise committed: get to their scrum-half. This player must have his concentration eroded by the pressure of your forwards. If the oppositon delay for a moment on compressing their line, our forwards must be half through on him. One player – our thrower-in – has a fairly clear run at him, and should be encouraged to chase him and then run deep. This aggression is possible only through commitment: let the jumpers look after the ball – you look after the scrum-half.

If the opposition move the ball from the line-out, they're likely to strike rather further out than normal, and cover from the line-out should, therefore, start a little deeper than normal, especially for those nearer touch.

There are times when conditions are so bad that the line-out becomes an embarrassment – when the ball is almost impossible to control. At these times, especially, this kind of pressure pays. It's still desirable for your jumper to jump – as an added disincentive to their jumper – but he shouldn't try to get the ball: just make it that much harder for their jumper to deal with it competently. The aim is to get it on the ground, and then to get it with the foot. Keep it going forward, keep it in play. Your thrower-in is the man to keep it in play: try to keep him between the ball and touch.

Once again, the overall aim on their ball is to convert the pack from open-mouthed gazing to simple, committed, action. Simplicity and commitment mean speed.

7. THE PEEL

In the line-out, the gain-line is only one pace away. It's, therefore, an excellent situation for getting the forwards taking the ball on themselves. One basic way of doing this is the "peel".

Teams try this at both ends of the line but the only time a peel to the front is likely to be successful is right on their line. There simply isn't enough space to make attacks there consistently successful. On their line, however, a determined ball-carrier aiming just inside the corner-flag stands a fair chance of success, provided the intention is adequately disguised. The simplest way is to put all your jumpers together further back. If their jumpers move to cover them you may then be able to use a "non-jumper" – who has practised diligently – to catch the ball and hold it out for one of your big men to take and crash over. If their jumpers don't move, then you throw to your power block.

If you wish to attack the front you're usually well advised to launch a feint attack to the open – by a peel, for example, or getting the ball to the fly-half running slowly – and then switch the ball blind, using the full-back, winger, and thrower-in as strikers.

Far more useful is the peel to the open. For this the ball must be thrown far back in the line, and there's something to be said, therefore, for taking one forward out of the line to keep the throw a little easier. The advantage of throwing to the second-last man is that it allows him to concentrate on the ball confident that he has support behind him. His aim is to stop the ball and let it drop – not to push it down hard. The ball collector has a much easier task if the ball is dropping slowly – it allows a greater margin for error in the timing of his run. It's also easier for him if the ball drops to him before he reaches the end of the line: he can concentrate on the ball rather than his opponents.

The ball collector, however, is virtually certain to be taken out. Even if the end man has managed to make a little room for him in stepping across to protect the jumper, the ball collector is not likely to get far. You must, therefore, discount him as a striker. The really important figure in the peel is the second ball-carrier, and much of the work in preparing the peel is to get him in precisely the right place at the right time. He's got to be right alongside the ball collector at the moment he passes the end of the line-out. If he's a yard back, the move may well break down.

The second ball-carrier must be picked with great care – speed of reaction, acceleration, and concentration are required. Where he starts from is less important than that he should be in contact and moving fast. What position – e.g. prop, lock, hooker – is equally unimportant: his qualifications are not positional but personal.

If you find difficulty in getting the right player moving from the front of the line, there's much to be said for having your second ball-carrier stationed at scrum-half. This gives him a clearer view, a shorter distance to run, and a better angle to run at.

The question of angle is important. If your ball-carrier tries to get across the gain-line fast he'll be running into their cover, and his change of direction will not improve his speed. He's well advised, therefore, to be moving fast when he takes the ball and get at least a couple of strides in on that line before seeking to go forward. From scrum-half, however, he can go forward without needing to change direction.

You may well find that experimenting with another forward out of the line, stationed near the fly-half, and running straight to straighten the drive and bring more momentum to the strike, adds to the effectiveness of the move.

It's futile, of course, confining a peel practice to those immediately involved: as ever, you should expect the worst, and play through second-phase. Peels tend to be successful in proportion with the number of forwards who get there quickly, in balance, thinking. You seek to develop the attack on the open, supporting as if you were doing a loop practice (see p. 52). Your scrum-half should get right behind the ball so that the ball-carrier if tackled can roll it straight back to him. The rest of the forwards must hope to handle but be prepared to ruck or maul.

Your halves must be summing up continually. The scrum-half may well find that gaps open up round the maul. The fly-half has got to be checking on whether the peel has involved any of their backs, and whether the rest have moved in – if so he'll spin it open, if not he may go himself. He's also got to take a look at the blind-side: it may have been left virtually unattended.

The peel is very much an attacking move, and is often most successful in setting up a scoring situation: use it in their half. There are a number of small advantages in using it on the left. It's also a convenient way of bringing your forwards into the game. You might use it first throw on the left in their half of the field as a declaration of intent.

Defence against the peel

The best moment to counter any close-quarters attack – at line-out as at scrum or maul – is at the moment it starts. Your jumper at the back should be committed to getting to the ball and pushing it back towards the middle of his line. If he fails to do that, the end man becomes the key figure. As the jumpers go up he must try to step back behind his immediate opponent, and concentrate on taking the first ball-carrier out of the play. If he can stop him at once, the opposition timing and support may be put out. If he can knock him backward, the initiative is passed from the attackers to the defenders: they are going forward. But every player must be reacting. The thrower-in should stay wide – just in case the attack is switched blind. The rest must get – with half an eye on their immediate opponents – into a cover pattern.

8. VARIATIONS IN THE LINE-OUT

Any variation you adopt in the line-out capitalises on lack of preparation by the opposition. Some variations have already been described:

1. movement of jumpers;
2. variety of jumps;
3. timed jump;
4. peel.

A most important one has been implied: altering the length of your line. Immediately you drop a man from your line, the opposition are forced to drop one from theirs, and are faced with a choice of which player to drop. The tendency is usually to drop the player at the back of the line – who may very well be a tackler you're pleased to see retire ten yards. Most teams are prepared for an 8-man line and a 7-man line – but not for a 6-man or a 5-man line.

The more people you drop, however, the more important it becomes to prevent the opposition simply drifting out and making attack impossible. You must, therefore, make sure that the players you drop form a compact, threatening, group so placed – e.g. in the 5-yard area or inside the fly-half – that they're available both as a real strike force, and an effective diversion. As a strike force they have one major advantage: timing. They can start to run, and cross the 10 yard line in full stride, because the thrower-in can time his throw from then, and put the ball in their path to coincide with their arrival. Try this from a 2 or 3 man line, say twelve yards from their line. Equally, the fly-half or inside-centre running against the saturated defence should be aware of the group, e.g. on the left touch and be ready to chip the ball in front of them.

Dropping players from your line allows you effectively to dispense with line-outs: you can simply throw the ball over the top. In the example above you were throwing it to a group on the move, but you can equally throw to an individual player. This is often the scrum-half, but there may be an advantage in dropping your scrum-half back and throwing to a very aggressive flanker running from scrum-half position. Variations on this kind of move, and the use of a timed jump, are obvious partial answers to the problem of limited size.

Very simple but effective variations on the short line are based on the idea of getting one of your players into space.

(a) On every short line, have your end player come into the line from dead astern. Quite often he isn't picked up and the ball can be thrown straight to him.
(b) Throw to the end player running back. He takes three or four quick steps back with the ball already on its way, and either checks and goes up, or simply lets the ball reach him. He can feed the scrum-half who in turn can either carry on running or pass.
(c) Line up with an obvious jumper at the end of your short line,

with a flanker immediately in front of him. If he isn't picked up by one of their jumpers, throw to him. If he is, he sighs, shouts "Change" and moves on the outside to change places with the flanker. The flanker runs backward and keeps on running with the ball on its way to him in space.

(d) Shorten your line and as soon as the opponents have shortened split the line, leaving a gap. The thrower-in immediately assesses and throws –

1. they've covered the gap; throw to the spare man.
2. they haven't covered the gap; throw into it for the first forward in the second group running forward.

Speed is the essence.

You obviously cannot throw over the top at every short line, but the likelihood that you will may give you an advantage throwing into the line. The people you put in the line should all be capable of jumping, and your thrower can look for an advantage there. You can employ a timed jump at 2. Once you've done that, he can take off as for a timed jump and as he comes down the ball is thrown at a timed jump to 3. Again if once the two man line is formed both your players take a step back you gain the possibility of moving forward or back for the ball – very simple, but very effective.

It isn't particularly difficult devising such variations. The important thing is not to leave them in a coaching vacuum – what are you going to do with the ball once you've secured possession? Incorporate them in your unopposed and situation practices, talk to the players and work out what for your team are the best bets.

The one place on the field where you do not think of using a short line is within ten yards of the opposing goal line – where the bulk of their pack can be closer to the action than the bulk of yours. One place where it is always considered but infrequently used is within ten yards of your own line – when, conversely, the bulk of your pack can be nearer than the bulk of theirs. If you are doing well on your own ball you won't need to: a good feed and a good wall give a fine defensive screen, and the more people you have between the ball and the line, the better. The idea of a two-man line, the ball thrown, two-handed from under the waist, to a catcher, stepping out from the try line ten yards out, who feeds the kicker is very attractive if you can't be sure of coping with the normal line. Most mistakes occur when it's not properly set up – e.g. when the actual kicker is expected to catch – or it's not adequately coached.

Response to a short line

Just as you prepare a set of lines to take advantage of lack of organisation in the opposition so you must counter your opponents' plans to surprise you. The easiest way to do it is to establish a "leaving order" of your players e.g.

1. prop (6)
2. prop (5)
3. non-jumping back row (4)
4. non-jumping back row (3)
5. front-jumper (2)

The second stage is to redeploy these players to maximum advantage. If your opponents are taking up organised positions, your players can match them so that the overall balance is undisturbed. If they simply retire from the line-out, you can arrange:-

1. prop . . . inside your fly-half, ready to move open or blind
2. prop . . . inside your fly-half, ready to move open or blind
3. back-row . . . just outside your fly-half, ready for a throw over the top
4. back-row . . . just outside your fly-half, covering 3
5. jumper . . . with 1 and 2

For 3 and 4, you should also consider replacing your scrum-half. The shorter the line the greater the probability the ball will be thrown over the top. Depending on the relative speed, aggressiveness, and size of your scrum-half and 3 or 4, you may elect to send the scrum-half back instead of 3 or 4. Near their line, for example, if they intend to throw long to a kicker, having a very aggressive flanker at scrum-half can cause them real problems. It's probably better to replace the scrum-half at 4, since you need a back-row player to counter the throw over the top to a forward running from the 10-metre area.

18
Supporting, Mauling and Rucking

The critical question facing every forward in the loose is: where can I most quickly get into the action? This is a matter of judgement – which is, perhaps, why so many coaches avoid coaching it.

The coach can help by giving guidelines, by setting up practice situations, and by focusing attention on it in all team practices.

The basic guidelines are straightforward:

i. Get your head up; guess what's going to happen; back your hunch.
ii. Make sure you get between the ball and your try line.
iii. Run off the man ahead of you with a sense of the need for the whole pack to provide width and depth in all support.

The good player is one whose judgement is sound. Some players are over-optimistic – they go too far forward, and find themselves outflanked in defence, or in front of the ball in attack: they fail to get between the ball and their try line. Some players are pessimistic – they go too deep, and rarely get into the action in defence or attack. Mechanical aids to loose play – neat lines in a diagram – are useless. The notion of "corner-flagging" focuses attention on the ultimate line of defensive running: if you don't catch them on that line, they've scored a try. The idea that a forward would automatically break from a scrum and mechanically set off for the corner flag is ridiculous. He has got to judge his line. The simplest general advice is that most movement in cover is crossfield, with immediate divergence forward or back in view of developments.

Very useful basic exercises are outlined in the first part of Team Practices (chapter 26), where the pack and backs work against each other, helping the forwards develop skill in following up a kick or covering crossfield. They encourage judgement rather than provide set answers. After each run you check with the pack how effective their running was, and how it could be improved. This allows the coach to drill home the basic guidelines.

Intelligent use of the group handling exercises described under Intensive Handling (chapter 7) are another way of encouraging imaginative running. If you keep hammering the basic needs for width and depth in handling attack, with the whole pack creating space to allow the attack to develop, you'll find that it rubs off in support play, both in attack and defence.

All forwards should be encouraged to play small-side touch rugby to help them improve their decision-making especially in terms of movement off the ball.

A certain amount of help can be given to forwards in attack if, as soon as the tactical decision is made, they are told what it is. This is normally relayed by the scrum-half. They need to know:

    i. the direction of attack;
   ii. the striking point;
  iii. whether there's to be a switch.

This might come out as "red-x-cut" – a movement left with attack at inside-centre following a switch. You can make up codes for yourself: keep them simple. This will certainly be a help, but can never replace the judgement from immediate feed-back of the individual player.

MAULING: A DEVELOPMENT OF SUPPORT PLAY

So far as attack is concerned, the delay implicit in a maul or ruck is a disadvantage even if the maul is effective. Ideally, the momentum of the attack should be maintained without check. When I first suggested this, it was well received, but perhaps without an appreciation of its implications. It implies that a great deal of effort should be devoted to handling and support to avert the need for mauling. The characteristic weakness in forward handling, for example, apart from inadequate preparation of the players for a handling role, is a failure to create space for themselves. By remaining in a tight bunch they make their assumption – that the pack's role is to maul – come true. The prime need for sustained forward attack is space.

Once a maul is likely, however, it's obvious that the pack must converge speedily. An isolated player has little chance of retaining possession against superior numbers. The only way to make mauling fully effective is to train your players to ensure that they only enter the mauling area in pairs. This means a need for the ball carrier to look ahead, and if necessary try to delay contact till a supporter arrives – by a change of direction or pace, for example – and for the nearest supporter to make an all-out effort to get to him so that they are setting up a wedge as they hit the opposition. Ideally, the ball-carrier will be able to drive on without delay because of the support being immediately available – this is superb in its drive and power, but the essential thing is that the ball does not get lost – the pair is more important than the single player's drive and power.

The technique of mauling is described under Personal Skills (chapter 10), because, of course, any player can be required to act as a wedgeman, as ball-carrier or first supporter.

The great need for the coach is to bring home to the pack the overwhelming importance of support – to see mauling as a contingency in open, handling, attack. He can adapt all his group handling practices to this simply by having a ball-carrier put the ball on the ground and turn to act as an opponent: the nearest players whip up the ball and form the wedge; the rest isolate them; the ball is fed back, and the handling starts again. This affords good practice in a powerful form of attack – rolling off the maul against an unprepared defence. The key figure is the second ball-carrier: drill him to offer immediate support, and fight to keep the ball alive. In team practices he will usually be the scrum-half, receiving from a forward, and feeding a forward.

MAULING: DEFENSIVE TACTICS

Although the side taking the ball into the maul should always have the advantage in getting it back – should see losing it as exactly equivalent to loosing their own put-in in the scrum – the opposing team must make every effort to deny them an advantage. This has three basic elements:

1. Dealing with the ball-carrier;
2. Setting up a defence to stop opponents attacking close to the maul;
3. Making sure the opposing maul is going backwards.

1. Dealing with the ball-carrier

This must be practised by everyone, and is dealt with under Personal Skills.

To isolate the ball, or the ball-carrier, calls for a very fast reaction, and clarity of thought. There are three basic methods, each with its own advantages. The first is to "*turn the ball-carrier*" – i.e. turn him to face his opponents, so that his own body isolates the ball from his supporters. This calls for some superiority in strength and size from his immediate opponent – if it isn't done fast, it isn't likely to succeed. The most efficient way to do it, is to pick him off the ground, swinging him by hip and opposite shoulder to get maximum leverage, and trying to keep his head up so that he can't fold himself round the ball. Once he's round, the ball is isolated and the next aim is to isolate him – to drive between him and his supporters. Once he's isolated, he's got to be attacked. As much downward pressure as possible must be exerted on the ball, and if that isn't sufficient, his hands must be pried off it.

The second way of dealing with him is for the *first opponent to slip in behind him* so that the ball is isolated from his supporters as it is from his opponents. The critical point then is whose supporters can isolate the ball-carrier, driving past so that the ball is in their half of the maul. Single-minded commitment is what's needed. The advantage of this method is that it allows a smaller opponent, who'd have difficulty in turning the ball-carrier, at least to isolate the ball. At worst, it denies the side in possession the chance of a clear feed.

The third and best way of dealing with the ball-carrier is to *knock him down* and put him on the ground. This is easiest if he's backing into you – you can use his energy to put him down. Grab his far shoulder and turn him over your leg so that he falls between the ball and his supporters. As soon as he's on the ground, get your hands on the ball. The big advantage of this method is that it puts the onus on the ball-carrier to release the ball.

2. Setting up defence from a maul

The odds are on the side that takes the ball into the maul getting it back. If the opponents have shown that their mauling (or rucking) is of a good standard, it's sensible to back the best bet and make sure that their use of probable possession is limited. The key to this is *never to overcommit*. You want as many players in the maul as will stop them driving forward, and use the rest to stop attacks close to the maul. It's convenient if your scrum-half always takes the blind side, but you can't depend on his being available – he may be in the maul – and so you must hammer home the idea of the spare forwards covering both sides and being intent on driving forwards as soon as a ball-carrier appears. The best time to stop them is before they get up momentum: hit them before they get started. It's always sensible for the defenders to get a metre or so wide of the maul and drive the ball-carrier into it.

3. Making sure that the opposing maul is going backward

Frequently a maul becomes static with the ball effectively locked. A concerted rucking drive can then minimise the advantage of the ball-carrier and deny the opposition good ball. If the ball is on the ground such a drive can often uncover it. The aim is to roll up the maul and deposit it beyond the ball.

The key word is "concerted". It is virtually useless to go in singly, though this is the great temptation as players arrive singly. In fact, the most important idea is for the single player to pause and wait for the next player or players to arrive – a matter at the most of a very few moments, but requiring concentration and discipline. Then binding together and driving straight down the pitch they can hit the maul effectively, in the same position and with the same power as in a tight scrum.

As in all contact, there's much to be said for the drive to be *forward and up*. The upward motion is an excellent way of helping the players stay on their feet. As players in front go down, it's highly desirable that those driving do not in turn go down: this means being prepared to keep on driving forward, walking on friend and foe alike. While you're practising, therefore, it's sensible to do this kind of exercise without boots on. Further details appear in the next section.

RUCKING

The alternative to mauling is rucking. We've already seen that the maul may be transformed into a ruck – when the ball-carrier finds an opponent's hands on the ball, and has to squeeze the ball down, or when in an effort to deny the opponents good ball, the pack make a concerted drive to shift the maul. Both highlight one great advantage of the ruck: that it simplifies the role of the supporting players. All too often in mauls the supporting players become obsessed by a need to get their hands on the ball, and omit to do anything else. Not infrequently this results in players on the same side wrestling futilely for the ball. Once committed to the ruck their job becomes simple – to drive forward and get beyond the ball. They're no longer in two minds – to isolate, or to go in for the ball. Their relationship to each other is much simpler: wait for the next man, bind with him, drive forwards and up parallel to the touch-line, beyond the ball.

It also highlights a new need: to look for the ball on the ground. If a foot comes in contact with the ball, it's got to be pushing it back – under control – but ideally the drive should leave the ball uncovered.

Neither of these maul to ruck situations, however, conveys the ruck at its most dynamic. Imagine the forwards inter-passing as they drive upfield, all thinking of support in width and depth, all ready to converge when the tackle is imminent. When the ball-carrier is opposed he goes on driving forward, trying to pick his opponent up on a shoulder, keeping the ball back and low. He fights to create time for his supporters to converge. As they do he rolls the ball back, and the supporters drive over it, sweeping back the opposition, and leave it for the scrum-half. They still have width and depth; they bind as they approach – pausing, if they have to – before driving forward, but maintaining that dynamic momentum that will take them over the ball. It's an impressive exercise!

You may find that your players cope better with the problem of staying on their feet, if they use their left hand arm to lock onto their first opponent's shirt. This gives them a post to support them. They aim to keep the ball in their right hand where the opponent can't touch it. Set it up as a discovery session, and let them experiment with ways of carrying it safely out of the way.

If your player is much smaller than his opponent he may find it easier to concentrate on a totally different approach: tell him to concentrate on being able to put his front shoulder on the ground. This sounds odd, but it's an excellent way of keeping the ball available.

These two methods are in no way contradictory: the only problem is how to get that ball back and both of these are effective. Nor does it in the least incommode supporting players: they still drive in to keep the opposition back from the ball.

I was surprised when Bill Freeman, that excellent New Zealand coach, came to Loughborough and demonstrated the teaching of rucking using exercises (two players standing, leaning away, while the third drives between them and heaves them forward, repeated in a continuous cycle) we'd given up six years before. I believe now that such exercises are over-academic. It isn't an exact science: it's applying basic principles with utter dedication that's needed. Now, I set a pack to defend a line of restricted length, and encourage the other pack to drive forward, get the ball on the deck, get beyond it, and attack again. It sounds hard, and there's always some blood about, but it teaches the truth of rucking.

You use it to add points:
—gather yourself, hips low, three paces back!
—hit him on the up (or: shoulder on the floor!)
—lift them off the ball!
—converge!
—control!

This last point refers to another misconception: the ball needs to be controlled in the ruck as in the scrum: The 'No 8' in the ruck checks the ball and waits for the call, taking it with him, till he hears it. This resolves many of the problems caused by over-enthusiastic, under-intelligent attempts to hammer it back.

The supposed strength of the maul and weakness of the ruck is that in the first the ball is kept in the hands and in the second it's put on the ground – where an opponent may get it. The critical factor is the immediacy of the support. *To ensure possession in either, fast support is essential,* but mauling may allow a little longer for the support to arrive; given that the support is available, rucking has the advantage of speed and simplicity. *A team that can ruck going forward and maul going backwards has the best of both worlds.*

Rucking exercises: the dynamic ruck

The first need for effective rucking is the ability to run with the upper body more or less parallel to the ground. This is a matter of habituation. *Simple running with the fingers brushing the ground* is hard work but effective. It can also be done in *ten-metre stretches* alternating with normal running back and forward over the half-way line. Emphasise the need to wait for a partner to arrive so that they can drive from ten-metre line to half-way together. Concentration on passing exercises with *the ball held below the knees* gets the body into the right position, and encourages the players to keep looking and thinking! Cyclic *picking-up* exercises have the same effect.

a. *Handling exercises:* see "group passing"

Develop these exercises into rucking exercises, with emphasis on moving fast, but in balance, *together*, into the rucking situation from the wide attack. Once the exercise is under way, the ball-carrier puts the ball on the ground and turns to provide opposition: nearest man scoops up ball, checks momentarily for support, and pushes the ball back as they hit the opponent.

b. *Cyclic exercise:* in fives

Ball-carrier runs forward, puts ball down, turns to offer resistance. Nearest player picks up, checks for support on both sides, then drives in pushing the ball back. Last man picks up . . . and the cycle continues.

c. *Shuttle exercise*

See the shuttle exercise outlined under Mauling. The ball carrier checks for support before driving (in and up) against his opponent. He keeps the ball back and low – about knee level if possible – ready to roll it back, or leave it behind. If he goes down he makes sure that the ball is behind him. His supporters check and bind as they approach and drive in and up over the ball. Concentrate on getting them to squeeze as they hit, and to keep their legs working after they hit. There should be a sense of the supporters arriving as a series of waves rather than as individuals.

d. *Rucking exercises:* the static ruck

When a ball-winning situation collapses into a pile of bodies, it's obvious what we should do: drive in, preferably bound, preferably parallel to touch, roll up the debris, and deposit it beyond the ball. In practice, once this situation is allowed to develop, it's often impossible to uncover the ball. The emphasis, therefore, must be on carrying out mauling and dynamic rucking efficiently, and in getting an immediate response to the tackle-ball situation: if we can train the players to do attacking falls almost as a reflex when the ball appears, and scoop it back, we're well on the way to avoiding fruitless confrontations.

These are moderately effective – but prevention remains better than cure.

The aim of this section has been to show mauling and rucking as a natural extension of the forwards handling in loose play, and coming into unavoidable contact with opponents. Very often, however, the player who comes into contact is a back. Every player in the team must know how to function in this initial contact, and that's why under Personal Skills (p. 84) there's a full description of what the player must do. If he can stay on his feet then the maul can be set up quickly and efficiently. If he goes down, he may still be able to feed the ball (see p. 85). If the ball goes down without his being able to do so the support players are faced with a ball-on-the-ground situation (p. 87). The coach sets out to clarify the player's reaction to these situations, and to incorporate them as starting points in mauling/rucking exercises. This is another easy and satisfying way for the coach to develop confidence in his own inventiveness, and to add something to the coaching of the game.

PART 6
Unit Techniques—The Backs

19
Half-back Play

Total rugby is possible only with accomplished half-backs, chosen as a pair to offer variety and judgement. My own starting point each season is to establish the halves – to improve them technically and to talk them into believing in their own decision – making capacity. It's remarkable how quickly both aspects of their play can be improved.

Between them, the halves provide or initiate the bulk of the team's "mix", and between them they must provide the abilities required. The four possibilities – passing, kicking, doing a move, or running with the ball – must all be available. Both must be fine passers of the ball, but this is comparatively easy to ensure; one must be a thoroughly competent kicker; one must be able at least occasionally to run the ball himself; and one must be able to initiate moves. Both must be prepared to make decisions and one of them should be recognised as the prime decision-maker. These, it should be stressed, are absolute minimum requirements.

As decision-makers, they must also be at the heart of the team's communication system, relaying information to the forwards and the backs. And, of course, communication between the halves is essential.

The efficiency of the halves is critical in turning possession into a positive advantage: they must take the initiative by making early choices and having the technical ability to carry them out.

POSITION OF THE FLY-HALF

The first need is to understand the positioning of the fly-half. It has four components:

Depth

The depth behind the gain line at which he takes the ball will depend on his intentions. Broadly speaking, the farther along the line the team intend to strike the deeper he must receive the ball. If he sees the chance to strike himself he'll take the ball flat, to minimise the reaction time of the immediate opponents; but if the strike is to be at outside centre he must create the space to get the ball out there. Nothing is more revealing of the inadequately prepared team than the fly-half who after a few tentative steps is forced into a tentative kick: he needs help with decision-making and positioning.

Lateral spacing

For the spinning game that's a vital part of total rugby, it's best for the fly-half to lie wide. It allows him to run onto the ball without the need to run across and it puts him into space outside the immediate pressure of the back-row. It needn't deprive the team of the chance to attack the short side: both the centres and the full-back should be able to function capably as fly-halves, and should practise with the scrum-half to that end. For other purposes, however, he may find advantage in positioning himself directly behind the scrum-half – e.g. to counter and take advantage of opponents wheeling the scrum.

Angle of running

Once he has established the point at which he wishes to receive the ball, the best advice for him is to cross the line of the scrum-half's pass at right angles. If he goes in to meet the ball, he increases the relative speed, makes it harder to take, and makes further difficulty for himself in passing; if he goes out, he makes the ball easier to take, but he makes life harder for his centres – checking them or forcing them to run out – and reduces his own chance of making a break. If he runs out consistently, the ic should lie wider and deeper so that he can run onto the ball effectively. If he runs out occasionally, it's most likely that the scrum-half is passing the ball too far in front of him.

Crossing the line of pass at right angles has a further advantage: it sets the fly-half up automatically for the action appropriate to the depth at which he takes the ball – running straight upfield off the flat ball, running slightly out for the deeper ball and so setting up an easy pass.

Speed of running

The fly-half must be able to choose the speed at which he runs onto the ball. Some passes he will want almost straight to him – if he's going to punt in attack, or drop at goal; some only slightly in front of him – if he's looking for a change of pace as a striker runs onto the ball; some that he must run onto – so that the whole back line is accelerated sharply. The scrum-half should know precisely what the fly-half needs on each pass: the communication is a necessary concomitant of the early decision, and the early decision is essential for effective action. If the fly-half sees an advantage in kicking then he must *decide* to kick and set himself up to do that as well as he can.

COMBINING THE HALVES

It's useful to get clear the respective responsibilities of the fly-half and scrum-half. The fly-half decides his positioning and the speed at which he wishes to move onto the ball; the scrum-half has to provide the ball required immediately it's available, on the appropriate line. If the coach finds that his fly-half isn't moving onto the ball then he checks if the fly-half is calling for the pass to come right to him; if he isn't then the scrum-half is at fault.

The critical factor for combining the halves is the distance in front of the fly-half that the ball must be passed to let the fly-half run fast and confidently onto the ball: any divergences from this are comparatively easy once a code of signals has been established.

It's impossible to establish this distance accurately if the technical level of the two halves is not consistent. The place to start is with the scrum-half: until he can deliver a consistent service, you can't plan further. I've never come across a scrum-half – no matter how good – who didn't benefit from short check-up sessions on his passing. I've met several who would have benefited enormously but were denied the chance. There's no doubt that the scrum-half is a player who can be helped enormously by intelligent coaching, and it's comparatively easy to do.

Basic spin pass off the ground

Start with the *dominant hand* – usually the right hand pass to the left – and a *standing target* – the fly-half standing on the line of pass. The scrum-half has to hit him waist-high every pass, and must be encouraged (as soon as he has grasped the basic principles) to account for each inaccuracy: he must be getting feed-back from his own performance every time he passes the ball, and like every other player he must in part become his own coach. It's a help if you use a line to pass along – it's not realistic in terms of angle of pass, but it's a great aid to the coach and the player in establishing technical efficiency.

(a). *Moving onto the ball*

Start with the ball stationary. Get his right foot immediately behind the ball – i.e. directly between the ball and his goal-line – with his left foot about six inches away. Encourage him to get low over the ball – knees bent, head low, eyes on the ball. His weight should be on his right foot, and evenly distributed from toe to heel. If his weight goes onto his toes he can find himself out of balance.

Next, get him to *move* into this position. As in any game, the ball's path can be considered as fixed: the player has to do the moving. Then start rolling the ball so that he has to move to get into position. This he can later do for himself by gently bouncing the ball off the base of a goal-post and getting his feet into position as he takes the ball. (A pressure practice described later generalises this movement onto the ball.)

(b). *Weight shift*

The next phase involves getting the body weight moving in the direction of the pass: so far as possible this movement must be parallel with the line of pass. The movement is initiated by the left foot being extended just behind the line of pass – in this case, the line on the ground acts as an invaluable check. It must be just behind the line of pass for three good reasons: so that the arms can throw vertically into the pass; so that the right hip should not be blocked as it starts to rotate; and so that there should be adequate resistance to upper body rotation. How far the foot is extended is a matter for compromise: a wide base gives power, a short base speed.

It's convenient if the left foot is pointing roughly in the direction of the pass rather than across it – it makes it easier to go into a dive pass if that becomes necessary.

To groove this movement of the leg, and the body-weight, along the line of pass is very desirable: it establishes the need to move the ball directly away in that direction rather than "winding up" to the pass. Most players faced with the need to pass "off the ground" will pick the ball up without positioning their feet and to get a longer contact – and so greater power – will take the ball back before going into the pass. *Given time, even the best player will do it, and rightly so.* But the good player has to be able to cope with immediate pressure – when there's no time to wind up. So the next stage is to establish a scooping action of the controlling hand.

(c). *Modified scoop action*

As is pointed out in the chapter on Intensive Handling, all the power and most of the accuracy of the pass comes from the hand behind the ball. Convincing the player of this is the first step in reducing the tendency to wind up into the pass. Get him into the outlined starting position behind the stationary ball, with his right hand behind the ball. Then get him to spin the ball one-handed, straight off the ground, to his target. The synchronisation of this with the movement of the left foot along the line is automatic in anyone who's going to be even an average scrum-half, and if the player you're coaching finds difficulty in it, find another player. (Passing to the right, however, you may find it useful to suggest that the arm strike starts as the right foot passes the half-way point on the passing base. This co-ordination of weight-movement and arm strike is what causes most weakness in passing "the wrong way".) This scooping action effectively prevents any pick-up or take-back off the ball, and speeds the delivery up greatly. Where there's no very strong tradition of rugby, however, the coach must take care not to be misunderstood: both in Trinidad and California I've met scrum-halves who consistently passed one-handed, as a result of this practice. It worked well in the right circumstances, but the coach has to prepare his player for the time when the circumstances aren't right.

(d). *Getting the forces accurate*

Length in propelling anything from throwing a javelin to hitting a golf-ball is a function of the player's contact time with the implement. It's essential, therefore, that the scrum-half's right hand should stay in contact with the ball as far down the line of pass as possible. A moment's thought will show that this has implications for what the rest of the body is doing. If the left foot – as it frequently does – strays across the line of pass, the right hip is blocked and the rotation is checked. If the head and shoulders come up, the contact time is shortened, and the hand will tend to move upwards rather than along – the usual cause for the ball going high. The head and shoulders must move virtually parallel to the ground so far as they can along the line of pass. For real power, the right shoulder must go right through the pass: towards the conclusion of the delivery the scrum-half's right shoulder blade should be visible from the front. This rotation is helped by the action of the left arm, which tends to swing wide: a follow through on the line of pass with *both* arms is a completely phony, and mechanically unacceptable, exercise.

Once the player is at ease with the scooping action and is developing some power, he can go back to a two-handed pass. Immediately he does so, he'll start picking the ball up again. Faced with this, the coach must be realistic: his aim is to encourage the scoop action, and *any* gain is to be welcomed.

It's desirable for the coach to move around as he coaches: he can see the accuracy of placing the right foot best from the front, but he can see the accuracy or inaccuracy of the right hand best from the target area. He can gain a lot by watching carefully what happens after the pass is complete. Any tendency for the body weight to move off the line of pass is informative. If it tends to fall to the right of the line of pass it generally means that the player has had his weight on his toes; if he tends to topple to the left, it generally means that the left foot isn't adequately far back. Balance is essential for accuracy – and this is what limits the length of contact with the ball: it must stop short of getting the right foot off the ground.

Coach and player must accept completely the notion that for every effect there's a cause, and that each cause of inaccuracy has to be tracked down: until the scrum-half is really consistent it's difficult to go further. However, careful, thoughtful work of the kind we've been examining is usually effective fairly quickly. Once the scrum-half is hitting the target accurately, we can move to the next stage: getting the fly-half running onto the ball. I believe strongly that "fly-half" should include in each team at least the inside-centre and full-back. It's a great source of flexibility in the team's play that all three should be able to function effectively at fly-half, and should be happy so to do. Once the basic principles are understood it's perfectly easy to get any player running onto the ball, and the extra time needed to coach it is small.

(e). *Establishing the lead*

We need now to establish how far ahead of the fly-half the scrum-half must pass to make him run onto the ball without overstretching. This is done by intelligent trial and error.

The coach acts as target for the scrum-half, and the fly-half is set the task of intercepting the ball by running onto it. If the ball reaches the coach accurately and without delay, the scrum-half is doing his job properly and the fly-half must adjust his position.

There are two basic rules for the fly-half to observe: that he must not move till the scrum-half has the ball in his hands, and that he should cross the line of pass at right angles. The first of these is designed to prevent creeping – which reduces the available space, can very easily reduce the choices open to you, and prevents any real acceleration of the line. The fly-half must learn to discipline himself in terms of position and of standing still – both much easier in first-phase than in second. The second point has already been discussed.

By trial and error we can establish how far behind the given line of pass the fly-half must start to run onto the ball. Ideally, we want him running on so that the ball comes into his fingers – in front of him but without his overstretching for it. Later, we can begin working on his taking it early and so moving it faster.

This distance has now to be drilled into the scrum-half's head. It's almost always surprisingly large – much more than you'd assume. The scrum-half must see clearly that this is the distance ahead of the fly-half that he must put the ball to make him run, irrespective of where the fly-half chooses to stand.

Variants on scrum-half pass

The pass we've described is the basic model which other things being equal we'd like the scrum-half to use. But part of the coach's job is to prepare his players for every likely eventuality, and in the scrum-half's case this may mean dealing with situations in which the standard pass isn't on.

The most common variant is the *pivot pass*. This is a way of using the strong side when you'd normally have to use the weak one. All it requires is that you do a normal pass, but do it with your back to the opposition. It occurs most frequently at line-outs on the left of the field. To get your fly-half clear of the end of the line, you need a long pass – longer than you can consistently make with your left hand

TIE-UP
SCRUM HALF → FLY HALF → INSIDE CENTRE

1

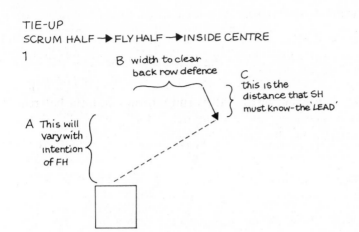

B width to clear
back row defence

C
this is the
distance that SH
must know – the 'LEAD'

A This will
vary with
intention
of FH

2 So in practice – SH aims for coach
coach handicaps FH till he runs smoothly onto ball

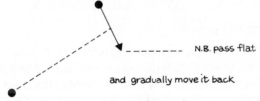

FH

COACH

in this distance FH is
trying to leave IC
for dead

SH aims to beat the FH – get it to the coach!
FH doesn't move till
ball is in SH's hands – DISCIPLINE!

FH crosses line of pass
at right angles.

SH

3 then mark the spot where FH passes

N.B. pass flat

and gradually move it back

4 then handicap IC from line of flat pass

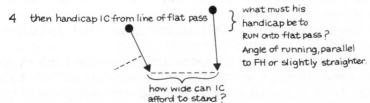

what must his
handicap be to
RUN onto flat pass?
Angle of running, parallel
to FH or slightly straighter.

how wide can IC
afford to stand?

providing the power. You set yourself up a pace or so infield of the catcher and facing the touchline: this will help you minimise the time needed for rotation. Your feet should be comfortably placed; your knees slightly bent to keep the centre of gravity low and provide power. As the ball comes to you, your weight should move onto your right toes to get a longer throwing base, and to allow you to pivot into the pass. As the pass starts you lean slightly forward from the hips so that the arms can swing through vertically. As the weight begins to move, your left foot moves out just as it did for the basic pass, but this time a little upfield of the line of pass. Once again you must get your right hand to stay with the ball – keep your shoulders low.

The tie-up with the fly-half can cause problems. The fly-half often starts to run when he knows the scrum-half must have the ball. But the rotation of the body takes longer to accomplish than the normal sweep pass. The result is that the fly-half receives the ball further forward than he expected. The way to cure this is to rephrase and reinforce the basic dictum – now in the form 'Don't move till you *see* the ball in the scrum-half's hands!'

Since the scrum-half receives the ball in the air from the line-out we've been describing, having the left foot across the line of pass is rather less important .– the right hip will not be so completely blocked. To be consistently effective, however, the left foot should be back, and the right heel on the ground as soon as the pivot is complete. Since there are times – e.g. at mauls and rucks – when the pass will be done off the ground, the scrum-half should aim at getting this right. Some scrum-halves prefer to use it from scrums as well, and the aim then is to get fast into position so that the right foot is to the right of the ball as it emerges, with the body already half rotated as described above.

When the ball is already in the open, or the scrum-half has to move some distance towards it, the *dive-pass* comes into its own. It's true that the dive-pass puts the scrum-half momentarily out of the game, but the importance of this is much exaggerated: if the situation arises he may have to use it, and so he should be helped to do it well.

It's easier to coach the dive-pass using a line – this helps establish that the body-weight is moving down the line of pass. Put the ball with its long axis lying along the line. The scrum-half starts a couple of metres behind it, with (for a pass to the left) his right foot on the line. He moves to the ball so that his right foot comes down on the line immediately behind the ball as his hands make contact with it. He cocks his wrists so that his fingers point back towards his right foot. Immediately he has his hands on the ball he's getting his eyes up to look down the line – this simultaneously gets him checking the line, initiates the upward movement that's to follow, and starts the arching of the back that helps power the pass.

He may have to drive off the right foot if he's under pressure but it's mechanically much easier if he can move forward onto his left foot and drive off that. The length of this left foot stride is a compromise between short and faster, long and more powerful. Whichever foot he drives off, the essential message is that he drives forward and up. He must get high enough to give time for accuracy in the pass. If he simply throws himself forward and down, the delivery action will be flurried and inefficient. I tend to stand alongside the line and put my hand out as a target for his head – and gradually take it higher and further away; you can also measure the distance from right foot at take-off to right foot at landing as another measure of the drive he generates.

As the body drives up, the back has to arch to give power. This has the effect of increasing the inclination of the body, which in turn will tend to produce a pass going too high. To compensate for this and get the body into a more horizontal position, encourage the player to get his driving leg high after take-off.

The hands should be kept as far back as possible until the actual moment of delivery – the straighter the arms are before delivery, the greater the potential power.

The pass we've described is the simplest in that all the forces are acting along the same line – there is no vertical rotation of the body to compensate for. You'd, therefore, expect the scrum-half to land with his body stretched along the line. You're liable to find though, that the dominant arm has a more vigorous swing and affects the landing position. Provided, however, that this doesn't greatly affect the flight of the ball, it's acceptable – it tends to appear only when the scrum-half is trying to exert maximum power. There are cases, however, when the scrum-half may wish to use a dive-pass incorporating rotation – e.g. from a line-out, when he's been facing the line-out as the ball comes to him. For this he needs to practice, as ever, getting his lead leg behind the line of pass and trying to complete his pivot and rotation before he takes off – i.e. for a pass to the left he takes the ball with his weight on the ball of the right foot and as he shifts onto the left foot pivots on the right foot till his shoulders are square to the line of pass. From there on the pass is as already described.

The last of the passes that the scrum-half needs is the *reverse pass*. Imagine a scrum, our put-in, from which he wishes to make a quick pass left. He sets himself up as for a pivot pass to the left – weight on the ball of the left-foot, left-foot to the ball as it emerges, right ready to shift out in front of the line of pass, his back to the scrum. Instead of his left hand going to the far side of the ball, however, it goes to the near side, and his right to the far side, both at the rear end of the ball with the fingers pointing back. He can then fire the ball either with his weight remaining on the left foot, or as it transfers to the right. This pass allows the use of the dominant hand either way, and it is extremely powerful. It's no more difficult to execute or control than other passes, but it's essential that it isn't used blind: the scrum-half really must look for the man running onto the ball.

Although they are identified with a specific position it's desirable that all players should be reasonable competent at least with the spin pass and pivot pass, and that back-row players should be a little more than merely competent. There are inevitably times when the scrum-half isn't available and success depends on a decent pass being given. Any moderate games player can learn to do these passes in twenty minutes without the need for individual attention, and the time is certainly well spent. The most important factors are the placing of the feet and distribution of the weight. Stand the players in 3s – one on the 10 metre line, and one on the centre line, one on the other 10 metre line. Start with passes to the left. Put each player's right foot on the line. When his turn comes he puts the ball on the line immediately in front of his right foot. He then scoops the ball one-handed straight to the next player, stepping out onto his left foot as he does so. Explain about the right heel, the left foot, the right hand – one at a time – and very soon you'll have a bunch of players who feel moderately confident. Then you can start a relay to bring some pressure and fun into it. As soon as the first man has passed, he dashes ten yards beyond the last man, and so on down the line. You can make up rules as you go.

For the scrum-half proper a little more individual attention is needed as you build up the pressure. For him, too, speed onto the ball is of the first importance: he has to learn to move fast and economically onto the ball. Getting his feet into bad positions and having to shift them is a time-consuming luxury he can't afford. He can do a certain amount by himself – bouncing a ball off the base of a goal post and moving into position – but he doesn't have much feed-back on the rightness or wrongness of the lead leg. A useful practice is for the coach to take the scrum-half and another player – not necessarily the fly-half – and half-a-dozen balls. Dump the balls on the ground and start the other player trotting in a circle round them. Then walk about and touch ball after ball with your feet – slowly at first, but gradually speeding up. The scrum-half has to get the touched ball to his partner as fast as he can. As with all pressure practices this is technically neutral: if you don't comment and coach it can do as much harm as good. As with all pressure practices, it's very hard work for the scrum-half, so have stops for a breather, and don't do too much at a time. It isn't a bad thing to build to a peak, and let down again so that his success continues even when he's tired.

Accuracy is equally important. A ball that is even slightly inaccurate deprives the fly-half of a free choice of actions. If he's going to be inaccurate, however, it's better for him to err by putting the ball too far in front than a little behind. At different times, I've hung car tyres from trees and painted numbered squares on walls to give scrum-halves a passing target. I try to fit in a short quality work-out with the halves at least once a week – frequently starting from scratch, with the fly-half intercepting a ball aimed at me. Unless the halves are functioning at a high level, there's little hope of the team functioning as a team.

20
Three-quarters in Attack –
Spinning the Ball

The first aim of the three-quarter line is to move the ball into space. As a staple activity for the team, it becomes rather more specific – to move the ball sideways to the point at which a strike has the maximum chance of being successful. Success is primarily scoring a try, and secondarily retaining possession for a subsequent attack.

For total rugby – involving all the players – it's essential that the backs should be capable of getting the ball to the wings. There's no question that the team will *always* do so – but it must be able to do so when it chooses. And at its most typical, total rugby chooses to do so often – its staple activity is to get the ball to outside-centre, and mount handling attacks from there.

In those distant, golden days when both back lines took up attacking positions – each set of backs aligned with its own corner flag, so that they attained an optimal defensive positioning only on their own line – it must have been rather easier to move the ball freely than it now is. (No.doubt, too, the centres found more gaps with increased space in which to run – at half-way, the gain and tackle lines would coincide, and there would be a premium on attack from your own half of the field. Kicking would be counter productive. Legislators looking for an elegant and easily administered method of opening the game up might well make this alignment obligatory!) One sign of the increased competitiveness and organisation of the modern game is a commitment to aggressive pressurising of their opponents·by the defending fly-half and centres. This has certainly made it more difficult to move the ball to the wings. It doesn't, however, excuse or even explain the inability of so-called first-class teams to do so. It can be done, for we do it every match.

The legislators have made several attempts to simplify the task – the most notable being their enforcing an eighteen-metre gap at line-outs – and I've heard reputable coaches declare that only from a line-out should you try to spin the ball wide. Even then, teams at the top level have difficulties, and these difficulties reveal that the problems lie at least as much with the preparation of the attackers as with the

184

pressure of the defenders. The players don't recognise what's needed, and perhaps lack adequate technique to achieve it.

The recognition has two components: an appreciation of the need to create and preserve space, and a commitment by players to the chosen purpose. It's evident that the further out we hope to move the ball, the more space we must create to make it possible. Broadly speaking, the more players who are involved by a decision, the earlier the decision must be made. If the decision is to spin the ball, the decision must be made long before the scrum-half has the ball in his hands. Most failures in attempting to do so arise from a failure to make this early decision. The commitment by scrum-half, fly-half, and inside-centre must be positive – there is no surer way of wasting space than for these players to adopt a "will I; won't I" attitude: each unnecessary stride with the ball loses some four yards of space. The commitment must be positive, too, in terms of moving the ball faster and further than the opposition expect. It's futile simply to move the ball from one one v one situation to another: each player must be seeking to provide a slight edge for the player outside him. The basic aim is to stretch the opposing defence, so that each defender has a little more ground to cover. This is another staple activity – leading to scores, and setting up the opposition for variations. You may not use it every time but you've got to be proficient at doing it.

You still see back divisions employing a very deep alignment, as in the diagram, tucked in behind the scrum, with the winger a long, long way from the gain-line. This is one way of buying space, but it isn't cost-effective. It has a whole list of disadvantages –

1. It takes the ball far back behind the forwards – any mistake is going to be difficult to cover, and may be costly;
2. it takes the tackle line back far behind the gain-line;
3. it gives the cover defence plenty of time to get across;
4. it's uneconomical in energy – the players further out have a long way to go before they reach the gain-line;
5. it's difficult to maintain satisfactory lines of running – paradoxically, it encourages both running across and, when players are being left behind, running so straight that the opposing defence isn't stretched: and
6. if either of the halves is checked and has to kick, the backs are too far behind them to be able to support the kick.

GETTING THE ANGLE OF THE LINE RIGHT

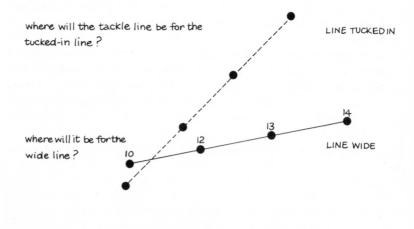

where will the tackle line be for the
tucked-in line ?

LINE TUCKED IN

where will it be for the
wide line ?

LINE WIDE

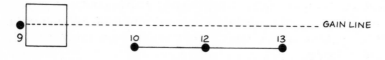

GAIN LINE

which would you rather cover against ?

The alternative method has virtually every advantage, though it calls for a little more technical assurance and coolness. Essentially, this seeks to create all the necessary space at half-back with the fly-half lying deep enough to get the ball wide. The line then lies in a much wider and shallower alignment. The diagram above makes clear the difference between the two alignments.

1. It relieves the fly-half and inside-centre of immediate pressure;
2. it keeps the tackle-line near the gain-line – so minimising the cover defence's chances of getting across;
3. it's economical in energy;
4. it makes satisfactory angles of running easy to maintain by the entire line, and facilitates stretching the opposing defence;
5. it's a much more flexible alignment for coping with late changes of intention, or when the pack unexpectedly lose possession.

It's worth pointing out that the precise alignment of the players is dictated by the varying speed and acceleration of each player – and it's unlikely to be a straight line, even if, as is most effective, there's a *gradation of speed* down the line, with the fastest players at outside-centre and on the wings. How to find this precise alignment is described below.

Although for different purposes, and as a matter of principle, it's essential that the line can function well at a variety of speeds, the one to emphasise in practice is the hardest one – when the line is moving as fast as it can. Here are basic rules for the line to adopt: they've got to be drilled home, by constant repetition, and constant monitoring.

1. Get into position immediately, no matter how shattered you feel

The most critical moments in any game are those at which possession is gained or lost: decisive action then is essential, and players must be in position to offer the widest range of choice. The typical mistake is not to get deep enough – with a resultant failure to accelerate, and a corresponding lack of strain on the opposing defence. You must work to preserve your depth and space from the man inside you.

2. Run slightly out

Players are frequently told to "run straight", but nothing (except running across) makes it harder for a line's passing to be fluent. The aim is to run slightly out in the direction of pass. This avoids the inside hip being blocked, and makes passing much more easy.

3. Nobody moves till the fly-half moves

Just as the fly-half must remain still till the ball's in the scrum-half's hands, so the rest of the line must remain still till the fly-half starts his run. A failure to do this is a certain way of reducing smooth acceleration to the series of halting passes.

4. Leave the next man behind before you get the ball

To get up real pace, each player must in your practices see the man outside him as a rival – the aim is to show how much faster he is than the next man. This has the excellent effect of making both of them run as fast as they can.

5. In practices, pass dead flat

This is valuable in two ways. It provides a check on the proper positioning of the players – you adjust each player's positioning so that he runs fast onto the flat pass. If he's running fast and the pass goes in front of him, he's got to move up a little in the preliminary alignment; if he has to check, then he's got to lie back a little. More importantly, the flat pass minimises the covering time for the back-row: every pass back gives them that much extra space and time to get across. This applies too, to the defender in a 2 v 1 situation: the flat pass gives him a minimum chance of recovery.

6. Pass with purpose – to give the next man a little more space

Just as the flat pass allows a precise positioning of the man receiving the pass, so passing with purpose establishes lateral spacing. Broadly speaking, if the ball reaches the next player with energy to spare, he should be lying wider. This is the key to stretching the opposing defence. Naturally, as with the flat pass, judgement of the actual situation comes into it: if the player outside you is slowed by fatigue or injury you keep the ball in front of him, but you keep it where he can reach it; if it's wet or the wind is blowing you must adjust your pass to suit.

7. Unless you or the next player are going for a break, pass at once: never "draw a man" unless the immediate break is on

This is the least understood of all the basic rules. Every pace the ball is carried towards the opposition surrenders two paces of space – one by you, one by the defender. Against a flat defence, man for man, to run at the first man is to give the second man a great chance to take man and ball: it's the standard recipe for the "hospital pass". You draw a man only when the player you're passing to is running into space.

8. You are responsible for the ball till the player you passed to has used it effectively: back up – pass and run

The player who passes the ball is the nearest man to the new ball-carrier – the nearest for support in defence or attack. If something goes wrong – if the ball goes down, or the player is tackled – he's got to go in and rescue the ball. The player outside the new ball-carrier will certainly have over-run. If the new ball-carrier is tackled but stays on his feet, support from the inside can lead to great attacking situations; if the pass on the outside is blocked, a pass back on the inside can upset the whole defensive plan of the opposition by disrupting its timing.

9. If tackled, you must fight to keep the ball available

Frequently, it's a back (and very often a centre) who finds himself at the centre of an incipient maul. That's why every back must practise mauling as assiduously as any forward. He must fight when tackled to keep the ball available for his own team – ideally the player who gave him the pass, for if *he* gets the ball it's most likely that the attack won't be checked by a maul. Keep the ball in two hands, where of course it ought always to be in a passing movement, and fight round to look for a supporter. See page 85.

10. The outside-centre must make a decision

Rule 7 – if there's nothing on, pass at once – applies up to the point at which the next man will be left carrying the ball. When the ball gets to outside-centre that situation is most likely to arise. The wide overlapping attack seeks to move the ball to him, and strike through him, the full-back, and the winger. By the time the ball gets as wide as this, the attackers are liable to be under pressure from the opposition. Indeed, unless they *are* under pressure they're unlikely to make a decisive break – the whole idea of drawing a man is to get under pressure so that a decisive break can be made. The outside-centre must have a variety of possible activities to choose from. He himself must have a fair amount to offer in terms of individual flair – he's got to be a runner, he ought to have an effective swerve, he ought to be big enough to stay on his feet in the tackle, and he ought to have some facility in decision making. The possibilities open to him are examined in the next section.

BUILDING THE LINE

The most economical way of using the time available for coaching the backs during the units practice is to split them into two sub-units. Start with the scrum-half, fly-half, inside centre tie up. While you are setting up and polishing their performance, the other sub-unit – the outside centre, full-back, and wings – can run through a separate programme reflecting their needs in attack and defence. These can be summarised as:

i. ATTACK – in which they play a major part

2 v 1: outside centre, full-back, and wing against the remaining wing – outside centre runs, feeds full-back, who draws the wing and puts his own wing away. (see p. 56)
> *or* outside centre misses full-back and feeds wing, who draws the other wing and puts the full-back clear on the outside.
> *or* outside centre misses full-back and feeds wing, who takes the other wing out and feeds the full-back on the inside.

Switches: outside centre swings wide and switches with full-back.
> *or* full-back swings wide and switches with wing.
> *or* wing cuts back and switches with outside centre.
> *or* any of these switches becomes a dummy switch. (see p. 51).

Kicks: outside centre grubber kicks for wing. (see p. 82)
> outside centre chips for wing. (see p. 82)

Counter-attack: back three take up defensive positions. Outside centre kicks to them, and then runs back to join in movement. Back three build up the counter-attack pattern. (see p. 247).

ii. DEFENCE – in which they provide depth

Kicking and catching: this is preferably done in pairs, starting easy and getting more difficult. A specific exercise is to practise touch-kicking, with one player on the field, and the other in touch. This can also be used for practice in bouncing the ball into touch, or grubber-kicking for touch.

Covering the overlap: use the initial 2 v 1 practices for the lone winger to practise turning inside his man and funneling him onto the full-back.

All of this needs coaching, and the coach makes time for it over a sequence of sessions. Make sure that they practise close to where you are working; that they have a written list of what to do; that one player is in charge. What they do in a particular session may reflect last week's weaknesses, the probable needs of the next match, or the intentions of the coach.

While they are working on this programme, the coach is laying the foundations for the fundamental ability to spin the ball along an accelerating line. Before they split up both back sub-units will have worked on basic handling with great stress on quality: putting the ball precisely where it's wanted, and establishing rhythm, length, and speed of passing, at gradually increasing running speed. They will have worked together in the intensive handling warm-up, and this is a final polish.

Even late in the season, it's worth occasionally starting again from scratch with the halves on the basic drill outlined on p. 178. You seek to redefine and sharpen the scrum-half's awareness of how far in front of the fly-half he must pass to get him running fast onto the ball. The inside centre can function as the fixed mark to which the scrum-half passes while the coach polishes the halves. When he's happy with their performance he adds the inside centre. The aim now is to establish the starting position for inside centre – how far behind the fly-half he stands, and how wide. Apply rules 3, 4 and 5, and alter the depth of the inside centre so that he runs fast onto the flat pass. The slower he is relative to the fly-half, the flatter he must stand. The coach is, in fact, repeating the exercise he has just carried out for the halves, but is putting the onus on the receiver rather than on the passer to judge the required "lead".

He then applies rule 7. If the ball is to go wide, nobody must waste space with unnecessary ball carrying. Check where the fly-half gave the pass, and put a marker on the ground. Encourage the fly-half, taking the ball on the same line, to get his pass away a little earlier – bring the marker back a couple of feet. Skill in this comes with accuracy of pass from scrum-half, and a deal of practice of the basic speed passing exercise (see p. 51).

How wide the inside centre stands is established by how hard the ball is going when it reaches him: if it's still got energy, he can move slightly wider, and, of course, a very little back.

Once the inside centre's position is established, you bring in the outside centre and repeat the process. Immediately you establish his position, you'll probably see that fly-half, inside centre, and outside centre are not in a straight line in their starting positions, even if there is a speed gradient out to the wing, with each player a little faster than the one inside him.

At this point, check on the angles of running of the front three. The fly-half is crossing the line of pass at right angles; the inside centre is running slightly straighter, but still slightly out; the outside centre is running parallel to inside centre. Make the point to the inside centre that if, in the match, the fly-half starts running across, he must move wider and a little deeper to correct the drift.

Now add your full-back, who must see himself as a third centre and a key striker. He has a tougher problem than the others in judging his entry, and starts his final move into the line as the scrum-half goes down towards the ball. Ideally, he is still running onto the flat pass: if the ball has to be passed back to him, it gives the immediate cover e.g. the opposing outside centre time to get across. He also has problems with the angle of his run: the great majority of full-backs come into the line so straight that they have difficulty in passing. If he intends the break, running straight is fine; if he intends to pass, he must move slightly out. He must get his head up and judge early what's required.

Both wingers join the line together. Their main difficulty is to overcome the fear of being left behind, and their main danger that of getting in front of or too close to the full-back. Keep making them think about space. As with every other line player, they will tend if they feel they are being left behind to straighten up and arrive closer to the passer than you want.

If you have worked in the right detail you will now have a line moving the ball fast and accurately, and be conscious of their acceleration. This is the basis of everything, the fundamental need for effective back play. Only when this is established can you afford to look at variations and moves. Every session we do, we get the line running sweetly before doing anything else with them.

Once the line's initial positioning is established, the players must discipline themselves to getting back into it. The basic practice is to spin the ball left, check, spin the ball right – and work on getting into position faster each repetition. You can then have them run against the pack (see p. 231), and re-emphasise rules 6, 7, 8 and 9. Specific practice of rule 8 is best provided in Defensive Unopposed – see p. 243.

The toughest situation is in the loose – see p. 265. Here especially, the fly-half's decision making, and his judgement of the depth at which to take the ball are vital. You cannot divorce judgement from execution: what is needed is intelligent commitment to the chosen action. A call has to be made, and every player contribute whole-heartedly to its execution.

21
Three-quarters in Attack – Moves

There's a rare pleasure for the players and the spectators in a well-executed move. That it is rare is usually the result of inadequate coaching that doesn't go into adequate detail in preparing the move, or in creating effective judgement in the players. Even the simplest move has to be thought out and practised in detail, and the players have to execute it with understanding, purpose, and judgement.

It's difficult, for example, to envisage a move much simpler than a loop between fly-half and centre, and yet to be moderately successful the coach has to help the players provide answers to these questions. *Please take a little while and try to answer them yourself.*

1. What indicates the move?
2. When should the decision be made?
3. How far apart should fh/ic initially stand?
4. What should their alignment be?
5. At what point should they initiate the move?
6. What should they do before that?
7. What line should ic move onto?
8. What must the opposing ic be convinced of?
9. How should the ball be transferred?
10. What line should the fly-half turn onto?
11. What's got to happen to his pace?
12. What is his purpose?
13. What will he do if he is checked?
14. Where should oc have started to get into an effective support position?
15. What should he be aiming for in his line of running?
16. Where should the winger be?
17. What cover do you have if the move breaks down?
18. Do you have an alternative form of attack once ic gets the ball?

Once the need to ask these questions is clear, the answers aren't particularly hard to find. The questions fall into eight categories, and several appear in more than one.

A MOVE IN THE BACKS

Bone – if you find a good move, try it in a variety of situations
You've got to work and work to establish starting positions and timing

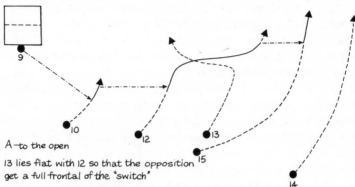

A –to the open

13 lies flat with 12 so that the opposition
get a full frontal of the "switch"

14 lies wider–to make room for 15 – and deeper because
12 is running across

12 judges when to start the switch and aims to get as far
across as possible – he doesn't go forward till when?

15 makes sure he isn't running too straight when the ball reaches him.
Ideally he's dead flat for the pass : why?

How could 14 and 15 elaborate the move? Most moves are far more effective
if there's a sting in the tail.

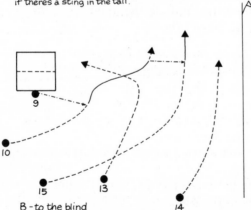

B – to the blind

here is the same move used on a blind side with the centres– split

10 gets a signal from 9 and takes the ball shallow
13 waits, runs with him, and runs at the opposing back row
15 checks that he's not running too straight
14 checks on space–he may have to come inside
your back row stay down till the ball's in front of them

1. TIMING – QUESTIONS 1, 2 AND 5

You'll find the move works best when the opposing fly-half is up a little faster in defence than his inside-centre, and that's when to use it. It's best called when possession is fairly predictable – e.g. your put in at a scrum. It's a ball carrying move so there's a slight advantage in using it moving right to balance the fact that passing moves – e.g. misses – are best done moving left.

The *decision* has got to be made early for, as you'll see, four players are involved and need to adjust their position, and the scrum-half and back-row need to know.

If you start the move too far from your opponents, they'll see what you're doing and snuff it out; if too near, you'll be tackled in possession: you must *judge* the point at which they don't have time to react and yet you have time to do the move.

The last two of these are general principles –

(i) There are always a fair number of players involved – you must *decide early* to allow communication and co-operation; and

(ii) *Judging* when you start the move is absolutely vital. If a team start running moves against you *change the pressure of your defence*: if you slow it down, and come up leisurely, you'll see them do their moves in front of you. In attack, therefore, you've got to *judge* when to start.

It's as well to see the actual decision as provisional, to have a "cancel" call if anything goes wrong, and to simplify your subsequent action (e.g. kick into the box).

2. PURPOSE – QUESTIONS 8, 12, 15 AND 16

Everyone involved in the move must act with clear *purpose*. These questions involve fh, ic, oc and winger – and the scrum-half and back-row are involved just as purposefully. It emerges first in their positioning (see below), and goes on to their line of running (see below), but in fact it takes in all that they do.

The basic purpose of the inside-centre is to convince his opposite number that he is the striker – he must look like the striker in his running.

The basic purpose of the fly-half is to get into the space behind the opposing outside-centre.

The basic purpose of the oc is to take his own opponent further out, to open the gap for the fh.

In a wider context, the move sets out to achieve one of the two basic purposes of all moves: to create a 2 v 1 situation in the backs (in this case fh + oc v oc). The other purpose is to get the ball back in front of the forwards.

In the widest context, the move sets out to achieve an overall purpose – to create an advantage for a single player, who must then exploit it by using his flair and judgement. The notion that "the move gives you a chance and you must make the most of it" has got to be accepted fully by the striker. Moves are no magic formulae for success.

3. POSITIONING – QUESTIONS 3, 4, 14 AND 16

The strike is being made between the centres so the fly-half should move onto the scrum-half's pass neither very shallow nor particularly deep (see p. 172).

The further apart the fh and ic lie the earlier they must start the move, and the more time the opposition have to react. They must, therefore, be rather *closer* than normal.

Their alignment must be such that as soon as ic has the ball he's in front of fh, so that fh can accelerate smoothly across and forward behind him. The ic, therefore, should initially line up *flat* with fh.

The oc knows that the fh intends to run outside ic – and he must, therefore, lie *wider* to stretch the defence. He knows the fh intends to run across field – and he must, therefore, lie *deeper* so that he can accelerate onto the ball without being forced to check.

The winger knows that oc intends to take his own man wider – so he will lie a little wider and deeper than normal from the oc.

I've expressed these in terms of positioning because that is simpler for the players; it could have been expressed in terms of running speed. The oc, for example, instead of lying deeper – which might alert an opponent – could start very slowly, and then accelerate onto the possible pass. I'd advise starting, though, with positioning.

A recognition of the spatial relationships necessary to the move is basic: it can never work at its optimum without it. If the fh has to check, or the oc has to check, the move will probably not work.

4. LINE OF RUN – QUESTIONS 6, 7, 10 AND 15

For simplicity's sake it's advisable to start as predictably as possible – the fh running onto the ball at a normal angle, and the ic running parallel to him. They continue to run on those lines till the time is right to start the move.

The ic must then straighten up and pose a threat on the inside of the opposing ic. This also facilitates giving the ball back to fh on the inside.

The fh should run flat behind ic and make no abrupt attempt to turn upfield – which would certainly slow him down: an easy curve behind the opposing oc is what he wants.

The oc starts off parallel with ic's line of run – a little further out and deeper than usual. As fh comes across he must move out slightly so that his opponent is tempted to come with him, and open the gap even further.

5.   PACE – QUESTIONS 8, 11 AND 14

If ic is running slowly he poses no threat and isn't a convincing feint.

If fh is going to get clear he must be running fast and must preferably accelerate at the point of decision. He may, therefore, have arranged with the sh for an appropriate pass (see p. 173).

If oc is going to be effective he must reach the possible point of pass running fast – if he has to check he ceases to be an effective threat.

6.   COVER – QUESTION 17

You must always seek to provide some measure of defensive cover for a move. In this case you have the full-back in position – but he might be employed as a second striker (see below). Your back-row will be in position – to cover and as alternative strikers (see below). Otherwise, you'd expect your blind-side winger to move across behind.

7.   ALTERNATIVES – QUESTION 18

You must always have alternatives built into your move, so that if something goes wrong you aren't stuck. The alternatives apply to possible actions by your intended striker, or the provision of other strikers.

(i)   The fh may find that the opposing oc comes in to meet him, or goes out to cover his own man: in the first case he passes to oc; in the second, he runs.

(ii) The ic may drive on as for a crash ball hoping to make a break himself, but most importantly to get in front of the back-row and get them handling.

(iii) Most moves work best if they contain two elements, the second being a further surprise to the defenders. The commonest of these is to use the move as a distraction to allow the effective entry of the full-back, probably inside but possibly outside the oc. An alternative would be fh going across field to do a switch or dummy switch with oc or fb.

This sounds incredibly complicated but it's effective enough to justify the practice that will make it work.

8.   TECHNIQUES – QUESTION 9

It's interesting, on reflection, that the last thing to be discussed here is often the only thing the coach offers in helping the players to do a loop – the mechanics of transferring the ball. This is precisely the same as in any switch – the ball-carrier (ic) offers the ball to the fh, turning towards him, and pushing it out to him. As with any technique, it's got to be grooved so that the players can do it with a minimum of concentration being displaced from the *purpose* of using it.

These eight headings should prove a useful check list for your own analysis of moves, for there obviously isn't space in a book like this for a detailed examination of even a few. A book which shows fine imagination in propounding moves – though not at all in establishing the working detail – is Van Heerden's "Tactical and Attacking Rugby". You may well find that exercising your intelligence and imagination on the moves suggested there is a good start for improving your ability to make moves more effective.

Certain broad guide-lines are fairly obvious:

1. You need moves for the overlap, and to bring the ball back in

MOVES - what do you aim to do?

CHOPPER 1   get it back to the forwards

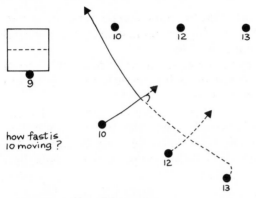

how fast is
10 moving ?

CHOPPER 2   drive into space

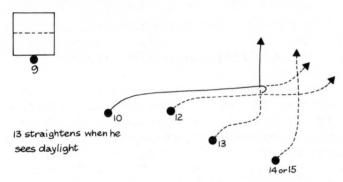

13 straightens when he
sees daylight

front of the forwards, and your moves should focus on your established striking points;

2. You've got to be clear what you're trying to do with a move. Two diagrams are shown above of a switch fh to oc, with totally different results. What kind of team would tend to use the first variation? the second?

3. The move must be congenial to the players involved – in terms of physique – you wouldn't use variation 1 above with a fragile player – and personality – not every oc relishes work close to the scrum.

4. Broadly speaking, passing moves – e.g. misses – are best done to the left: the general principle is play to your capabilities.

5. You need a few moves – not many – but they must be rehearsed again and again so that the players are completely at home with their requirements. Running through them half-a-dozen times simply isn't enough.

EXTRA MAN

Quite the simplest way of creating a 2 v 1 situation is to introduce an extra man – the full-back, or blind-side wing, or a visiting forward.

A very common, very effective, example is the full-back operating as a third centre in the wide overlapping game. This is a typical feature of fifteen-man rugby, and suggests two basic elements of that game:

1. Stretching the opposing defence laterally; and
2. Striking wide, with oc, fb, and w as potential strikers.

This helps focus the coach's attention on two basic requirements – that his team can get the ball to oc whenever required (see p. 201), and that the outside three should work on methods of striking. They must be conscious of themselves as a small attacking team – a strike force – within the team, and work intensively on the 2 v 1 situations they hope to create. They can also work on switches, dummy switches, and misses (see p. 190).

In general, however, there are two questions to be answered about the extra man:

1. Where to introduce him; and
2. How to introduce him.

1. Where to introduce the extra man

Look at the figure opposite. On introducing the extra man we improve the odds as follows:

$$
\begin{array}{llll}
4 : 4 & \text{becomes} & 5 : 4 & \text{on (crossfield)} \\
3 : 3 & '' & 4 : 3 & \text{on (split centres)} \\
2 : 2 & '' & 3 : 2 & \text{on (sh goes blind)} \\
1 : 1 & '' & 2 : 1 & \text{on (fb acts as fh)}
\end{array}
$$

The improved odds on the short side are one reason for the

THE NUMBERS GAME

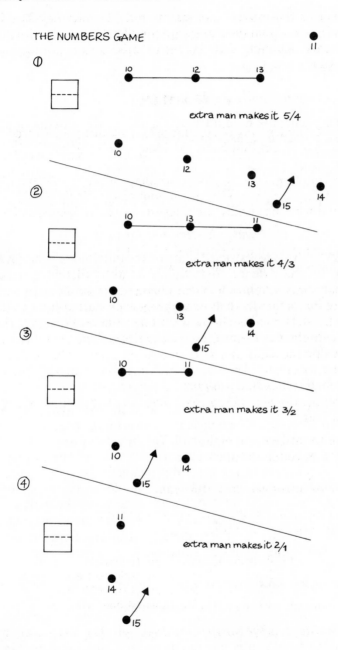

extra man makes it 5/4

extra man makes it 4/3

extra man makes it 3/2

extra man makes it 2/1

effectiveness of attack on that side. It's also, by its closeness to the pack, easier to support or cover an attack there.

There are three basic mistakes that account for most failures in attacking the blind-side:

(i) Attacking too narrow a blind-side

Attacks generally need adequate space in which to develop. It's pointless launching a back attack on the blind unless you have at least 15 and probably 20 metres to play in. You may, on the other hand, launch a very effective diversionary attack on a narrow blind-side provided you've arranged for the ball to come back quickly and then be spun away (preferably to the left) crossfield.

(ii) Attacking the blind-side from too far back

By definition, the restricted space on the blind side can be covered quickly by the defence. Attacks on it must, therefore, seek to minimise the reaction time of the defence. The single most critical factor in this is the depth at which the attack starts – if the fh takes the ball deep, the odds are long against the attack succeeding. This is in line with the basic principles governing the depth at which the fh takes the ball (p. 172).

(iii) Lack of immediate support by the back-row

Although support should be easy at such close quarters, it isn't always forthcoming. The typical mistake is for the back-row to start moving forward in front of the ball. They must stay down till the ball is level with them and then get across behind it. This is simply a specific application of the general principles of support running.

The odds suggest that the team should work on split-field situations – see p. 257 for "up the sides and down the middle" – as having advantages in attack complementary to the wide strike and the close strike, and that the fb should be trained to operate as a fly-half at least in the blind side situation.

2. How to introduce the extra man

You can improve the extra man's chances:

1. *By enlarging the gap for him* – make sure that the player on the outside of the gap is moving away, and that the player in the

inside runs fairly straight and – if the overlap has been established – draws his man;

2. *By creating a diversion* – so that the opponents' attention is diverted. Quite our most successful move over the seasons has been "Bone" – named after John Bone, one of our full-backs – which consists of a dummy switch between ic and oc with the full-back coming on the outside (see diagram p. 194). Another effective move, of course, is miss one – missing first centre – which gets the ball to oc faster than expected, and puts out the cover's line of running (see p. 224).

3. *By creating a change of pace* – if the line is moving fairly slowly the extra man can come in with a substantial injection of pace. This can put him clear of the opposing pressure defence, but he needs support on the outside if the ball is to clear the cover defence. The ability to vary the speed of the line is dealt with under half-back play (see p. 174). It occurs automatically when the ball is carried cross-field before the full-back hits the line – one reason for the success of Bone.

22
Three-quarters in Attack – Flair

Flair – that quality of personal performance that goes beyond coaching – is a precious resource, and it's got to be effectively used. All too often the player with flair is not given the help that will maximise its effectiveness: he is allowed to develop an exaggerated reliance on it; he is not given the help that lets him use it with judgement; he is not given the full co-operation he needs in setting up the situation; he is not given adequately organised support.

1. JUDGEMENT

The player must be helped to recognise the situations that allow his flair to work to best advantage. It's in his own interests, and those of the team, that he doesn't trust blindly e.g. in his elusiveness: trying when it's not really on alerts the opposition to the danger, frustrates him and takes the edge off his performance, improves his opponent's morale and decreases his. He's got to be taught the virtues of patience – of waiting for the right moment to come, and then delivering a really effective thrust. He needs to recognise the value of establishing a rhythm, a pattern of play, that lulls his opponent and keeps himself fresh, so that when he breaks the pattern it's decisive.

2. CO-OPERATION

The team must work together to create this optimum situation for the player of flair. This is basically a matter of giving him the ball when, where, and moving at the pace he wants it and of establishing this as one basic intention with those responsible for his getting the ball. Wingers, for example, often are players of flair who rarely see the ball because of a lack of commitment in getting the ball out, or a lack of expertise in moving the ball, or a failure to recognise that some situations make it easier to give him the ball than others. All three of these points are part of the coach's responsibility. He can establish in the centres' minds, for example, that in given situations they must be prepared to move the ball at once without dilly-dallying over the possibility of a personal break. He can work on establishing the judgement of space in the halves, and the accuracy of passing in all the backs, that will get the ball to the winger in space. He may examine in detail midfield situations in which the number of passes involved is smaller – and the chance of success, therefore, higher. And he can examine miss-moves.that have the same effect. He's got to make the other players – and the winger himself – aware of the conditions that the winger is most able to exploit. This is usually a matter of angles of running, involving examination of starting positions, and of how far from the opposition he wants the ball. Set even a gifted player up wrong, and he won't do much.

3. SUPPORT

It's as short-sighted to expect the gifted player to finish off the action, as it is to expect a move to lead straight to a try: it may happen, but it's not a good bet. The gifted player, like the well-executed move, will probably give you an initial advantage – he may well, for example, be able to get past the first line of defence. This is an extremely valuable contribution – it probably means that the entire team can move forward. But it will be of small value if it isn't expected by the rest of the team, and especially the immediate support, or if they aren't equipped to get into effective support positions. The personal gift comes in various forms – to take two polar examples, one player may run like a snipe and be very hard to predict, another may be able to ride tackles, stay on his feet, and keep the ball available. You may, as coach, be able to organise an almost mechanical support play for the second; for the first, you must have got your supporting players thinking ahead. That is always the best bet for the supporters' future.

The important point is to make sure that support is available for the gifted individual, and to make sure that he is aware of the support. He has to recognise the real criterion of success – that the team secures a real advantage: to beat one man and keep the ball available is success; to beat two men and lose possession is failure. He has to pride himself on being a complete player rather than a great jinker, or swerver or whatever, and the key factor is judgement.

It's fair to say that there are some players very talented in specific directions whom it is difficult to fit into a team. In almost every case, it's because of a failure to convince them of the need to be complete players. The greatest service a coach can do such talented individuals is to convince them that they need to be and that they can be complete players, and to work hard on extending the range of their skills.

Sometimes, of course, it's not possible to convince them. The coach then has to consider his duty to the team as a whole. This is particularly important at half, for a talented kicker at scrum-half, for example, who is reluctant to modify his game, will impose a pattern of play on the whole team: if you play him, you have to build your team and team tactics around him. It may be possible to play him in another position where his particular gifts or attitudes are more effective. Sometimes, however, you have to put the interests of the fourteen other players first.

In the paragraphs above I've concentrated on flair as it is most strikingly displayed and most commonly understood – the flair of the runner. Selectors especially, however, should not be blind to other kinds of flair, less obvious but equally valuable. Your effective runner is often set up by the quality of 'passing and timing of the player inside him, who does nothing very startling but creates fluency in the line. He and the runner complement and complete each other as has been suggested under Selection. So, too, you may fail to see the player – often a back-row – whose talent is turning up in the right place, and moving the ball on, again without pyrotechnics but to great effect.

23
Kicking

TACTICAL KICKING

Kicking, especially in its tactical form, is one of the fine arts of the game – at its best, it shows the judgement, precision, ease, and effectiveness that are the hall marks of the best athletic performances. It's an essential part of the mix even for teams committed to handling rugby.

1. It's the simplest way of overcoming the basic difficulty of the game – getting the ball over the gain line and in front of the forwards. It does so with minimum risk of making mistakes behind the gain line, and with a minimum expenditure of energy.

This is particularly important during those phases of the game where any loss of concentration is liable to be punished. Typical moments are at the opening or close of each half, or immediately after you have scored, or when the team, having gone into a lead, are getting slightly complacent. At such times it pays to simplify the game, and concentrate on getting the pack moving forward.

2. It's an extremely economical way of moving play into valuable space – the striking zone where the opponents' line is within effective attacking distance, and the risks involved in handling are much reduced.

The value of distance gained down the pitch can be set out notionally in a diagram (p. 204). This is based on the notion that a metre at either end may lead to a try, and a metre at half-way is neither here nor there. Economy of effort in getting the ball into an area where the ground is more valuable in front of you than behind you is sensible tactically, is good for your pack's morale and bad for theirs. Playing the game in the opposition half of the field is a sensible guide-line – though, like all guide-lines, it's an aid for the apprentice tactician rather than the craftsman. At the start of the season with tactically inexperienced halves, or an untried back-line, you can suggest the guidelines on the right of the diagram as a reasonable basis. If you are coaching well, however, your players learn to read the game with greater insight as the season goes on.

TACTICAL KICKING DIAGRAM

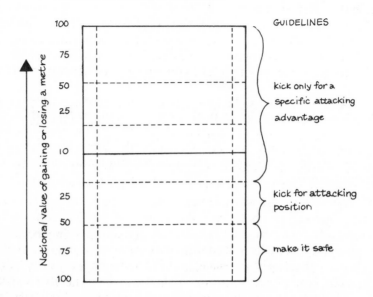

3. It's an effective way of creating a situation in which handling is easier. Difficulty in handling comes from the attentions of two pressure groups – the front three (fh and centres) and the back-row. Both of these groups can be slowed down by intelligent kicking that poses an alternative problem. If the ball is consistently put over the heads of either group – e.g. chips over the front three, preferably to the full-back's weaker side, and back into the box over the back-row – will help create conditions in which neither group can commit itself early to pressurising.

4. It's an effective way of probing weaknesses in the opposing back-three (fb and wingers), and of imposing pressure upon them. By kicking high you can force the back-three into lying deep – opening the way to attacks wide using miss-moves, with the opposing wing out of position to counter the handling attack. You can create the conditions where mistakes by the opposition set up excellent attack situations. By kicking centrally you limit the chance of the catcher's making an effective, long, touch kick. By kicking to the weaker side – i.e. usually to the player's left – you can make it difficult for him in the time available to kick at all. At a scrum or maul with a workable blind-side, the opposing winger is caught in the dilemma of whether

to lie up for a handling attack or back for the kick into the box – and the halves can expect this.

5. This becomes even easier if there's a strong wind or rain from behind the attackers. In this case it's highly important to play as much of the half as possible in the defenders' territory where scores are likely, since in the other half you may well be kept far from their line.

6. A final way to use kicking tactically is as a means of transferring the focus of attack with minimum reaction time for the opposition to cover the new threat. Typical of this is the kick back over the midfield scrum or maul when the fly-half's initial movement has already forced the opposing pressure groups to commit themselves on one side. This can be even more effective if the kick comes from inside-centre.

The key to all tactical kicking is early decision-making. Failure to make decisions, or to make them early enough, leads to that most depressing of spectacles – the kick that is forced upon you by lack of decisive action, and by your opponents' pressure. There's a world of difference between the kick you chose to make, and the kick you make because you've got into a position where you can't do anything else.

Most tactical kicking is best done when you've set it up. It calls for the same procedure as any other decision. As soon as the scrum or line-out or maul develops, you are examining the possibilities – the point on the pitch, the weather conditions, the line-up for the opposing defence, the morale of both sides – and reaching your provisional decision. Then you communicate to all those immediately involved. The fly-half, for example, on deciding on a tactical kick, must let his scrum-half know so that the ball is passed to him standing – balance is a key factor in consistent kicking, and kicking on the run is an altogether more complicated and difficult exercise. He needs also to alert those immediately concerned with reaching the kick or the catcher – there's no point, for example, in kicking for three-quarters who are lying back as for a handling attack, and are giving the opposing catcher yards more space then they would if they were lying up flat.

The skilled player has a fair tolerance of inaccurate passes, but if his kicking is to be at its best he must get the ball precisely as he wants it. This allows him to set himself up for the kick – to get his hips at the right angle, and to have the leisure to concentrate on his kick.

In most situations, tactical kicking is an exercise in precision – the direction, length, and height of the kick must all be under control, and understood in terms of a defined objective. The direction is implicit in the decision – it's never just "a kick" – and length and height depend on the purpose. If you want your players to arrive at the same time as the ball, you've got to establish in practices the right mixture of length and height to achieve it. If you want speed and great accuracy – e.g. for a kick to touch when the rhythm of an attack has broken down – you may want a very low kick bouncing in the field of play and rolling into touch. If you're kicking for a player following up, it's best to keep the trajectory low so that the ball rolls forward rather than bouncing up: if the bounce is right, it's marvellous – but if it's wrong the whole momentum of the attack can be lost, and that's the important thing.

The players following the kick must be just as purposeful as the kicker. If it's a group of players, they must be quite sure of their function – see e.g. the forwards (p. 233) – and support each other intelligently in width and depth on the line of the landing point. If it's a single player he's got to set off intelligently – e.g. to get between the ball and touch in kicks into the box, and keep the ball in play. The basic rule is to start fast and arrive in balance, to deal with the ball or the catcher. In apparently 50/50 situations, the attacker has the advantage: it's easier for him to go up to meet the ball and if he can't catch it make sure he knocks it back to his supporting players. When the catcher has the advantage, the aim is to limit his choice of actions. If you're sure of the tackle, make it; if you're not, get outside him and push him towards touch, narrowing the angle for his kick.

As an aide-memoire to the kicker, it's convenient to think in terms of four basic areas for the kick.

1. *Into the box.* This is overall the most effective kick since it gets the ball in front of the forwards, creates a shift in the direction of attack and limits the possibility of counter attack. It's most easily done by scrum-halves from the scrum as on either side of the field they can use their right foot for it. The box is also the best place to kick from a heel against the head in a defensive situation – if you kick open you may not force your opponents to turn, and instead present the ball to them with space to move it.

2. *High up the middle.* This, especially in difficult conditions, imposes maximum strain on the opposing back-three, and makes it most difficult for them to make ground on touch-kicking. It's also, especially in difficult conditions, a useful alternative to touch-kicking in defence. There comes a point where simply getting the ball into touch isn't enough – if the attackers can sustain their attack they will probably, in the long run, score. A player who recognises this should consider the possibility of kicking long down the middle and so moving into attack. The critical question is the depth of the opposing backs: in your own half it's imperative that your kick be long enough to make them all turn and go back. Given that – and the need not merely to relieve but remove the pressure – it's worth trying.

3. *Behind the opposing centres.* A staple method of creating the space to handle. This is usually best done moving to the right – partly because it's a marginally easier kick for the right foot dominant fly-half, mainly because it creates difficulties for the right foot dominant opposing full-back. The aim is to put the ball over the centres and to the full-back's weaker side.

There's an advantage in performing this on the run. The very fact of your running gets your centre moving in the right direction and forces your opponents to come forward in case you handle. This opens up the ground behind them. Timing your kick is a matter of judgement: too early and your opponents may be able to turn and kill the ball; too late, and they may be able to charge down the kick. Technically, the kick is more difficult than a kick at the halt. Put the ball at right angles to the long axis of your foot – you need the best possible target. Think of bringing your knee up to get the height. Keep your toe down so that the ball rolls on when it lands. You can practice this running at the posts and chipping just over or under the cross bar. Keep your eye on the ball once you decide to kick.

4. *Diagonal kick.* Aimed to put pressure on the opposing open-side wing, and bring your own winger quickly into the game. The longer the kick, the less sure you can be of its accuracy, and the more time your opponents have to react. This kind of kick is, therefore, best employed from a midfield scrum when the opposing winger has come up flat with his centres.

Kicking as described above is an essential element in the team's mix. No team can function without it. Every half-back must work to improve his skill in it – a half who can't kick accurately and preferably long is a big handicap to the team.

On the other hand, nothing is so easily abused as kicking, and nothing is so ditchwater dull as a team whose sole method of going forward is kicking. It's typical of the play-safe syndrome that kicking is the major and often the only weapon in attack. Typically, the coach concentrates on the pack's getting possession, and leaves the use of it to a fly-half who can kick. Typically, too, such a team lives on the other team's mistakes – they win, as it were, by default, and by good goal-kicking. The impact on the backs and on the game has been looked at in the introduction.

NON-TACTICAL KICKING

Most incidental kicking in the game is based on the need to keep the ball alive and going forward when the player is under pressure. It's certainly an easier skill than those of swerving and side-stepping, and becomes essential when support running isn't intelligent or intensive, or when the defender's positioning cuts out these possibilities.

The most important case is when some error has checked the momentum of attack. Broadly speaking, wherever timing is very important – e.g. in setting up a move – and the error has made the timing difficult, it's sensible to simplify the situation by kicking. To continue with the move is simply to put the next player in an odds-against situation, and will probably lead to a breakdown behind the gain-line. So far as possible, however, the kick has to be purposeful in length and direction – once again, the player who consistently thinks ahead is far better off than one who starts to think only after he's gathered the ball. The neatest solution is often to bounce the ball into touch as the present generation of French midfield players are so adept at. This needs practice – two or three minutes of such practice each time you go out is enough. The best bet otherwise is to put the ball in front of your forwards – so limiting the chance of counter-attack. The next – dependent on how much space you've got – is the high kick up the middle.

A second important case is the kick that opens the way for the next man out to run past his opponent onto a rolling ball. This is particularly valuable from outside-centre for the winger, when handling has failed to create an overlap. The opposing winger is faced with the difficulty of marking his man and being uneasily aware of the space behind him: if he's up to take his man, and the full-back is slow in covering him, the grubber in behind him can be devastating. In any kick of this kind, the winger aims to run wide and keep the ball in play – pushing it on for himself, or back behind the full-back for his centres. A place can be made for this kind of kick in normal handling practices – indeed in any handling practice by the backs it's as well to build in variety as the ball reaches the outside-centre, full-back, wing area: if you haven't created an advantage by the time the ball reaches outside-centre, he's *got* to have some ploys to keep the ball going forward.

The general criteria of success also serve as guidelines for the kicker:

1. Wherever possible the defenders creating pressure should be forced to change direction and preferably turn round.
2. The kick should be judged to create a reasonable chance of regaining possession or imposing a weak counter:
   (i) it is aimed to put one attacker or group of attackers into contention;
   (ii) it is aimed to put one defender or group of defenders under stress;
   (iii) it allows adequate defence against counter-attack;
   (iv) all players recognise the need to stay onside, or put other players onside.

In the course of team practices probable kicks should be built in. This is easily done in programmed unopposed: you specify a cross-kick from the right wing, or a grubber from outside centre, or a chip back from inside centre, to give practice to both kicker and supporting players, just as you would with tactical kicks.

PART 7
Team Defence

24
Team Defence

To the connoisseur, defence is as satisfying as attack. There's a real pleasure for the player and the coach in a team defensive effort in which everyone has a part to play, and which may well lead to a resumption of attack against an overstretched opposition. Properly, defence always shades into attack and must be regarded as positively as attack is: when we've got the ball, we attack their line; when they've got the ball, we attack them. I remember as a twelve-year-old standing at the back of a line-out and muttering small Presbyterian prayers that their fly-half would get the ball, so that I could get him: defence should never be defensive.

There are three basic elements in team defence: pressure, depth, and cover. If you keep them separate in your mind, you'll get a simple, strong, very effective picture of defence.

THE FRONT THREE

Pressure comes from the front three: the fly-half, and both centres. Their aim is to deny their opponents space, deprive them of the initiative, gain possession beyond the gain line. They also seek to limit the distance the ball moves across the field – to stop it at, and preferably before, outside centre.

Here are the imperatives for the front three:

1. Get into position immediately, however shattered you feel

The most critical moments in any game are those at which possession is gained or lost: decisive action in attack or defence at such a moment can turn a match. Discipline – and it's always self-discipline when you get down to it – is at the core of success in defence as in attack. You still need a leader, and the most effective leader in defence for the front three is inside-centre: he's ideally placed to marshal the trio and talk to them. He's got to get that front three into position fast.

216

2. Commit yourself

Whenever the odds are in favour of the opposition getting the ball, you position yourself to pressurise them. If we *do* get the ball, then the scrum-half and forwards can launch our attack. What we don't want is our front three in intermediate, uncommitted positions – not in position to defend, not in position to attack. Even if we are on their line, the best thing to do if they are likely to get the ball is to make life as difficult for them as possible: they must all be aware that you are there, and that the slightest hesitation will let you in. You pressure them mentally as well as physically.

3. Give them as little space as possible

The defence line and the off-side line coincide. Leave as little margin for error as your skill and balance allow. Every foot you are behind that line is a foot more space for them.

4. Keep inside your opponent

A key idea in defence is to deprive your opponent of choice. In this case, you must deprive him of choice in direction of running: force him to run outside you. This ensures – if you judge it properly – that he has to run further than you do. Judgement comes in estimating how far inside him you must stand to prevent him coming inside, and how far inside him you can afford to stand to deny him the chance of running outside you. If he's very quick, you'll have to stand wider – and run a greater risk on the inside (but point 8 below covers this).

Keeping inside your opponent, therefore, doesn't mean being inside him initially at say a static first-phase situation. All the opposing back-division will be running slightly out since it makes effective passing 100% easier. You must be inside him as you approach the tackle area, but you can afford to let him run out towards you, and into that situation. All of you will appear to be outside your immediate opponents before the ball becomes available (see p. 12).

5. Go up in line

The front three must move up as one man. The absolute imperative is that you must never go up faster than the man inside you. If he isn't going up as fast as you'd like, you can tell him so afterwards, but at the time you go up with him. If a player goes up faster or slower than the other two then a dog-leg appears in the line, and that dog-leg is the most basic form of gap. As soon as it appears, skilful opponents will take advantage of it.

I believe that the fly-half is always best employed going up on his man. The odds are that his opponent won't be looking for a break himself, but nothing is more likely to prompt the thought than a fly-half who's giving him space. It's possible for the centres to go up, running off a flanker; it's possible for both the centres to come in one, so that inside-centre takes the opposing fly-half – but a miss move by the opponents leaves that for dead. In every way it's healthier that the fly-half should see himself as one of the front-three committed to pressure.

6. Pressure them by balanced aggression

A key idea in games is "start fast, arrive in balance". There's no point in emulating the bull who may once in a lifetime catch the matador, but all the rest wastes in futile rushes. Start fast by thinking ahead and being ready to move. Keep glancing at the ball as well as at your opponent. Check that your starting position allows you to get off the mark fast – weight forward, feet comfortably close, nothing in tension. Keep thinking: the man *and the ball*. Keep checking that you're keeping position relative to the man inside you.

7. Take the man who comes to you

It's best to think in terms of a zone defence rather than man-to-man. Switches and dummy switches depend on the defenders being lured out of position by chasing "their own man". Think rather: whoever comes this way is my man.

8. Support the man outside you

The high work-rate maxim "do it and run" applies here as well: see your man pass... and support the player outside you. This supplies a great deal of strength and allows your partner to concentrate on the outside. It's the equivalent of the shuffle of the defence in sevens. It's also the best bet for setting up counter-attack: if your partner makes the tackle, you're the nearest player, and *must* get your hands on the ball.

9. If a break is made inside you, turn with your man

The only time a player (and this includes the winger) can afford to go in to meet a runner at the expense of leaving his own man is when he's sure of taking man and ball. To go in without that assurance – which is possible only when the player has looked ahead and predicted what's about to happen – is usually a dead loss. At best it may force a pass; at worst, it leaves an opponent running into space. Unless you're so close to your line that allowing the ball-carrier to run on will lead to an immediate try, it's a far better bet to turn inside your opponent and so prevent the ball reaching him. The aim is to funnel the runner onto the deep defence (and specifically the full-back). However, not infrequently having turned you can simultaneously blank off your opponent, and reach a tackling position on the ball-carrier.

10. The tackle is the first stage; the aim is the ball

Any notion that getting the ball is a concern solely of the forwards is futile: everyone has to see getting the ball as important – more especially since immediate action by the nearest player is the most effective way of getting clear possession. So the tackle isn't simply a matter of stopping your opponent, though that is always the overriding aim. You're trying to stop him in such a way that the ball isn't available for his team.

A centre who can ride your tackle and stay on his feet is an ideal starting point for second-phase play. He must be prevented from keeping the ball available: knock him down if you can, and if you can't, smother him. And remember: if you *can* get the ball, you must. You should have immediate support from the player inside you – the nearest player on your side.

To be sure of your tackling is essential in the front three. Certainly, it's one of the key qualities I look for, especially at inside-centre. Most difficulties arise not from lack of courage, or lack of desire to make effective contact: they arise from not setting it up correctly – not thinking ahead, not making allowances for your opponent's speed, and coming up out of balance. The only danger comes from loss of concentration. You can hit your opponent low – just above the knees – or high, with your shoulder in his solar plexus: you cannot hit him at his hips. If he sways into you with his hips, he can hurt you. The odd crash tackle can be very effective – but you must make it where he is less powerful and solid than your shoulders are.

11. Work-rate

If the pressure is effective, you'll find that your opponents kick a fair amount. If they do, you must get back to offer support to your back three. The outside-centre, especially, ought to be able to get back fast, to offer help in defence or counter-attack. This eleventh point, in fact, reiterates the first: discipline and work-rate are the bases of good play.

The basic aim of the front three, as defined above, is pressure. There are times, though, when it's most effective not to drive forward on your opponents. If you think of a team that's getting a fair amount of ball against you, and is setting up moves in the backs, you'll see that a constant tempo in your defence may be to their advantage: it allows them to predict, and it simplifies their timing. If you then come up in line at a slower pace you'll find that they start their moves too early. This allows you to see what they're doing before you're committed – you get them to commit themselves first. You don't lose too much if you do this: they will always have more ground to cover before reaching the gain line than you do.

Defence practices for the front three

The essential things to be drilled home are less concerned with the actual tackle than with organisation – positioning and timing. Tackling practice is better done in the kind of practice outlined under basic skills – practices where you can build up a high tackle rate and limit contact power. To build up contact power use a tackle bag and a crash-mat indoors. The method is to move the take-off mark further and further from the bag, so that players have to generate more energy and drive to get there. Then I encourage them to get the elbow of the tackling arm well forward, so that the shoulder is in a very strong position. The head should be tilted well off to the side, and the eyes fixed on the tackle point.

Once this kind of tackling power is established, the aim is to get them thinking very clearly about positioning and timing. The only way to do this is against the 2nd XV backs, and the only contact needed is two handed touch on the shorts. I've met mad theorists who claim you ought to have flat-out tackling in practice, but a touch of experience would correct their ideas. It's a joint practice, so there's much to be said for arranging that the pressure on the attackers should increase from a fairly low level to something approaching match pressure. The first thing to look at is lateral spacing – so placing them that *at the tackle line* they'll be inside their opponents. Initially, the attackers simply spin the ball and continue running. The defender goes up as if his specific opponent were running for a break, staying level with the player inside him. Gradually you can move the defence line forward and encourage the defenders to move up more rapidly but still in balance. As soon as you feel that each is covering his immediate opponent adequately, introduce the idea of supporting the player outside, so that as the attackers move the ball, the defenders go up and then out. You can then ask the attackers to vary their play and test the adequacy of the zoning by the defenders. However, I tend to delay this till the forwards are available to provide cover defence.

This is a preparation for effective pressure defence. There is an alternative system, however, that can be employed whenever the ball is consistently being moved wide. I christened it a 'drift' defence, and the term is now used everywhere.

A drift defence starts with each player lying wider than normal. The aim, without broadcasting the fact, is to allow our stand-off to tackle their first-centre, our first centre to tackle their second centre, our second centre and wing to tackle their extra man and wing. This allows our full-back to concentrate on depth defence, and allows our full-back and blind-side winger to continue their cover against a multiple overload.

Many teams employ this method at line-out. The space between the lines often encourages the side in possession to spin the ball wide. For our stand-off and centres to continue trying to pressurise is not merely futile then, it's counterproductive: their going forward prevents them from obeying the first rule of defence – get between the ball and our line. In effect, they contribute to being outflanked.

It isn't, however, of use only at line-outs. Whenever the opposition are consistently moving the ball wide – if they're sensible, employing a miss move – the drift defence comes into its own.

Evidently, drift defence is buying strength wide at the expense of strength in the area of stand-off: who takes the opposing stand-off if he runs? The answer must be one or other of our back-row. After their immediate duty (see pp. 135–139), their first priority is to cover inside the stand-off before adopting their normal cover running. Nevertheless, this is the area that the side faced by a drift defence must be prepared to attack.

Evidently, too, it's more difficult to exert pressure on the opposition. We'll always be forced to run more across than usual, which prevents really hard tackling, and gives an extra advantage to the really swift attacker. I wouldn't recommend the use of drift defence except when the opposition are consistently spinning it.

Setting it up is easy. Get the players to adopt their normal positions against the 2nd XV backs (or the forwards!) and get them moving up together while the ball goes through each pair of hands in the opposing line. Put a spare man wide in the opposition, evidently ready to join the line. Move the stand-off out half the distance to first centre, and so on down the line. Walk through it, with each defender taking his new opponent. Then trot through it till they're all happy. Don't at this stage encourage the opposition to throw in unexpected attacks: the aim is to get the defence confident in their new roles before going further.

Next bring in the back-row explaining that the new system, by providing cover wide, should help cut down on the amount of running the flankers will need to do. Get the opposing first centre to lie deeper, and their stand-off to carry the ball forward to carry the ball forward. His aim is to force our stand-off to choose between checking to take their stand-off, or continuing to chase the first centre and let the stand-off run. Let the back-row see this, and then continue the practice with them providing cover. It's all very simple.

I first saw this applied almost unconsciously by the Fijians in the early '70s. The North were spinning the ball wide to our excellent winger Keith Fielding, but by the time the ball reached him there were two, three, and on one occasion four Fijians in front of him. They got there without effort, just drifting across to cover. Hence the name.

THE BACK THREE

The back three have two functions: to provide depth in defence, and to set up counter-attack. The depth they provide is two-fold – against kicks and against running. In both they work together. When the ball is in the air one player must call for it. If two call for it, the player who is deeper should take it: if you call, and you hear a call behind you, it's his ball. But always there must be cover for the player catching the ball – get round behind him so that you can support him if he makes a mistake, or if the chance to counter-attack is there.

The central defender is the full-back. He must position himself in terms of width and depth. The width – i.e. where he positions himself relative to the ball – depends on his speed. Ideally, he'll be moving across field inside the ball as the opponents pass it. He may find, though, that if he isn't quick he may have to lie outside the ball, so that he can cover kicks to the open side. This leaves him vulnerable to a break on his inside, and to kicks back over his head. Taking into consideration his role in attack, it's obvious that speed is needed in the full-back just as in his two team-mates, the wings. His depth, again, must be a compromise: for tackling he'd like to be close to the point of break, and take his man immediately he comes through; for kicking he'd like depth – it's always easier to run forward onto the ball, and it gives him time to cover effectively. It's best if he allows the cover defence to do the early tackling, and commits himself to covering kicks, and taking the later tackles. He's also got to think of the kind of kicking used by his opponents, and of the conditions on the day. A wind in your face means that you need to get deeper; a wind on your back that – with a careful eye on the way the opponents are using ball – you can move forward.

The open-side wing has two jobs to do – to cover against the long diagonal kick, and to be up to tackle his winger if the ball reaches him. He's best advised to move up steadily as each pass is made – starting when the fly-half passes. As he moves up, the full-back moves across to cover the space he's left. As the full-back moves across, the blind-side wing moves across in turn to cover the space left by the full-back. The three work as a single unit. If the opposing winger beats his man, the full-back should be there to cover him, and if the winger beats the full-back, the blind-side wing must be there to cover the full-back.

All of this demands that the wingers must be able to concentrate throughout the match – the days when they could comfortably rest or look at the crowd have long gone.

The blind-side wing has a great deal of work to do. He is in a difficult position, since a single pass may put his immediate opponent in possession, and a single kick can put the ball into the box behind him. It's a foolish scrum-half who isn't aware of the blind-side wing's dilemma at every scrum, especially near the left-side of the field when his right foot is available for the chip into the box. Broadly speaking, the right wing should be more aware of the kick, the left more aware of the pass. The blind-side flanker must be ever attentive: he is the critical player in supporting his winger against the passing situation. The full-back, directly behind the scrum, provides the support against the chip.

The blind-side winger, immediately the ball goes open must get back to join the rest of the back three – getting his depth first, and then moving across-field. This gives some measure of protection against a delayed kick back across the forwards to the opposing wing.

COVER

The third element in team defence is cover. This is provided by the whole pack moving cross-field and creating a defensive pattern with width and depth. The basic guidelines for this are exactly the same in defence as in attack, and have been covered earlier in the book.

There are one or two specific points that help:

1. The last hope running line against a handling attack is for the corner-flag – but if you can't make that, you may be able to force a score far out.
2. If you are the leading man in the cover, you keep going out – what looks like a switch may be a dummy: if it's a switch, the players supporting you will take him out; if it's a dummy, you must be there.
3. Any miss move by the opposition means you must run deeper.
4. If there's a two-man break – e.g. outside centre and winger – the cover must provide for both: the second man must assume the winger will get the ball, and run deeper.
5. Far and away the most common error is for the back-row to go forward and get outflanked: as soon as your immediate job is done, aim where you are sure of getting between the ball and your try-line.

However, there's no substitute for your judgement. Back your hunches – it's the only way you're going to develop that judgement.

For the coach, in all unit v unit or team practices, the rule is –teach your principles, and talk to individuals: keep them thinking, improving, learning.

The one place where you can drill your players is in the immediate defence at scrums, line-outs, and mauls. Absolute alertness and clarity is essential there. You'll find details in the appropriate sections.

Team defence has got to be tight knit, with every player playing for every other. This is especially important for a team that believes in attack, and plays with a sense of adventure. There has to be the same elan, the same sense of constant support, the same willingness to play fifteen men in defence as in attack. But remember, *never try to play rugby going backward under pressure – kill the ball, set up a maul, get reorganised, then play rugby.*

PART 8
Team Practices

25
Varieties of Team Practice

The culmination of any structured session is work designed for the team as a whole. Indeed, one way of planning a session is to start with what you want the team to be able to do at the end and build the session towards it. Certainly the team practice must run smoothly. It is no place to start on activities that concern only a few, and keep the rest standing about, or to expose weaknesses in the units. What you try on the team level has to have a very high chance of success, likely because it has been prepared for, and necessary because team morale is linked to it.

On the other hand, the team practice is still a coaching situation and it must be used that way. This means that for the most part, and certainly early in the season, you will be working with limited aims and in depth. You will tend to examine a limited number of activities and be prepared to rerun them until the performance has reached a satisfactory level.

When you call the team together you have a whole set of possibilities on which to base the practice.

1. *Unit v Unit* – basically the forwards working against the backs to test basic competence.
>   e.g. the backs spinning the ball and introducing moves against the forwards' covering pattern;
>   the back three counter-attacking from a kick against the forwards' covering pattern.

2. *Unopposed rugby* – the team working in attack or defence to establish basic forms of both, and especially to establish support patterns. This can be kept realistic because of the constant recurrence of predictable situations.

3. *Semi-opposed rugby* – the team working against a limited number of opponents, and so under limited and possibly conditioned pressure.

4. *Situations* – since the game consists of predictable situations much of the detail of team tactics can be built up by establishing the team's most effective response, in attack and defence, to representative situations.

e.g. a scrum, our put-in, or the middle of the opponent's 25 line. These situations can be examined in unopposed or semi-opposed practices, and reach their culmination in inter-team practices.

5. *Pressure practices*– once the team can cope adequately with a variety of situations, it's possible in unopposed, semi-opposed, or opposed practices to present them with a series of situations, and to increase the pressure on them by increasing the speed of movement from situation to situation.

Team tactics

In the final section on team practices (below p. 259) there are some suggestions of the kind of guidelines that the coach might offer his tactical decision maker. His grooming and preparation for the job is one of the major concerns of all team practice: he has got to be assimilating not merely the technical requirements for a particular team pattern but the match context that would indicate its use. As well as establishing high technical standards, therefore, the coach must constantly be encouraging the fly-half – who is by far the player best positioned to assess and control the situation – to develop the habits of mind that will allow him to make effective and early decisions. At every first-phase and every practicable second-phase position he must be able to communicate a provisional decision within moments of the check. This is possible only if his concentration and alertness are continuous throughout the match. The decision-making process has already been outlined on page 15 above. The coach has to make and keep him aware of the three broad categories of information mentioned there. Of these, the third – a knowledge of the team's basic pattern of play and the methods appropriate to particular situations on the field can be embodied directly in the work that the coach sets the team. The other two categories are largely a matter for discussion, and they seem to be best dealt with either in fully-opposed situation practices or in team-talks. It's highly desirable that though the bulk of this tactical education is addressed to the fly-half every player in the team should learn to think in the same way. This is partly because all can then contribute to team talks and the development of team tactics, and partly because all at some moment in the match may be faced by the need to make a quasi-tactical decision. You can see this clearly, for example, in the discussion of counter-attack on pages 247-8.

The first step – getting the player to recognise and accept his necessary role as decision maker – is often the crucial one. The abilities required are not uncommon, but are left dormant for lack of encouragement and stimulation. He must see himself as a leader, and take a proper pride in the quality of his judgement. In all team practices he should be habituating himself to this role. How the coach fosters his thinking I've tried to suggest by taking particular examples of team practices and working through them in some detail.

In all of this the aim is to encourage a habit of mind, on the field and off – where mental rehearsal is a valuable element of preparation. The moment at which the player produces something of his own better than the coach had imagined is the real moment of success.

It's important, too, to ensure that the rest of the team commit themselves to the decisions made. Nothing is more destructive of coherent rugby – or any team game – than lack of voluntary discipline. There are, of course, moments when an individual player's judgement prompts him to take an immediate and real advantage. What must be avoided is tentative hanging on to the ball in the hope that an advantage will appear. Their chance will come: unless there's something very evidently on for them, they've got to cooperate. This is made easier if all are involved in the tactical discussion in team talks and tactical preparation on the practice field. And every player must be encouraged to take pride in his judgement.

26
Unit v Unit Practices

When the units first come together, it's useful to test one against the other. It's a comparatively simple situation to deal with, and gives both backs and forwards a chance to start making decisions against a friendly opposition. It's also a useful experimental situation, testing the efficiency of what's been practised, and often suggesting useful improvements.

1. CROSS-FIELD COVER

This is an exercise designed to get the forwards thinking about the general principles of their movement across-field when the opposition have the ball.

The pack kneel down in scrum formation between touch and the five-metre line. The opposing scrum-half has the ball three or four metres in front of them on the five-metre line, with his backs in position outside him. Initially, the backs will be using right-hand-dominant passes, and will be told to spin the ball to the wing, and put him clear of the defence.

The coach counts "1-2-3-4-5", starting his count as the scrum-half touches the ball. At "1", the back-row can go; at "3" the locks; at "5" the front row.

Each run ends up with a "score", or the pack setting up a maul. It is immediately followed by discussion of what happened e.g. Are the *pack* obeying the fundamental rules? i.e.

1. get between the ball and your line;
2. run off the man ahead of you, giving him support in depth – in case our opponent goes outside him – and width – in case our opponent comes back inside him;
3. get your head up, look at the opposition, back your hunches.

Are the *backs* making the ball do the work? If each player can safely put the ball a yard further, then the winger has four more yards of space in which to get round.

Once this basic form has been used, the coach can start encouraging the backs to try other possibilities. For example:

1. The outside-centre goes as far as he can with the ball before passing – this creates a second target for the pack, and gives the winger a little more space. The front runner for the pack must go for him: what must the rest do to cover the winger?
2. Inside-centre and outside-centre do a dummy switch – this will probably check the cover, and give slightly better odds on the overlap. What must the covering pack learn from it? That the front-runner mover checks for the switch, but goes on to take the outside runner, that the players behind him must be in balance to take the runner coming in, and that those running deep, must run a little deeper in case the overlap comes off. At this point, too, the back-row can start scrutinising the opposing backs, and making their predictions of what's likely to happen judging from their positioning.
3. The backs can do a switch between inside-centre and outside-centre – have the forwards' predictions worked? and for the backs, which centre is in the better position to decide on switch or dummy-switch?
4. The backs can do a miss move – this will probably result in the pack suddenly being forced to run deeper than they had intended, and may well suggest to the backs the desirability of using miss-moves in the opposing 22, where the opposing pack cannot run very deep.

When the coach is satisfied that the pack are running intelligently – which he may well feel coincides with the time that the pack stop trying to get closer to the scrum-half in the starting position – he can alter the starting point to a mid-field scrum. Immediately, the back-row defence (with one of the front-5 subbing for the scrum-half) must start operating their immediate action plans (p. 135). The practice then goes on in the same way, with the coach commenting and whenever possible complimenting between each run.

2. UP-FIELD COVER

A second excellent unit v unit practice deals with following up a kick – e.g. a high kick from half-back, or an up-and-under penalty.

In this the back three – the full-back and his supporting wingers – take up defensive positions with the full-back on the line of the near post.

The pack kneel in scrum formation between touch and the five-yard line, some thirty yards out – the actual distance will depend on the scrum-half or fly-half's range with a high kick measured against the running speed of the pack, and is one of the things that the coach will hope to establish.

The pack's actions are controlled by the coach using the same 1 to 5 count from the moment that the ball is kicked. The first thing that each member of the pack has to do is gauge the line of the ball; the second for the pack to get between the ball and their goal line; the third to move forward with enough width to prevent the back three going round the outside and enough depth to be sure that the catcher, who may beat one man, cannot beat the pack.

It's usually best to start without the centres, so that the pack face the worst possible situation, and so that the back three have a reasonable chance of counter-attacking (see p. 247 below). But whether the back three can counter-attack or not, they face the situation that will occur match after match – the high ball in the air above them – and get adequate practice in positioning, calling – if two people call, the one further back takes it – and catching. They are also faced with the decision – should they try to counter-attack, or play safe? (see p. 247).

Once the pack have faced the problem of covering without the centres, the latter can be brought on. Since the decision is to kick they will, of course, lie up flat: their aim, to pressurise the back three. It's useful for the coach to arrange for the receiving catcher to kick the ball back over the heads of the centres occasionally to bring home to them the need to turn and get back fast if it should happen in the match, even although in the match their own back three would be giving depth to the whole move.

Again, once the coach is satisfied that the attackers are moving intelligently, he can change the situation to that of following up a penalty – e.g. an up-and-under. He can then establish in what precise area of the field this is likely to be the most effective way of using the kick. The forwards can begin their run in their follow-up pattern as they will in the match, with the line of the kick as the axis of the pattern. The coach will find, if he leaves the kick to this point, that most players find great difficulty in kicking the ball high down a given line (see p. 77) and he'd do well to have established the best kicker earlier in the practice and given him some coaching (see p. 83).

In both of these follow-up practices, it's best to play to a "score" by the back-three, or possession by the forwards followed by an attack from their backs. Initially, however, the pattern must be established, and the coach will find it more effective to concentrate on that. Later he can introduce the ways in which the forwards can gain possession – how to deal with an opponent who has the ball (see p. 99), how to do an attacking fall (see p. 89), how to set up a maul (see p. 85). Then he can introduce the backs in the second-phase attack, with the tactical decision being called on each replay according to the positioning of the back three. This helps the fly-half acquire the habit of looking to see precisely where the opposition are positioned. A useful variant on this in all unopposed or lightly opposed practices is for the coach to represent the bulk of the opposing defence – he moves into probable positions, and the team must attack in a more lightly defended area.

It's as well in any opposed practice to remind all the players that they are members of the same team, or at least club, and to moderate the aggression. The practices just described can be substantially carried out using two handed touch as a substitute for actual tackles. When you introduce tackling make it abundantly clear that there will now be tackling.

27
Unopposed Rugby

The various forms of unopposed rugby are a very valuable – I'd say an indispensable – aid to coaching, provided that:

1. They are a direct preparation for the pattern of rugby you intend to play in your matches;
2. They are seen as coaching situations – opportunities to improve individual, unit, and team performances; and
3. They are complemented by a balanced programme of other work.

The aim of unopposed team practices is precisely that of any practice that seeks to reduce the pressure on the players: it allows full concentration on the performance of the techniques. They are practicable since in any of the given recurrent situations in the game the formation and behaviour of the defence is predictable.

It's very important that any team practice should be successful. One of the aims is to encourage confidence in the team, and the growth of mutual respect between the various units. What we don't want at this stage is a succession of errors, or more stoppages than those at the end of each exercise. Errors will occur, and a vital part of preparing unopposed work is to drill home the need to deal with them effectively. But the first aim is to create a sense of the team working effectively together. To this end, whatever you incorporate in your unopposed programme should already have been worked on during the session. If you intend to use a back move in the programme, for example, it ought to have been practised during unit skills. At this stage an error by one player affects fourteen others: we want to get rid of errors while as few other players as possible are involved.

It's evident then, that unopposed has to be an integrated part of the whole session – one that appears to rise naturally from what has gone before. In practice, this means that the coach has to consider the session as a whole, working in part from the needs of the team backward, and partly from the needs of the individual and units forward. I feel very uneasy when team practices are divorced from the whole session.

This can be taken further by using the basic technique practices as elements of the unopposed. When the forwards handle, for example, they can be using "left and right" (see p. 53); when the maul is set up, it can be done by a player putting the ball down and turning (as on p. 106) to offer resistance; when it's to be a ruck, one player puts the ball down and offers resistance, one falls on it, the rest drive over (see p. 106). This has a further advantage in speed of communication, when I say "left and right", the players know exactly what's wanted.

As with all coaching, it's important to insist on quality standards. Simply to go through the motions does have a place – at a very low introductory level – but by the time we reach team practices we ought to be functioning fairly effectively. What's now needed is precise, crisp, work. The team must be absolutely clear on what's wanted, and must expect to work till the pattern is adequately established. This can only happen if there is constant monitoring of what happens, and if the coaching produces an improvement at each scrum. With the players working at a high level of concentration and performance you must limit the number of repetitions and give very specific guidance on how to achieve the improvement.

A number of points call for very careful attention from the coach. The single most important point is the positioning of the halves. Without opposition, it's fatally easy for the fly-half to take the ball too shallow – in a position where he'd have in the match to go himself or kick – and then try to spin it wide. His appreciation of depth is the most fundamental thing he has to learn, and the coach must constantly correct him or praise him for the position he adopts relative to what he's got to do. (see p. 172).

Again, a basic aim is to involve the forwards in handling attacks – but it's got to be realistic, with each player contributing to the forward drive and ball speed. This means hammering home the basic support themes of depth and width – of working to get into useful and interesting positions where he can run fast onto the ball and be able to move it fast (see p. 53).

A third point to check is that everyone – and especially the full-back on tbe blind-side wing – is fully involved: there's rarely a moment when a player cannot be making a positive contribution, offering support or cover. Keep checking what the players not on the ball are doing.

The whole exercise is conventional and certain specific *conventions* are very useful.

1. The scrum

For this the forwards kneel in scrum formation, and the ball is fed back by the scrum-half. The hooker counts 1-2-3-4-5, starting his count as the scrum-half regains possession at the back of the scrum. At 1 the back-row can break, at 3 the locks, and at 5 the front-row. This simulates the slow break-up of the real scrum.

2. Rucks and mauls

It's best, as suggested above, to adapt a known practice to this. Make sure that it doesn't simply become a rest: the scrum leader has got to be encouraging them – "walk forward", "pick him up". The critical point – and one highly desirable in the match – is that the ball is not fed back till the scrum-half calls for it, and that he doesn't call for it till the player he's passing to is ready.

3. Dropped ball

It must *not* be dropped, but if it is treat is as a maul situation: fall, offer the ball, set up the maul. It's very important that play doesn't stop because a mistake has been made.

4. Ball on the ground after a kick

Treat as for a dropped ball.

PROGRAMMED UNOPPOSED

This is based on a sequence of events dictated by the coach. Basic principles underly the preparation of such a programme:

1. Link-up

The forwards feed the backs and the backs feed the forwards. Except for specific purposes – e.g. making sure that the outside-centre must go for the ball if the winger is tackled – the ball shouldn't simply be put on the ground when it reaches e.g. the winger. The aim is to get the forwards to see themselves not as drudges moving from set-piece to set-piece but as rugby players able to run and handle. The coach must see to it that the backs are alive to the notion of handing the ball on to the forwards.

For this to happen, the support patterns have got to be established (see p. 161). Emphasise the need for team communication and for observing the basic support laws. Look for individual forwards and check whether they are getting into effective positions. Are they running too shallow? running too deep? running with an eye to the man ahead of them?

2. Speed into position

The critical moments in attack are the moments of regaining or retaining possession – you must emphasise the need to get into the *right* position *fast*. This applies to all the players, but in unopposed keep an eye specially on the fly-half and centres. If they aren't in position they immediately diminish the number of options open to them.

3. Decision-making

Even in programmed unopposed, where the sequence is set out, you must expect your tactical decision-makers to be at least announcing decisions. One way of ensuring this is to leave options open – e.g. "when the ball comes right for the first scrum, I want to see a move in the backs" – so the decision-maker has to decide, and the communications system has to work.

4. Continuity and direction of attack

Continuity – the sustained attack – depends on getting first to the breakdown point and doing the right things (see e.g. p. 87). After this has been built up in technique and pressure practices it can be incorporated in your unopposed practices.

So, too, the basic patterns of *extending* your attack, of keeping your attack swinging right or swinging left away from belated defenders until you reach the critical point of attacking the *short side* or switching back open and *stretching their defence,* these have to be built in so that the whole team but especially the decision-makers get a sense of team rhythm.

5. Establishing the mix

Your unopposed programme must reflect the mix – that balance of attacking methods appropriate to your team – so that passing, running, kicking, and moves all get an appropriate share. This won't, of course, all happen initially in one session – but all should be represented in a sequence of unopposed sessions.

Moves, for example, are essential to your rugby, not an optional extra, and the whole team must be confident in their use, aware of their weaknesses, clear about support patterns. So you must build in your moves for every unit in the team, and for your penalties. You may leave considerable discretion to the players which move they use at any given moment – and if you have doubts about the decision, get them to account for it at the next stoppage – but you can prescribe e.g. "a back-row move", or "an overlapping move", or "a get-it-back-in-front-of-the-forwards move".

With these ideas in mind we can now proceed to set up a programme. Initially, it's got to be limited in length – e.g. a single second phase. If it doesn't involve all the players actively and in an interesting way, you may find it more satisfactory to prescribe a separate exercise for them – e.g. although a winger will certainly benefit from moving across to cover the full-back, it's not adequately rewarding to ask him to repeat it ten times.

Programmed unopposed is wholly concerned with attack, and it's sensible, therefore, to start from an attacking position and end with a score. It's the first stage in situation work in which you work out with the team its best attacking methods from a given point on the field. Let's say, then, that we start with a scrum, our put-in, on the opposing 22, eighteen metres in from the right touch, both centres on the open side.

In a situation like this, we might exploit the blind side, and then switch play across field to stretch their defence. The basic elements are

1. the backs attack the blind side;
2. the forwards handle and maul;
3. the backs spin the ball wide.

1. From the various possibilities open to us we select one. We'll have the fly-half take the ball blind, the full-back come in as extra man, and the ball go on to the wing.

The aim is to use the better numbers situation (see p. 201) to punch down the blind-side, and to get the forwards in support either to handle or if we're stopped to keep possession. Either way we should pull their defence across, and open up the field for second phase.

The points we'll have to emphasise as coach:

(a) early *decision* and *communication*;

(b) *positioning: fly-half* stays open till ball is on its way back; takes ball *shallow* to attack blind-side; *full-back* stays behind fly-half and starts running (wide first and then moderately straight) just before fly-half; *winger:* must lie a little deeper so that he won't over-run the ball – the fly-half is coming *across*.

(c) *execution: fly-half:* runs till challenged then feeds full-back; *full-back:* must be up flat with fly-half to deny the opposition further time to cover – we'll have to work on this, varying his start position and timing. If opposing winger comes in, he'd feed wing; if opposing winger stays out he'd go himself, and look for support from the forwards; *winger:* must run fast onto the pass – we'll have to work on this varying his starting position and timing; he must keep the ball in two hands, and keep it in play.

2. The forwards must get across to support the blind-side move. Initially, though, they must make strenuous and intelligent efforts to avoid the *wheel*: if the wheel takes place, the fly-half should cancel the move. This means locking the scrum, getting as low as possible on the right, and real concentration by the hooker to speed the heel.

The shove must be *sustained:* it may keep the opposition down a little longer, and should rock them back on their heels. We don't want our back-row going into the blind until the ball has passed them: keep pushing,

(a) *positioning:* the key ideas are *width* and *depth*. We want, if possible to have the forwards behind the ball and on either side of the ball-carrier and we want the forwards who break later from the scrum giving depth support, so that if the ball goes down we have cover.

(b) *execution:* as the ball passes them, the back-row and scrum-half move wide to get the width and then move forward. If they go forward first they will probably be out of the play.

The players nearest to the ball-carrier shout to let him know they are there: shout *his* name – it avoids confusion.

If space is available we'll go for forward handling – using as much width and depth as possible (see p. 53); if cover is there we'll concentrate on making sure the ball comes back. For the purposes of the exercise, we'll put in four sharp passes left and right (see p.

53), the last ball-carrier will put the ball down and turn to act as opposition, and we'll set up a maul (see p. 105).

The coach checks the support pattern, the speed of passing, the fact that they "walk forward" in the maul. While the maul is on he glances left to check the speed into position and alignment of the backs, and encourages the full-back to get back fast for the second phase.

3. If the blind-side drive has been successful we've scored – but we practise what happens if we haven't.

The ball comes back from the maul when the scrum-half calls for it, and he calls for it when he's checked that the line is in balance and ready to go. If the ball comes back before the line is ready, he'll have to make an immediate decision – to go himself, or to chip blind, for example. The coach must prepare him for this, and if in the practice the situation arises, then he's got to make his decision and execute it. *We never want our players to stop judging, deciding, acting: the programme we're working through is a staple for the team, but if it's likely to break down we must have positive alternatives, and people ready to execute them.*

(a) *Positioning: fly-half* – as ever his judgement of the situation is crucial, and should immediately affect his own positioning (see p. 172). In this situation it's unlikely that his opposite number will have been drawn into the maul. If he has, and the opposing three-quarters have moved in one to cover, there'll be a gap wide – so we'll spin it; if a flanker has gone to fly-half – we'll attack him; if the full-back has moved up, we'd chip over the top. The Coach uses the practice to point this out: we've got to coach judgement and decision-making as well as the mechanics of the game.

For this practice, we're going to spin the ball wide, trying to stretch their defence so that a gap appears. This means that the *fly-half* will take the ball fairly deep, and out on the open-side.

Centres: at any second-phase situation, the temptation is for the centres to lie too shallow, which effectively retards the acceleration of the line: make sure they're in place both in width and depth to allow stretching and acceleration. Usually I make the inside-centre responsible for alignment.

(b) *Execution:* we're looking for quality in moving the ball (see

p. 187). We want the ball to reach outside-centre with time for him to make good decisions. In this case, though, we'll give the ball straight to the winger and let him score.

Once the players have got the basic pattern, we can begin to develop it, and elaborate it. We *develop it* by creating more opportunities for the forwards to handle and give possession from mauls. A key notion in total rugby is that the forwards should see themselves equally as e.g. props and players in the loose. We need to establish the self-discipline that gets the forwards into effective support positions even when they're weary. We want to build up their work-rate – which means "scrum – and run; maul and run; pass – and run" – so we don't want them in the unopposed above to give the ball back from the maul, and stand applauding as the winger flashes over the line: they must *be* there in case he gets stopped. We want especially to create a sense of small team unity in the back-row – a real pride in the way they support the ball-carrier and each other. We tend to aim, therefore, for at least two handling movements by the forwards in each programme.

We *elaborate* the programme by examining the different possibilities in each of the basic elements. In the two back movements – 1 and 3 – of the programme we're looking at, we can easily incorporate moves. For example, when the ball goes blind, the fly-half can do a dummy switch with the full-back with the full-back coming back inside to check the opposing back-row (see p. 194); when the ball comes open we can add a dummy switch between the centres (see p. 194) and encourage our full-back – weary from his recent exertions – to make the extra man. We try, in fact, to incorporate those elements of our particular mix appropriate to the starting situation.

At all times we must see the programme as a learning/coaching situation. It's useless if we don't go on making individual performances better – calling attention to weaknesses, and suggesting – or working out with the player – ways of improving. To this end, you may run through the programme half-a-dozen times. It's useful to start off on your own goal-line and call the 22 the opposing try line; and repeat attacking the 10 metre line, the half-way line, the 10 metre line, the 22, so ending up performing the programme really well in the opposing 22. You should also, where practicable, switch from side to side of the pitch. In this programme it is practicable – though you'd have to check on the scrum-half's pass, and expect the final spinning of the ball to be slightly less effective since it will entail left-hand-dominant passes right down the line. On the other hand, it means that a wheel on the initial scrum will work to your advantage, tending to take the bulk of the opposing pack away from the blind-side drive. When you try it, you can, of course, build the simulated wheel into your unopposed, as you would in setting up back-row moves to take the ball left after being wheeled.

What has been outlined here is a fairly typical unopposed programme. It starts from one of the recurrent situations – e.g. scrum, line-out, drop-out, kick-off, tap penalty – at which you can predict possession, and within wider limits, the behaviour of the opposition. You build in the basic patterns suggested by your overall strategy, and use it to explore possible tactics. You monitor very carefully the probabilities, so that players don't try to run through the opposing pack, or ignore the tackle line. You insist on quality – and should have prepared for it in the rest of the session. You keep on coaching and commenting – getting the players to think ahead and make decisions. If you do this, you'll find that the programme does much more than establish a single pattern of play – it helps establish basic principles in the minds of the players.

DEFENSIVE UNOPPOSED

Programmed unopposed is all about methods of attack, and an attitude to attack. We also need a method of encouraging high work-rate and efficiency when we are actually going backwards. The situation that fits in most easily is where one of the backs is tackled behind the gain line, so that the pack has to go back to maintain possession or limit our opponents' gain. This is easily simulated, and leads to a very intensive pressure practice I call defensive unopposed.

We start from a simulated scrum facing upfield on the centre of the 22. The ball is played back and spun out left or right. When the coach blows his whistle, the ball-carrier puts the ball down, and the player who gave him the pass nips in and picks up. The first forward takes the ball off him and the rest of the pack maul on him. The two backs concerned get swiftly back into position. When the scrum-half sees that the back division are ready, he calls for the ball, the ball is spun out, the coach whistles and the cycle is under way.

The coach can vary the distance from the pack and the depth at which he elects to whistle and give a great deal of intensive practice in support running in a short time. He must, however, carry on coaching – watching individual players and checking that they are using their heads as well as their legs, watching the build-up of the maul and the continued drive – "walk forward" – as the ball comes back, watching the positioning of the backs so that there's genuine acceleration onto the ball, and so on. Mistakes are never welcome, but at least in this kind of practice they are what the team are working on, and they do ensure that mechanical running is avoided.

This is a very high-pressure practice and the coach should limit its duration – start off with three whistle-stops, and gradually in succeeding sessions extend it.

Defensive unopposed is an excellent situation to drill home two imperatives on how to handle the retreating situation:

i. the first aim is to stop the ball going back – don't hand the ball back unless the player behind you actually calls for it;

ii. don't play rugby going backward: set up a static situation that allows time for decision-making and safe execution.

CONDITIONED UNOPPOSED

Programmed unopposed breeds confidence by laying down in advance what is going to happen. The match situation, however, has a much higher content of the unexpected – basically, the difference between the expected efficiency of the opponents and their actual performance. The whole team, therefore, and especially the tactical decision makers must be put in situations that call for quick, effective, decisions. For this we need a form of the exercise that builds in the unexpected – so conditioned that individual players or units can create the unexpected for the rest of the team to react to. The coach's job is then to monitor the decisions and encourage the whole team to appreciate the reasoning behind them, and, of course, to improve the execution.

He can do this in two ways – by telling one part of the team what is going to happen, but not the rest, or by leaving it entirely to the players working within a few stipulations or completely free.

The first form, by its nature, will tend to be limited – playing it through second-phase will be adequate. Say, for example, that we have a scrum on the centre line with a blind-side of twenty metres on the right. The tactical decisions have been made and communicated.

The scrum-half, however, has been told separately that the scrum are in difficulties and he'll have to attack by kicking. This immediately creates an unexpected situation for the rest of the team. How are they going to react? The way in which they do so is the starting point for coaching. Has the back division moved immediately into its defensive position, giving pressure from the front three, the depth from the back three? Has the pack created width and depth on the line of the ball? Has the scrum-half put the rest of the team onside? If he's slow, the job will have to be done by someone else – who? And who will fill the resultant hole?

So far as the execution is concerned, we can start with the kick, its range, height, and direction. The scrum-half can go through this, thinking about the need to get it up quickly so that the opposing back-row can't charge it down, about the need to keep it in play, about the need to keep it more or less in front of his forwards, about the need to put it high enough to let the pack get into contention for it. It may well bring home to him the need to get out and work on particular kicks, working in real detail – kicking immediately the ball reaches him, from low down, with the ball across his foot, and his foot going where he wants the ball to go.

The coaching continues with comment on the rest of the performance – e.g. have the front three got into line before applying pressure? If they chase as individuals they're backing outsiders – spectacular if they make the tackle, but unlikely to be successful.

The actual mechanics of the practice will be as in programmed unopposed – the first player onto the ball will secure possession, if in doubt falling on it and looking to feed the mauling pack. The ball comes back when it's asked for, and by that time the decisions about the second-phase play must be made. The forward-leader may well have decided, however, that this particular situation is ideal for the pack to set up a drive from the maul – if the kick has been placed in front of them, there's a good chance that they will outnumber their opponents and be able to attack successfully. If they do, the coach lets them drive and then whistles, the ball is put down and the ex-ball-carrier turns to act as opposition, the maul is set up and the resultant ball can be used by the backs from this new and again unexpected situation. How effectively do they use it? The coach can then talk through the decision with the decision makers.

The second stage comes with the coach stipulating a starting situation and perhaps a closing situation: whatever shape the attack takes, it must end with a particular form of score – e.g. a score by a forward on the right touch-line. This last stipulation postulates an opposition that has left its left flank unguarded. It might equally be weak at midfield – and the score has to be between the posts, and so on.

In the final form of this exercise, the shape of the attack – or the defence, for any mistake, intentional or unintentional, will give practice in defensive play – is left solely to the pack-leader and the back-leader, who shape the events between them. The pack-leader creates the unexpected by calling for mauls or drives, and the back-leader shapes the attack from there. All the basic priorities for programmed unopposed apply, and only when the rhythm of the team is adequately established should this form of unopposed be undertaken. Again, it is only a coaching situation – the coach has to be in there commenting, questioning, suggesting, if it's going to be genuinely useful.

COUNTER-ATTACK UNOPPOSED

The ball that your opponents give to you by way of badly judged kicks is the starting point for a characteristic feature of total rugby – the handling counter-attack. This counter-attack almost inevitably starts with the back-three, the full-back and wings, whose job in defence is precisely that of giving depth against breaks and especially kicks. They must be guided into an appreciation of the factors that govern the profitability of attempted counter-attack, and given practice to build up confidence in their procedures. But the rest of the team are vitally involved, and the final success of counter-attack is often governed by their judgement and work-rate. You need a form of unopposed practice that will give everyone a clear idea of his role in the team effort.

What the coach must first do is establish basic conditions for launching a counter-attack, and a ground plan of how the attack is to proceed. The final aim, as in all help towards decision-making, is the independent judgement of the players, but initially a few key-factors can be very helpful.

1. Position on the field

The coach may initially suggest that if there's any doubt we should not try to counter-attack from inside our own 22, since a mistake there is hard to retrieve.

Broadly speaking, too, counter-attack is most difficult from a kick into the box when the ball starts off more or less directly in front of the opposing forwards.

In either of these situations, at least initially, safety is the sensible priority.

2. Indications

There are three helpful indications that counter-attack will work:

a. The catcher can go forward himself

This is the most reliable gauge of pressure. It's possible to counter attack successfully with the catcher simply giving a pass to a supporting player, but all too often this means that the supporting player cannot accelerate onto the ball, and/or cannot choose his direction of run.

b. The catcher has immediate support

You can expect the catcher to beat one man – especially if his opponent has ignored the basic precept "start fast, arrive in balance" and arrives out of control – and this may open up fresh possibilities. It's generally best, however, to see immediate support as a requisite.

In terms of the practice, this means concentration on getting the back three to work as a team, on an early call, and on a determined effort to be behind the catcher when the ball arrives. This simultaneously gives cover for the fumble, and allows acceleration onto the pass.

Of the other players, I expect the outside-centre to arrive first, closely followed by the back-row. The whole team, but especially these players, must make a real effort to get behind the ball as early as they can. A team that watches the ball go back to the back-three and stands waiting for them to bring it forward is never going to be a consistently successful counter-attack force.

c. The disposition of the opposition

Counter-attack will always have a better chance when the opponent's kick is a result not of choice but of necessity – when pressure has deprived them of the initiative. If they have prepared for the kick and the front three, the back three and their forwards are all in the picture, then counter-attack has a very limited chance of success.

The back-three must keep thinking ahead so that they know the situation that led to the kick, and they must use the time while the ball is in the air to glance at the way the opposition is coming forward.

3. Direction of attack

Ideally, we want the counter-attackers to play with the same confidence, judgement, and fluidity as a good sevens team, but once again basic precepts will be an initial help. The most useful precept is that you feint at strength, strike at weakness. What this tends to mean is that the catcher and at least one supporter run at the opposing pack. The aim is to discourage them from spreading cross-field – to keep them narrow when they should be wide. This preserves at least part of the field as a possible attacking area.

When judgement dictates, the supporter switches play towards that area (see p. 50). By the time the switch takes place supporting players – the centres and a wing, at least – should be out there, deep enough to be able to accelerate as a line onto the first supporter's pass.

This can be set up as a unit practice before the team come together. Do it on a small scale, with the coach throwing the ball to the full-back, and at a walking pace, until the basic pattern is established. The front three take four or five paces forward to simulate pressurising their opponents, and then move back into support position. Gradually increase the scale and speed of the operation. This small practice will simplify the introduction with the team.

4. Disposal of the ball

Setting up this basic form for counter-attack is equivalent to establishing an efficient form of a move – it is designed to give your striker an increased chance to use his abilities. As with moves, it offers no automatic key to unlock their defence – simply improved odds for your raider.

It's yet another case where judgement is called for. Before the switch is made, the players running into support positions, and especially the first of these to receive the ball, have got to be engaged on the assessment of the situation.

(a) *Look* – he must have his head up and be looking at the opposition defence, getting facts about them.
(b) *Judge* – he must be sorting these facts out into what is significant – evaluating the possibilities they offer.
(c) *Decide* – he must by the time the ball reaches him have made his choice so that he can set up the attack properly.
(d) *Communicate* – his decision must preferably be early enough to allow communication with those immediately involved (though in a fluid situation he may well find he must depend on their reading the situation in the same way that he does) so that all can
(e) *Co-operate* – effectively.

This kind of thoughtfulness has to be built up in the players by constant encouragement as is discussed on p. 244.

The decision is on which of the four possibilities to employ – to pass, to kick, to run, to use a move – and by running through these possibilities in the unopposed situation the coach can help them choose with confidence.

If the counter-attacking player has become isolated – by any of the chances that arise in a match – his choice is restricted to kicking or running. Once again his decision can only be effective if it's based on thinking ahead, and the scope of his choice is limited by his personal abilities – can he chip accurately ahead to find touch or keep the ball in play? Can he kick, perhaps left-footed, back to his forwards? Can he kick high and perhaps deep to expose the opposition's lack of depth? By bringing these possibilities to the player's attention the coach can perhaps motivate him to improve his kicking skill and, mutatis mutandis, his running and evading skills.

5. Counter-attack practices

Setting up an unopposed practice to exercise counter-attack is moderately easy. It can be done either as a practice on its own or as an addition to programmed unopposed.

For the first of these, start off with a simulated scrum just inside the 10 metre line with the front three up in defensive positions along the 10 metre line. The coach tosses the ball in the air to simulate the opposing scrum-half's pass. As soon as he tosses it, the front three go forward to touch the half-way line and then immediately get into support positions for the counter-attack. Immediately the coach catches the ball he puts in a deep kick to the back three – and the whole team goes into counter-attack.

Once again – this is a coaching situation: it's the quality of comment from the coach and from the players that makes it of value.

The second form of the practice simulates the situation where your team is attacking, the ball is put down, and an opponent kicks it through. The coach sets up a programme, warns the team what's going to happen, takes a spare ball onto the pitch with him, and at an appropriate moment kicks it through at the full-back. The full-back should have immediate support from the blind-side wing, and together they drive forward acquiring further support as they go. This also allows the full-back practice in the situation where the ball reaches him without support and he has to take the ball forward before kicking it in front of his forwards – again something that requires practice to be consistently successful.

SEMI-OPPOSED RUGBY

Although the name suggests a form of practice in which the team is opposed by half a team – e.g. a team working against a pack – it tends to be used to cover all varieties of limited opposition.

Limiting the opposition is a basic form of conditioning a practice, a further confidence-building step before the full pressure of the match. Besides limiting them in numbers the coach can limit what they are allowed to do. At its simplest he might station four of them, arms linked, at the point where this programme calls for a maul – to give some contact, and to sharpen the supporting players' awareness of the need to get to the mauling point fast. This can be made more realistic by having only one opponent at the mauling point, and the rest at an appropriate distance away, so that they provide opposition of the standard needed. Put them further away and the team's job is easier; closer and it becomes harder.

The coach can also give a free roving commission to this limited opposition – always ensuring that they play within the laws. In a programme beginning with a simulated kick-off, for example, they can pressurise the initial maul and then work as a back-row trying, within the laws, to disrupt play. It's as well to emphasise their acting legally, for they're obviously tempted to make up for lack of numbers by low cunning and mayhem.

Much more interesting forms of semi-opposed, however, are possible, and in my experience the best of them pits the team against a pack and half-backs. This can be conveniently done with the 1st team against the 2nd, with the spare back division working elsewhere on the field. Each team in turn plays against the opposing pack and halves.

The practice starts with a scrum on the 22, with the pack and halves attacking the near goal-line.

When they get possession, either at the initial scrum or at a maul, or at the coach's direction, they are forced to attack in the forwards. The scrum-half and fly-half must do their best to get the ball in front of their pack by running or very accurate kicking, and the forwards have to set up handling movements from back-row moves, or rolling off mauls. They win if they cross the line.

The full team score by putting two men clear before they reach the 22. Their aim is to get the ball efficiently and quickly into space, and to make sure that ball speed exceeds the running speed of their opponents.

This gives very intensive practice to the two packs in attack and defence in all normal aspects of the game other than line-out. The coach may have to impose conditions if one pack is markedly stronger than the opposition, but there's no reason why he shouldn't even it out e.g. by switching front rows. The backs have room in which to gain confidence, and the pack's halves have to concentrate on attack close to the forwards.

The intensity of the effort required from the packs imposes a time-limit on the exercise – I use it to the point where fatigue or frustration becomes evident, and then switch. And again, this is a coaching situation: you need breaks within the exercise to do some actual coaching and commenting.

If you intend to devote part of the team element of a structured session to this kind of work it obviously pays to incorporate within the skill and unit elements an adequately conditioned preparation, so that the semi-opposed practice goes well. It wouldn't pay to go into such intensive work until the skill level, especially of the packs, was reasonably high.

So, too, must be the coach's control of the players. He is, in fact, creating that kind of confrontation which in play-safe rugby can lead to violence. It's best, therefore, to use a certain amount of conditioning, so that the sharp edge of confrontation is blunted.

SITUATIONS

The final stage before playing a match is usually seen as a practice match. For those coaching or playing at a fairly high level, however, practice matches are of limited value: there's no guarantee that they are going to improve technically the play of the teams. They may benefit the stronger team in terms of confidence, but at the expense of the weaker. Besides which, the time can be better employed working in detail on what is most often, remarkably, left to chance – the establishment of team tactics.

It was suggested earlier (page 4) that the basic strategy of the team, the notion of the kind of rugby they are hoping to play, starts with a vision in the coach's imagination. The vision in the imagination of the coach committed to total rugby, for example, is that of a team playing flexibly to meet the problems posed by particular opponents and conditions but always aspiring to fifteen-man handling rugby. But within this basic sense of how they intend to play, there's a need for a realistic appraisal of how the team is going to react tactically to particular situations.

By the nature of the game, basic situations are bound to recur in the match and throughout the season. Team tactics are largely based on a clear understanding of how the particular players in the team are best equipped to deal with these recurrent situations.

The tactics must cover both attack and defence. Much of the attacking tactics can be worked on in unopposed and semi-opposed practices, and particular facets of defence and counter-attack can be dealt with as outlined above. The real test of their efficiency, however, comes with their exposure to a full-scale opposition.

Rather than play a practice match which leads to a fairly random set of situations played through only once, with poor opportunities for coaching and improvement, it's therefore in the team's interest to work, if possible, with a full opposition on the chief recurrent situations, repeated several times and treated both in attack and in defence.

The aim is to establish what, in a particular situation, the teams are best equipped to do, and to work to make it as effective as possible. As part of the general development programme for the team, the coach is always-trying to extend these possibilities, and offer greater variety of attacking and defending measures, but establishing what *at this moment* it can do is an indispensable aid to decision-making on the field.

Decision-making is most effective when it concerns a limited number of possibilities – enough to give variety and keep the opposition guessing, enough to provide alternatives when the opposition can cope adequately with a particular one, but so limited as to allow quick, easy choices. Establishing the right number of possibilities, and developing them to the point where each can be undertaken confidently is part of the coach's job. He can err in providing too few choices – as happens in play-safe rugby – or in offering too many, inadequately developed.

Apart from the right number and adequate preparation of methods, he must also help his team to appreciate the factors that indicate one choice rather than another at a particular moment. These factors are basically the strength or positioning of the opposition, but will also include the actual state, physical and emotional, of team players actively concerned.

At this point in Summer School courses, it's interesting to survey the course-members and say: "Right, think back to last season. Your team's been given a scrum fifteen yards from the opposing goal-line, and fifteen yards in from the right touch. What scoring possibilities were open to them, that they'd worked on and trusted and were actively conscious of?" When the thinking has gone on for thirty seconds, it's too late: the ball is in the fly-half's hands, and the time for decision-making on the tactical level is past. In that time the whole process – looking, judging, deciding, communicating, cooperating – must be complete. What situation practices do is to simplify the task, and to create a habit of mind that's sorting things out even before the referee's whistle goes.

Some time later at Summer School, usually in the bar over a quiet drink, the follow-up question is raised, of the coach's controlling the team, and the game, and converting it into a kind of chess. Some very proper fears are expressed of an American Football situation – somewhat exaggerated – of the looking being done by trained observers posted on top of the stand and in radio contact with the dug-out, of the coach judging and deciding, of communication taking the form of a substitute sent on with orders, and the co-operation being that of a set of zombies going through pre-ordained movements. I do remember an occasion, sitting in the West Stand at Twickenham for a U.A.U. Final, when at a particular moment Mike Titcombe asked "What'll they do now?" and I explained what we'd probably do, and it actually happened. He turned and said "My God, it's like chess". It was, but only in the sense that people who've thought about a subject – e.g. a move in chess, or a tactical decision in rugby – will often come to the same conclusion: it was the sensible thing to do. So far as the mental side of the game goes, coaching sets out to encourage the habits of mind which the gifted player uses almost unconsciously, and to bring them within the range of a greater number of players. A problem faced by talented players who turn coach is, in fact, that what seems sensible and obvious to them is by no means obvious to the people they're coaching. What complicates the problem is that to a great extent the process in the talented player is intuitive and he almost certainly will find it difficult to explain what prompts him to his actions. Before he can coach he has to make the process conscious and articulate it.

Considering set situations is a concrete way of solving this problem and of encouraging a like habit of mind in the players. Indeed, it allows the players to make a real contribution. You put them in the kind of situation outlined above and you say – "Well, what can we do here?" so far as attack is concerned, or "Well, what are they likely to do here?" so far as defence is concerned. Isolated from the pressures of the match even mediocre players can make useful suggestions, and these can be tested out. Out of this comes an appreciation of what is needed to make an action work, and what circumstances will make it a poor bet. It may be as simple as establishing how much space is needed on the blind to allow a move to work, or a recognition that an orthodox back-row attack to the right on our own ball is unlikely to work if the pack is being wheeled. The great thing is that by recognising such facts in the calm of the practice, the players are less likely to waste possession in the match.

There's no question, so far as I'm concerned, of prescribing what should be done in the given situation. It's simply a way of getting all the players to be aware of the possibilities which are likely to be effective. In this, as in everything else, the coach is trying to reach the point where he becomes superfluous, where he can safely leave it to the players, and examining situations is simply an easy path to that point. Initially, the players may depend on it but the great aim is to get them thinking more intelligently and imaginatively than the coach ever did.

The situations you deal with in unopposed, semi-opposed, or opposed practices must justify themselves – i.e. they are certain or very likely to occur, or they are particularly crucial, or they are representative.

They must deal with all the major restarts in the game – kick-offs and drop-outs, scrums, line-out, penalties. To be realistic they've got to be continued through second-phase, and this in turn covers the maul or ruck.

The coach cannot treat this full-scale situation, except in a few cases (e.g. short penalties involving the whole team), as an initial learning situation. Whatever can be done in smaller units – e.g. the fly-half kicking into the box, a back-row move to the left, the full-back coming in on the blind-side – should be covered before you reach this stage: you don't want half the team standing about.

Although you are dealing with specific points on the ground, and looking at specific possible actions, many of the situations may already be covered by broad principles set down by the coach. For example, the fly-half may have been given basic guidance about kicking (see p. 208), so that he will tend to kick for touch in his 22, kick for position from ball obtained behind his 10 metre line, and open it up beyond that. The coach may have pointed out that you tend to continue attacks checked at mauls and rucks in the direction you were going. That if you continue the direction of attack towards the right touch, you are opening the whole field up on the left to stretch the opposing defence with right-handed passes on the next phase. That you tend to feint at strength, strike at weakness. That broadly speaking it's sensible to pass to the left, and use moves carrying the ball to the right. That it's not a good bet doing miss moves to the right. That some moves can be set up initially more easily from line-outs than from scrums.

And, of course, you will begin to formulate general guidance for your actual team as you examine the specific situations. For penalties, for example, you can establish the profitable kicking range of your kicks, the optimum up-and-under area, the place where particular short penalties can best be used, the places where you'll kick to touch, who is best used for kicks to the left touch and who to the right, whether a pass should be employed to give a better angle, and so on. This leads to a general appreciation and so to better decisions. And, of course, for maximum effectiveness each of these has to be worked on with the whole team to establish the best follow up patterns, the requisite support, pressure, depth, and width. In general, once these guide-lines are established less time need be spent thinking what the team is going to do and more on the actual performance. It allows quicker action in the match – and delay is always an advantage to the defenders – and it allows full concentration on the execution.

All the examples used so far have been of attacking play, or at least of using possession we expect to get. Defensive play is equally important but tends to be more general in character – i.e. it isn't greatly altered by position on the field. Much of it can be dealt with in small units – e.g. the pack running crossfield against the backs, or the back-row and halves working on immediate defence at a simulated scrum against the opposing back-row and halves. Some of it can be simulated in unopposed – when e.g. the coach at a simulated scrum shouts "ball lost" and the team has to get into defensive formation and prepare for counter-attack, or at a kick-off, when the coach puts the ball where it's not expected.

Defence, like attack, however will benefit from being faced with situation practice. It's just as important that the players can deal with the opposing drop out, or short penalty, or kick into the box, or move, as they should be capable of using the attacking possibilities that they present. Situations played against an opposing team afford the best possible test for defensive arrangement, expose weaknesses, and give a real opportunity for improvement.

To cover all the basic situations in at least a representative form, it's convenient to think of a line running parallel to touch down the centre of the field. This, with the two 15 metre lines, divides the field, into four (p. 257). This covers a blind-side on the left, a blind-side on the right, and both split-field situations. In practice, these are approximate positions, and for specific purposes – e.g. a right-footed, drop at goal, or an attack on the blind that needs a little more space – we'll make necessary adjustments.

For convenience, we can use the 22s, 10 metre lines, and half-way line to complete a grid, and use the intersections to establish our representative positions. To cover the most critical situations, however, we have to add two more imaginary lines about five metres out, parallel to the goal lines.

We now have a complete grid whose intersections give a good

TEAM PRACTICE GRID

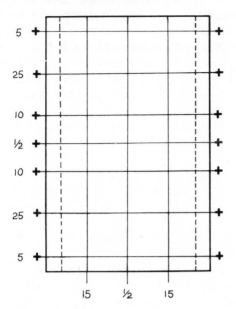

coverage of all the likely points for a set-piece – i.e. any set-piece position will approximate to one of them. The grid has various functions – as an aide-memoire to the coach, as a starting-point and prompter to experiment and devise new ways of attacking and defending, and as a fine basis for revision and pressure practices. To go round the circuit, up the sides and down the middle, affords an excellent range of starting points, each calling for decisions. In unopposed, semi-opposed, or opposed it gives the chance to play a whole variety of situations. Pressure can be built up by imposing time limits – how far can we get in four minutes? can we beat our record for going down the middle? But as with all pressure exercises this can be done effectively only when very sound basic forms of the activity have been established.

As a starting point for the use of this grid it would be a useful exercise for the coach to go through it in terms of penalty kicks, planning precisely what his particular team should do at each point. The whole team is, of course, involved in terms of support and defence. Immediately the kicker is faced with the precise problem there is motivation for him to practise and the coach to coach. You can establish the accurate range of your place-kickers – which is in the kickers' interest and the team's – and work out from there the points at which different tap penalties, and up-and-unders, and kicks to touch, can be used. You will find that the grid helps you be thorough in covering the possibilities.

28
Tactical Guidelines

Apart from the positive side of tactics based on the possibilities open to your particular team at given situations, you have to offer guidelines to the players – and especially, of course, the tactical decision-makers – for coping with or exploiting the situations outside their direct control, in particular the attacking or defensive power of the opposition, and the weather. This is one of those aspects of coaching rarely examined – it's usually left to the imagination and growing experience of the player – mainly, one suspects, because as coaches we haven't given it adequate thought. It's broadly speaking true that a team's tactics in uncoached rugby are a simple expression of the players' limitations.

1. DEALING WITH OPPOSITION PRESSURE

(a) Pressure from opposing front three

1. Fly-half takes ball medium-deep with centres lying up, runs and chips over the opposing centres to the outside of the full-back;
2. Attack the blind-side – taking the ball shallow and where possible bringing in your full-back;
3. Play miss moves – i.e., fly-half to outside-centre, or inside-centre to full-back;
4. Use change of pace – fly-half runs onto pass slowly (see p. 173) and full-back comes into the line at speed between the centres, with outside-centre moving out;
5. Kick into the box;
6. Encourage scrum-half and back-row to attack close to scrum or maul.

The most obvious answer to overall sustained pressure in your 22 – the fly-half taking the ball deep and kicking – is limited. Unless he has an exceptionally long kick, he will tend simply to relieve pressure but not gain the initiative. Under sustained pressure, especially in your 22, the time comes when a decisive attempt to take the initiative, even at some risk, is a better bet than what increasingly tends to be the vain effort to hang on. The fly-half must keep aware of the morale of his pack, and, when the pressure begins to tell, go into attack rather than simply make it safe.

(b) Pressure from opposing back-row

1. Engage them by attacking close to the set-piece – e.g. peeling off mauls, and line-outs, and attacking in the back-row from scrums;
2. Holding the ball in the tight;
3. In line-out, throwing long to keep them engaged, or using a push-down to set up a maul;
4. Take ball wide at fly-half or inside-centre, and kick back over their heads;
5. Use switches between fly-half and inside or outside-centre to take the ball back inside them, or dummy switches to check them while the ball is carried into space.

Broadly speaking, effective pressure groups do not expect to be taken on, and may not be well prepared for it – if you show a willingness to run at them in numbers (e.g. back-row attacks supported by the whole pack) you can take them out of their stride.

These pressure situations are at their most intense at set scrums. In most respects, the ·situation at a set scrum is the archetypal situation in rugby – all the elements present in line-out, ruck or maul are present here in a higher degree. Being able to cope with them and if possible turn them to advantage is the best gauge of a team's ability.

In most matches, the set scrum offers the highest probability of a good ball, and so the soundest basis for decision-making. It also offers various split-field situations which provide predictable advantages in introducing an extra man, and the possibility of drawing the defence across and switching play to the far side of the scrum. These are substantial advantages which repay attention in training sessions.

The proximity and organisation of the opposing defence make early decision-making vital: it's not only pointless but dangerous to play off the cuff at scrums. Lack of decision and inefficiency in execution are liable to be punished, and this has led some coaches to take refuge in statements about the need to simplify the play – by which they mean kicking possession away. There is, in fact, virtually nothing that you can do, say from a line-out, that you cannot, with adequate coaching, do from a scrum. Indeed, the extra space available from line-outs is balanced by the depth of the opposing defence, and the extra time that the defence therefore has to cover the field. If the risks at set-scrum are greater, so are the potential gains. A basic rule in coaching is that you prepare for the most difficult situation: if you can cope with that, the rest is easier. The coach must prepare his team to attack from the tight, and the first set of guidelines offered aims to help them deal with the pressure situation, and if possible turn it to advantage.

One further variety of pressure needs to be looked at:

(c) Opposing front-three coming up together but slowly

1. Take the ball wide, then chip back (e.g. from outside-centre) to the forwards;
2. Adjust the timing of your moves – i.e. delay the strike till you are in a position where they'll find it hard to react fast enough to stop you.

If you play running rugby and employ moves, your opponents may decide to hang back with the aim of putting out your timing. If you simply spin the ball, they can then drift out so that there's a majority of defenders out wide. You aim to exploit this by taking the ball as far forward as you can wide, so that their front three and cover are pulled across, and switch the focus of the attack behind them by a chip back to the forwards.

A mechanical use of moves will tend to break down against such a defence – typically the players go into the move too early, and the striker is faced with an undisrupted defence. The key is judgement – taking the ball forward to the right point before actually initiating the move.

2. EXPLOITING WEAKNESSES IN THE OPPOSING DEFENCE

(a) Opposing front three lying tight

1. Fly-half runs for opposing inside-centre; inside-centre runs

for opposing outside-centre; outside-centre runs into space;
2. Use miss moves – fly-half to outside-centre, inside-centre to full-back.

If they lie tight – close together – there's bound to be space outside them, and the aim is to put a player clear in that space. If their open winger is lying close in as well, you look to put your winger clear – and this can be done by diagonal kicks, e.g. from outside-centre, or by moving the ball faster and further than they expect. The long diagonal kick can be very effective if their wing is lying close on their own goal-line – but make sure your winger is ready for it, up wide and flat to maximise his advantage.

Of the two basic actions outlined above, it's sensible to use miss moves out to the left. In general, see end of next section.

(b) Opposing front-three lying wide

1. Fly-half runs wide and inside-centre runs parallel to him before either straightening for the crash ball (if his own opponent has stayed wide), or coming back inside for the switch (if his opponent is coming in to close the gap);
2. Use "Strawberry" – the open winger slicing back in to take a short ball from inside-centre. This becomes much more effective if fly-half has arranged to run onto the ball slowly so that it's easy for the winger to get into position, and he comes into the line with a distinct change of pace;
3. Bring in extra man – e.g. full-back or blind-side wing – between the centres;
4. Fly-half runs at his opponent, and curves back inside to feed the back-row.

Some teams adopt these extreme forms of defensive positioning on principle – e.g. to avoid the chance of a break fairly close to the pack – some because they are aware of weakness – e.g. if they are notably slower than the opposing backs they will tend to lie wide. A consistent pattern of attack will also tend to impose or at least encourage one or the other – if you consistently run the ball wide, they will tend to drift wider; if you consistently bring it back, they'll tend to close up. The good fly-half will seek to exploit the space created by these alignments – but he's got to have his head up and be looking for them, have methods clear in his mind for exploiting

them, and have effective communication with all those involved –
never forgetting the back-row.

(c) Opposing front-three dog-legged

1. The player whose opponent is lying back runs for the inside
   shoulder of the opponent one out from him – e.g. fly-half for
   the opposing inside-centre. If he comes in, give the pass; if he
   stays out, get behind him and give the pass as soon as you
   can.

This is the basic "gap" that all front three players pray for. A
typical case is where the opposing fly-half hangs back, and the
opposing inside-centre rushes up. Once the initial break is made, it's
always sensible to move the ball on – especially if it's the fly-half who
makes the break. Keep your eye on your opponent – if he hangs
back, there's always something on.

These various categories of bad alignment are easy to spot –
provided your tactical decision-makers have got their heads up, and
know what to look for. The first time they spot it they may not be
able to take advantage of it – but it clues them in for the future.

3. RELATIVE WEAKNESS OF AN OPPOSING PLAYER

1. Get the ball to your player when, where, and at the pace he
   wants it.

Most teams will possess a player who they feel is likely to be
capable of taking his man on; all too often they make no special
plans to exploit his skill. You have to establish the three basic needs
– when, where, and at what pace does your particular striker want
the ball? If he's elusive he may want the ball late to minimise the
opponent's reaction time; if he's quick, he may want it early. If he
comes inside, he may want the ball set up for him to come inside; if
outside, he may want the ball outside his man. If he's capable of
abrupt acceleration but limited in top speed, he'll need to be given
the ball moving fairly slowly. It's up to the coach and the other
players to recognise these needs and be clear how they are going to
meet them. Equally, he must be given support – if he can make the
initial break, players should be behind him to carry the attack
on.

4. EXPLOITING WEAKNESS IN THE OPPOSING BACK THREE

(a) Exploit the winger's placing

Every winger has two jobs in defence – to mark his own man, and to provide depth – and his initial positioning must be a sensible compromise to give him a chance of doing both. This is much more difficult on the blind – where the attack is very quickly mounted – than on the open, though once the ball reaches outside-centre the difficulty is just as great on the open: does the wing come up to guard against the handling attack or stay back to guard against the chip behind him?

If he commits himself to one and neglects the other, then you can exploit his position. Whenever you have a scrum on the left with a fair blind-side, check where the opposing winger is lying – if he's lying back, get the ball to your winger, preferably from scrum-half; if he's up, chip into the box. So too, outside-centre can choose to pass or kick.

What the winger in defence needs, of course, is the assurance of support from his full-back so that as he moves up the full-back moves across behind him. (See also 2a and 2b above.)

(b) Pressurise the full-back

In a badly organised team, the full-back, who should feel that he's a member of a tightly-integrated back three, is often a lonely figure. The fly-half can assume that he's right-footed by preference and when he kicks try to put it on his left. He can guess at his speed and manoeuverability and adjust his kicking to exploit suspected weaknesses. Once he's within range he can kick high to assess his reaction to stress.

This is not, by choice, how I like my team to play – it's based more on the other team's weakness than on our strength, and aesthetically it's much less pleasing. But it can be done better or worse, and there's some satisfaction in seeing it done well, by accurate kicking with well-organised support running, as one element in our mix.

(c) Exploit excessive depth

If there's a strong wind behind you and you've been kicking tactically, the opposing wings and full-back may all lie deep:

1. Chip short on their centres;
2. Use miss moves to get the ball wide fast.

5. OPPOSITION PRESSURE IN THE TIGHT

Run with the wheel

The big development of scrumming has been the eight-man shove, and the consequent tendency to wheel the scrum. This wheel is always clockwise, and tends to take at least two of the opposing back-row round to their left: you can take advantage of this by attacking where possible to the left of the set-scrum.

If the wheel is through 90°, you may well find, however, that the no. 8 and left flanker are effectively out of the game; they will be off-side if they break. The only difficulty to be met is that of the scrum-half's passing with their flanker threatening him. The simplest way of meeting this is for your no. 8 to feed the scrum-half standing back (see p. 131).

6. SECOND-PHASE BALL

Good second-phase ball means that you are running against a disorganised defence, and possibly a defence with one of the front-three under a maul. To exploit it you need

1. to know where the advantage lies;
2. to react faster than the opposition.

You must get your head up and look at the defensive alignment. Has someone been taken out? If they've lost a player, they'll either all have moved in and the gap is on the wing – spin it for the overlap – or there'll be a gap midfield – set up a break. This isn't the concern simply of the halves – all the backs must be looking for the advantage and moving to exploit it.

The easiest way of losing the advantage in second-phase, other than kicking it away, is to run across. If the ball comes back fast, you may well find that everyone starts running across because they haven't got wide enough or deep enough. This is where fast reaction comes in: it takes discipline to get fast into position, especially late in the game, but it's the only way to be sure of capitalising on possession in the loose. Work to be in position before the opposition are. If you're inside-centre and your fly-half is running across – probably because the scrum-half is putting the ball a little too far in front of him – do your best to get much wider and rather deeper initially so that you can straighten the line of attack for him. This applies in any situation, but it's rather more likely in second-phase. But in most second-phase situations every player would usually be better for being a shade deeper and wider!

Good second-phase ball also diminishes the threat of cover defence: it's unlikely that the specialist back-row will be in position – they may well be under the maul. Once the initial break is made, you can expect to penetrate deep, which helps sustain the momentum of attack. This second-phase play is at its most devastating in its continuity – it allows no relief from pressure. Every player must be imbued with this notion; he must work to support, to keep the ball alive, to go forward. With this in mind, it's even more important that the nearest player, whoever he is, goes in to get the ball at the tackle. Any check will break down the flowing continuity.

If no immediate advantage has been gained in terms of opposing backs being taken out, the sensible course is to *continue the attack in the same direction*. This avoids running into stray characters who haven't yet reached the maul.

This means that you'll be running into progressively narrower spaces. Any backs on the open side of the maul should, therefore, be preparing for the switch – so that when the *change of direction* occurs, the ball can be moved fast and accurately. This needn't immediately follow a maul: you may attack the blind, see that the odds are against you, check, and get the ball back to the open. Don't jeopardise possession and ball speed. Running across is always dodgy – if you are extremely fast, you may get away with it, but it's not a good bet. What is needed is the line in position ready to move the ball away. Once again, the basic precept – get a shade deeper than you think necessary – allows the acceleration that's needed to maximise the attack.

Attack always gives the player a lift, and makes high workrate easier. *High work rate* is the overall key to success in loose running. The game resembles, of course, sevens, and calls for the same qualities of running, support, and getting your head up to look at the opposition. The best preparation for this is small-side touch (see p. 60), which gives every chance to improve judgement of informal situations, and to improvise. Most of the guidelines suggested there apply to play in the loose.

The more flexible the team is in the loose, the better. Forwards who can see the ball is already under control may do better to get out behind the centres than to go on blindly to the maul. Keep making judgements; never run mechanically (see also p. 161).

One clear matter for judgement is the use of space: you can have too many players for a given space as well as too few. If you get into this situation, use miss moves or dummy switches to simplify the situation, or run to take out an opponent and pop up a pass.

7. USING THE WIDTH OF THE FIELD

One effect of driving on the attack in the same direction after each maul is that it opens up the width of the field for the subsequent switch. This is most advantageous if the preliminary movement is towards the right touchline so that you can really stretch the opposing defence with right hand dominant passes. As this preliminary drive develops, the backs should be creating more space for themselves to get the maximum effect on the move to the left.

8. GETTING THE BALL AGAINST THE HEAD

If we get good ball against the head we can expect to cross the gain line before we reach the tackle line, provided we act fast. Either the scrum-half or the no. 8 ought always to go for the break in this situation (see p. 132).

9. GETTING THE BALL IN THEIR 22

Every team works hard to reach the opposing 22; once you get there you must have ways of crossing the line. You can develop these in your work on situations (see p. 252). Which one you choose, however, is a tactical decision: get your head up and look at the opposition. Have they over-committed against a particular form of attack? Have they left another area vulnerable? Have they altered the spacing of their front three? Is there a space wide?

This must be done fast and the back-row told of the best bet. Otherwise, they may themselves launch an attack without a tactical overview of the whole situation. A dummy attack by them, however, is a useful diversion (see p. 133). If the scrum is very close to the line, there's always the possibility of a push-over try, best attempted after a half-wheel to detach some of the back-row. (In defence on your own line, it's always best to go for an eight-man drive and to try to keep the scrum fairly straight.)

In the backs, remember that the hardest place to defend is the blind side, and that in the 22 a miss-move may make it impossible for the opposing cover-defence to get across.

On penalties remember that the opposition will expect you to kick at goal, and if you have your kicker poised he can come up, tap the ball to himself and get across the line while the opposition are still retiring. Some tap penalties, too, are especially well-adapted to making a short gain. For example, the "phalanx" – in which the forwards form a dynamic maul and march toward the line.

10. USING THE WIND

You must use the following wind intelligently – employing the basic guide-line for tactical kicking (see p. 208), so that you keep returning with minimum energy expenditure to the striking area in the opposition half. Conserving energy in this way is essential since against the wind next half you'll need all the energy you've got.

Naturally, too, a swirling wind increases the chances of mistakes by the opposition and so creating good attacking situations. Once again, the ease of the actual kick (p. 77) shouldn't be divorced from the response of the whole team in its pattern of following up – identical on the axis of the kick to the basic elements of all defence: pressure, cover, and depth.

Apart from kicking for position, the following wind can force the opposing back three to lie deep and so open the way for attacks on the flanks – a quick miss move with the full-back in, and the winger running into space. One danger, in fact, is to allow the wind to dominate your thinking, so that you stop examining the precise situation, or in particular what opportunities for handling exist.

In windy conditions, passing demands extra care and common sense – you don't, for example, lie wide apart or try miss moves. Your lying close will tend to bring the opposition defence in tighter, and create more space wide. This can be exploited by diagonal kicks – short, toe-down, low trajectory into the wind, longer and more flighted with the wind behind. These kicks must be in behind the opposing winger, or so placed that your own winger has a good chance of reaching them first.

The prime concern with the wind in your face is to stop the opposition getting the ball – the forwards may need to concentrate a great deal of their energy on first-phase. You may well find that pressurising in the front three becomes a waste of effort, and in positions where they are likely to kick you do better by keeping in line and coming up slowly. The back row may well continue pressurising in the hope of mistakes, and because their fly-half may be a little closer to them and the pass a little less certain. Naturally, though, you adjust to the precise conditions.

Kicking against the wind places a high premium on sheer precision – drilling the ball low across the wind, with the toe down, and going for certainty rather than long-shots.

In defence against the wind, the wingers must support the full-back, and the front-three work hard to cover the gaps on the flanks. Basically, this means moving out when your opponent passes the ball, not content simply with supporting the next man, but on getting into the gap. This again is easier if you are not pressurising but hanging back. This is most effective from scrums and mauls when you are already near the gain-line: at line-outs, when the opposition are less likely to kick, you need to be moving forward to limit the chance of their running, but with the additional space you will find it easier to cover across as well.

The back-three should always be aware of the wind, since it dictates the depth at which you take up initial positions – deep with the wind in your face, more shallow with the wind behind you.

11. KICK-OFF AND DROP-OUTS

These are typical recurrent situations in which most teams rely on stereotyped procedure, designed apparently to minimise risk. They can, in fact, offer useful possibilities of attack or at least substantial ground advantage provided that the players are clear about their plans and confident in their execution.

1. Place kick at centre

Kicking the ball in the normal way to the opposition forwards is almost always followed by their gaining possession. Any coach expects his own team receiving the kick in these circumstances to secure possession virtually every time. It pays, therefore, to examine the alternatives, and establish these as your normal tactics.

a. Kick to your backs

Provided your team is organised for it, kicking open to your backs is far more productive You need a secondary kicker: we tend to employ our hooker, since if we do kick to the forwards we want him to be out of the fray. He stands, facing the same way as the expected kicker, and has the prior claim: if he decides that the kick open is on, he takes it. You need players to go after the ball, and these will normally be your centres and wings. You need cover, in case anything goes wrong, and these will normally be your open flanker, who lines up on the open side, some five metres from the ball, and the hooker.

The hooker – or whichever player you depute for the job – must practise his kicks to the point where he can stay cool and calm. He inspects the open side of the field at his leisure and, if he decides the kick is on, takes it at his leisure: if he has to hurry, the kick isn't on. He gets the same advice as your goal-kicker (see p. 79). He will usually be kicking for your winger, who starts out on the touch to give him the maximum chance of keeping the over-long kick in play, but is basically concerned with getting to the ball. The centres give him immediate cover and support on the inside; the flanker covers him behind.

If the hooker or his deputy is a good kicker there's also the possibility of finding touch. Few teams have more than one player to cover the entire open touch-line. The coach must weigh up the advantages of using an unexpected player in the hooker's position against disguising the projected surprise attack. Every season we score tries direct from this kick, and very, very, rarely do we find ourselves worse off than from a "normal" kick.

b. Kick to their posts

A second kick that leads to a better than average situation is the long drive downfield that goes dead, or is touched down for a drop-out, or evokes a touch-kick from the mid-field area. This again is consistently more successful than the normal kick.

KICK-OFF DIAGRAM

It may, of course, lead to a counter-attack. If you imagine, however, a situation exactly corresponding to the kick-off, but as part of loose-play, you'd have little hesitation in preferring the kick deep into their defensive zone rather than a kick straight to their forwards.

For this kick, once again you need an organised follow-up pattern providing width, depth, and cover. Counter-attack will develop only if you haven't arranged for this. If the catcher looks up to see an organised, balanced pattern covering the field, he'll tend to play safe; if he doesn't, you'll be able to capitalise on it.

c. The "normal" kick

The only time there's a tactical advantage to be gained from the normal kick is when you can guarantee an accurate kick, and have trained forwards to go up for the ball and push it back. Put your jumper wide so that he can run in with his eye on the ball, and arrange – as in following up all normal kicks – for a support pattern that offers width and depth. You don't, in any aspect of loose play want a thin line of support players.

You need to minimise the importance of any mistakes, and in practice this means preventing the ball moving infield. Your open flanker should start off wide (as for the kick to the backs) and come in on the opposing fly-half's blind side, as the latter watches the maul and his scrum-half. The hooker can cover the area between maul and open flanker.

It's sensible, if you expect the opposition to kick, to form your forwards up on the left; if to handle, on the right. If there's a strong sun, use it. If it's in your face, kick, if you can, towards it; if it's behind you make the opposition face it.

2. Receiving kick-off

To discourage the kick to the backs, you need at least four players ready to cover the open. Your hooker can mark the centre, your open flanker about half-way out on the ten yard line, your outside centre some fifteen metres behind him, and the open wing out on the touch-line in front of the 22. If the kick is to the forwards, the hooker and flanker go across to the maul only if there's a problem: if not they can drop back behind the centres.

The remaining forwards cover the probable kicking area. Since the opposing kicker is often using your front-ranker closest to touch as a target man, it pays to have him three or four metres behind the line. It may also pay to have your locks in front to catch the ball, so allowing both them and the props to carry out customary line-out functions of catching and blocking. The most effective maul to use is that in which the catcher gets right round with his back to the opposition. What's most important is that he doesn't go forward towards his opponents and away from his support, and that supporting players are on the move as soon as the ball is kicked.

It's useful to use kick-off as a starting point in your unopposed, to give practice in seeing the ball early. If two players call for the ball, the player further back takes it. The call should be heard at the back of the stand. The ball is fed back only when the scrum-half calls for it.

It's very useful to split the reception area notionally so that all the players are aware of how the ensuing play will go. If the kick doesn't reach the fifteen yard line, we've got a usable blind-side, and we'll attack that from the maul. The no. 8 goes wider on the blind-side to support the scrum-half, with the winger outside him. If the ball goes to the deeper of the locks or behind him, we can handle or feed the ball back at once for a touch-kick. Everyone deep, therefore, must have a player to pass to.

Any unopposed patterns you run from a kick-off must be sensible. Especially at the start of the game, when the opposition are fresh and quick to profit from mistakes, it pays to play within your abilities. You may well think, then, of putting the ball back into the box for your wing and pack to chase rather than in spinning the ball cross-field.

3. Drop-outs

Nothing in rugby shows less tactical intelligence than the standard drop-out from the 22. Looked at objectively, the idea of kicking the ball straight to the opposing pack only a few metres from the 22 is ridiculous: if your fly-half made a habit in loose-play of doing so, you'd drop him. And when you consider that the opposing XV have three-quarters of the field to cover, it's even more ridiculous. The basic reason for relying on this kick is lack of preparation for anything different, and lack of confidence in the players.

The plan we follow is very simple and effective: its aim is to get the ball as far away from our 22 as we safely can. Two players are deputed to take the kick. As soon as the touch-down is likely they get into position, one on each side of the field, half-way to touch, far enough back from the 22 to minimise the risk of a charge-down. Immediately the ball is dead, it's thrown to the nearer of the kickers who, with the full backing of the team and the coach, selects his spot, far down the field and away from opposition players, and kicks for it. Every other player works to get back behind him to allow speedy action. Both wings make every effort to chase the ball, and the whole team works to get into the basic follow-up pattern. The best bet, however, is to look for touch near the half-way line.

This is precisely the kind of situation where speed and discipline pay off – in any game the team that moves fastest from attack into defence, or defence into attack, has a substantial advantage. Discipline is the key word, for when both teams are weary, it's the disciplined team that recognises that the little extra effort will reap big dividends.

This is eminently true in receiving the ball from the drop-out. You can inhibit the long drop-out if your players provide immediate depth and width. As always in loose play, it may not be the customary players who provide it – they may be involved in attack. But intelligent players thinking ahead can foresee the need, and provide the cover.

If the opposition delay the drop-out, get back into the normal kick-off reception pattern, with your open flanker out wide, and the hooker at the centre, and apply the same basic rules.

PART 9
Fitness for Rugby

29
Fitness for Rugby

The amount of time to be devoted to the physical preparation of players for rugby is inevitably a matter of compromise. The rugby coach needs a keen appreciation of the various requirements of his players in terms of *basic conditioning, immediate pre-season testing, in-season sharpening, and specific and general strength work.* On the other hand, he cannot afford to devote more than a little of his own time to supervision of such activities. The team's efficiency is the product of its effective work-rate, governed by this physical preparation but conditioned by its freshness and attitude, and its technical and tactical expertise. The coach's specific function is the last element. He must, therefore, set quality standards in physical preparation, devise effective methods of attaining them, encourage personal and group commitment to specific strength work, and where possible delegate much of the actual supervision to particular players or helpers.

HIGH WORK RATE

High work rate in rugby corresponds to the basic pattern in the game – a capacity to produce a sequence of high energy bursts punctuated by moments of rest. It corresponds to a sequence of sprints rather than to a steady state middle-distance run.

The team as a whole can impose a pattern on this by a conscious effort in the match to concentrate on high energy output for say three minutes at a time followed by a conscious effort to diminish energy expenditure and consolidate the gain of the previous peak. This is one function of the leaders on the field – the captain, pack-leader, tactical decision-maker. To be able to produce this sustained, high-pressure effort at the beginning and end of each half, or to reply to a score, or to consolidate a lead – and these are the critical moments – makes a team much more effective in energy use.

For the individual team member, provided he's adequately prepared, the same kind of concentration on the next five minutes rather than the game as a whole is useful in getting a higher work rate. "Burn it up in the first five…and the next…and the next" is what he must aim for, confident that at the end of each five he can produce the same kind of effort for the next five.

In essence, high work-rate consists of "do it…and run" – and the "do it" refers to every aspect of the game. The player who tackles, and lies there for a moment congratulating himself, or misses a tackle, and lies there cursing is a sure case of low work-rate. A fly-half who watches his opponent pass, lets his concentration slip, and fails to support the man outside him, is a case of low work-rate – and so on throughout the team and the game. The coach must convince the team that there's never a moment when you can stop thinking, and – except when the ball's dead – never a moment when there isn't something you can contribute to team play.

The physical preparation of the team through fitness and strength work is one element in high work-rate. The other is the attitude of the team to the match: if they aren't raring to go, it's of little consequence how fit they are. A large factor of this is freshness. The coach can help by judging the mental and emotional needs of his players and providing a flexible, varied, interesting, and if possible entertaining programme of work. He can, if the fixture list is taxing, make sure that his whole squad is involved and that players have a certain amount of time off. He should note that some players not technically first-class can bring a great deal of commitment to the team, and spark it to greater efforts. He can encourage commitment in his players by getting them to see each match as a chance to show what they can do, and by making them focus on the challenge ahead: a psychological charging of the batteries. Commitment to the team is, in fact, the second major factor. The coach has to create a sense of each player's importance in and to the team, and build up pride in the player and in the team. At a high level in any sport there's got to be an element of dedication – willingness to give a major part of your leisure time to a concentrated physical, mental, and emotional preparation for the big match – and the coach must foster this as a long term investment. If some degree of this commitment is not present long before the match, no team talk in whatever style is going to be effective.

The nature of team talks has already been discussed (see p. 32). If the coach has got the right captain, the right pack-leader, the right tactician, he should leave immediate pre-match comment to them.

PHYSICAL PREPARATION: RUNNING FITNESS

Basic conditioning for any active sport takes the form of an extended out of season programme of fartlek-type running. This "speed play" is an enjoyable, cheerful, version of parkland or forest running in which' the runner adjusts his output to the available terrain and his immediate condition. The aim is to get variety of activity within the middle third of energy output, trying to maintain a moderate output at all times, though occasionally slowing to a walk if that means being able to extend the period of exercise. Varying terrain – different slopes and surfaces – are used to provide variety of challenge. Varying activities (with a staple of normal running) provide mental variety: hopping, skipping, frog-jumping, running backward, striding, trotting, driving up hills – there's an endless variety of activities to break up the time.

For the work to be effective, it should last about 45 minutes, be done twice a week, and be carried out over some two months before the immediate match preparation begins. It will be supplemented, in all probability, by alternative summer games – tennis, for example, or athletics. What is important is to establish and maintain a fundamental aerobic fitness.

Immediate pre-season training

When match preparation begins, it's useful to consider the immediate pre-season training rather as a test of fitness (and a selection criterion) than simply as a way of getting fit. This is an admirable incentive to out-of-season work.

Once match-preparation starts, it's useful to work always in mobility peer groups with an element of competition. The fitness session will come at the end of a structured session, when the players are all very adequately warmed up by working with a ball. The fitness work itself, however, is best done as a pure activity with no distractions from its prime concern: to establish the fitness state of the players. So far as possible we do this on a 400 metre track, and encourage the players to wear track shoes.

A typical immediate pre-season sequence conducted on successive days would read:

Day 1 : 10 x 100 m
In the first two 100s, player A leads and player B tries to stay with

him running as easily as he can – in particular trying to relax his arms and trunk.

In the next two 100s, the rôles are reversed.

In the fifth 100, both are together on the line, but player A has the right to start, and it's a straight race. In the sixth 100, the rôles are reversed.

In the seventh and eighth 100s, A and B have worked out handicaps and race.

In the ninth and tenth 100s, A and B on their handicap marks are running against the rest of the squad similarly handicapped.

Note: The group need not be restricted to two players, but it is useful to make sure that players from the same position are working together. The interval between runs is flexible, based on the time they take to walk back, and the delay caused by other starts. The coach ought to make it very clear that he can see the efforts being made, encourage them to greater efforts, and encourage them to run right through the finish.

Day 2 : 6 x 200 m

Split the players into fours, fives, or sixes, of the same basic mobility, and each group into half. A and B start on one side of the track, C and D on the opposite side. A and B set off on their 200. When they reach C and D, the latter set off, and A and B trot across the middle of the track to be in their original starting position when C and D arrive. The sequence then continues.

1 – 4 : the players alternately lead, with the partner staying with the leader running as easily as he can.

5 – 6 : straight race

Day 3 : 12 x 100 m

As for Day 1 but with two additional squad handicap races at the end.

Day 4 : 3 x (2 x 300 m)

This is the main fitness test. In the groups of four, the players repeat three times the basic unit:

trot 100, run 300, trot 100, run 300, rest.

On each of the first four 300s, the players lead in turn with the rest staying with them as easily as possible. On the last two 300s, the players are racing.

Note: So far as possible, the players are encouraged to keep moving through the trot phase – even if it's only at a walk. After each basic unit the players are allowed two minutes rest, timed from the arrival of the last runner.

Day 5 : 3 x 400 m (trot 40, sprint 40)
This marks the transition to in-season work. Once again in fours, the players trot 40, sprint 40 to fixed marks round the track. At the end of each 400, they have a two minute rest. We are now looking for quality work, with a very fast pick-up.

In-season training is concerned basically with keeping the players sharp. It takes a variety of forms, depending on weather conditions and state of mind. However, the staple form that we use is the sprint pyramid. This consists of top-quality sprints between paired players, together on the starting line, and alternately having the right to start. This gives an initial advantage which the leader fights to preserve, and his partner to erode. We do it on a concrete path, slightly uphill, with lampposts at 25 yard intervals. After each sprint, players walk back to the starting point.

The standard session is comparatively short:
(6 x 25) + (4 x 50) + (2 x 25) + (1 x 100): 600 yards
We occasionally, for special events, step it up to:
(8 x 25) + (6 x 50) + (4 x 75) + (2 x 100): 1000 yards

The key to the effectiveness of this is quality: it has to be a set of flat-out sprints, with the players walking back without pauses. Its great organisational merit is that it takes a short time to complete.

How often you have such fitness sessions is a matter of judgement. Except very early in the season, we would very seldom – if ever – do a pyramid more than once a week. Playing twice a week, as we do, there are many mid-season weeks when we do no specific fitness work at all. This is partly because we cannot spare time from technical work; partly because at some times the players simply do not need it. Occasionally, though they may not need it, we have a major session simply to unify the team and confirm team spirit: there's nothing like enduring together, cheering each other on, to bond the team.

Coaches are occasionally forced to work indoors on fitness work. Unless you have a very big hall to work in, it's difficult to make your running effective – the players cannot reach top speed. The following exercises, however, are useful to provide basic exercise. We use them to punctuate other activities – handling and resistance work.

Lines

Most gymnasia have court markings that provide excellent

shuttle run check marks. Starting at the back line, the players go out to the first line and back, out to the second line and back, and so on. This creates a need for starting fast, and, just as important, arriving in balance for the turns.

Line running can be used as a basic structure for the indoor session. We work on a time basis – e.g. 30, 45, 60 or 75 seconds – and usually arrange it as a pyramid – e.g. 30...45...60...45...30. If there are many players, they work in two groups, but within each group, it's flanker versus flanker, centre versus centre, and so on. They aim to beat their opponent, and get a little further each time.

Waves

Split the players into two lines across the gym, one say four metres behind the other, both facing the coach. Make sure that rival players are one behind the other. Both lines start trotting backward, and when the coach whistles, sprint forward with the back line trying to catch the front line. As soon as the first line reaches its starting point, both lines trot backward again...and the exercise continues. Then switch the lines. You can complicate this by having a call for each end of the gym, so that there's an element of decision in their reaction.

Up and down

A very effective exercise, this involves moving from a prone position at one side of the gym to a prone position at the opposite side – and trying to beat every other player on the way. Once again, they run specifically against players in their own positions. They lie prone, heads inward, on the edge of a basketball court. When the coach yells "run", they pivot onto their right side (to avoid collisions) and dash across. Do eight, one after the other, and the players will know they have been working. These, too, can be used as a basic recurrent feature – e.g. 4...6...8...6...4.

PHYSICAL PREPARATION : RESISTANCE

In addition to this basic preparation for a running game, the players must be generally conditioned so that they can meet the pressures and demands of a hard contact sport. In the early part of the season and occasionally throughout the season an indoor "sweat session" has much to commend it. Doing it indoors helps create a high concentration of effort and togetherness – suffering together is an excellent bonding agent for the team and the club. If you can get them singing while they are suffering, so much the better.

To achieve intensity, the session needs to be carefully designed so that when one muscle group is exhausted you can immediately move to another without a drop in tempo. The effort must also be sustained so that there's a contribution to cardio-vascular fitness. You can reach deep only if you are doing sustained work over a period. Our sessions last from 45-60 minutes.

Within the overall design, it's highly desirable that individual parts – e.g. work on the abdominals – are the responsibility of individual players. This gets them involved actively in team preparation, and opens up the chance of greater variety.

As suggested above, the whole session can be punctuated by a set of running exercises – e.g. 30...45...60...60...45...30 seconds of line running. You will need an initial stretching/warm-up period of about five minutes, and can space the running out in accordance with your projected length of session – e.g. for an hour session, ten minutes between runs. These ten minutes you then fill with activities. If you think of each activity lasting, 30, 45 or 60 seconds according to its nature, you can then work at the number of activities you will need – a minimum of about fifty. Using a time base – how many star-jumps can you do in 30 seconds? – can be alternated with a numerical base – get your partner on your shoulders and do three sets of ten half-squats – or a distance base – carry your partner in a fireman's lift the length of the gym. You try to group your most strenuous activities in the middle of the session, and avoid powerful resistance at the start. You may start and end with individual exercises, and use the rest for resistance work in pairs, or groups. So far as possible each section can deal with a single kind of activity – e.g. wrestling, scrum position, carrying, and so on. You may incorporate resistance + running exercises: e.g. push your partner over the centre line, run to touch the wall, push your partner...and so on; midway between line-running.

An approach to resistance work has been outlined under Basic Preparation. Individual and group exercises can be constructed in essentially the same way, and are equally easy to devise.

PHYSICAL PREPARATION : WEIGHT TRAINING

The provision of weight-training facilities at the club should be a high priority, partly because they are an added attraction, mainly because it's fast becoming an essential part of preparation. Every player can benefit from increased strength, for strength means speed as well as power.

Conditioning for general speed and strength

1. bench press	1 set of 10 start about 135
	aim for 180 lb
2. sit ups	15 × 10 lb 10 × 15 lb 8 × 20 lb
3. step ups	3 sets of 20 × 95 lb
4. arm curls	3 sets of 10 × 65 lb
5. leg extensions	3 sets of 12 × 75 lb (each leg)
6. leg raises	3 sets of 10 ×25 lb
7. press behind neck	3 sets of 10 × 65 lb
8. rowing	3 sets of 10 × 65 lb
9. pull-ups	3 sets × maximum

The weights mentioned are merely guides to an acceptable level. Start with the poundage you can handle, and build up. Aim to work out at least twice a week. For three people working together, the session above will last 45 – 60 minutes. For at least the first session have an instructor to check on correct movements and safety measures. For variety, you can occasionally try a basic setting of 60 seconds for the first set, 30 seconds for the second, 15 for the third, and go for maximum repetitions in that time.

Power schedule

Once the general conditioning has been done, the player – specifically, the front five – can go on to a power schedule aimed at the major muscle groups, and designed to increase muscle bulk and power. This involves reducing the range of exercises, limiting the number of repetitions in a set, increasing the number of sets, and increasing the weight being moved. Typically, he will be working on only three or four exercises, doing five repetitions, and five sets. The aim is to concentrate all the available energy on improving the performance of the major muscle groups.

Over the first three sets, the player builds to his maximum and maintains it over the last two sets. When over three workouts he has achieved this maximum he adds 10 to 20 pounds, and continues. A basic workout –

Squats – to parallel position				
set 1	set 2	set 3	set 4	set 5
230	270	310	310	310

Bench press				
200	220	240	240	240

Good mornings				
200	240	280	280	280

One specific power exercise that has shown outstanding benefits is aimed at improving line-out jumping. The player in question used a diver's belt loaded with 30 lb, and in each workout aimed at two sets to exhaustion jumping to touch a basketball backboard. This led to an extraordinary 44% improvement in his standing jump, and a marked improvement in his match performance.

All weight training needs commitment by the player, and must be in great part self-motivated. Forming groups to work together is an external help, and the coach's appreciation of the effort a further inducement. Once the player has begun to improve – and this is usually both sooner and more dramatic than expected – the need for external motivation declines.

It would be difficult to overestimate the need for top-class fitness: it can transform individual and team performance. It's the basic difference between success and failure. It's the basic difference – as the scoring pattern of their matches confirms – between the All-Blacks and their opponents. A Loughborough lad who went out to New Zealand and played top rugby there says 'We didn't know what fitness is' – and we certainly worked harder on fitness than 90% of teams. What we need is cost-effective ways of attaining it – methods that work fast, and don't restrict the time available for becoming a more accomplished player, a more accomplished team.

This comes down partly to quality of work: only the player can really tell how near to the limit he operates in training, and it's important that he becomes accustomed to operating near that limit. Partly, it comes down to quantity of work – measured in extended intensity of effort, rather than simply number of repetitions.

Here's a form of conditioning that certainly gives this extended intensity of effort:

1. Group your exercises as for a circuit:

	eg1	2	3 and so on . . .
legs	star jumps	touch-toe	rebound jumps
abdominals	sit-ups	jumps	sit-ups, feet off
		knee-bent sit-ups	the deck
upper body	press-ups	press-ups,	press-up, clap
general	fall-down,	hands wide	hands
	stand up	burpees	sit-down, get up

2. Do each exercise 8 times; repeat 6 times; repeat 4 times. (So that you perform each exercise a total of 18 times). Build up to 12,10,8. (So that you repeat each exercise 30 times.)
3. Start with 5 such groups; extend to 6 or 7.
4. Within each group aim to establish a known order of exercises and eliminate pauses. Seek full commitment.
5. After each exercise group do sets of 22m sprints.
Group A . . . 8 sprints. Group B . . . 10 sprints. Group C . . . 12 sprints. Group D . . . 10 sprints. Group E . . . 8 sprints. (So that you perform a total of 48 sprints). You then aim to do 10,12,14,12,10, and so on.
6. Start each sprint with the players paired with another player of the same position: it's a selection exercise.
7. Start with all players lying on their backs, in the goal-area, with their heads to the try-line. At the signal, they race to the 22, and drop into the same position, heads to the line, feet pointing towards the half-way line.
8. Aim to reduce pauses, insist on full 22m sprints. By way of a change, move from 22m sprints to 40/45m sprints between goal-line and 10m line, or do a pyramid 8 to 22m line; 6 to 10m line; 4 to half-way; 6 to 10m line; 8 to 22m line.

You can adapt this basic form to contain a wide variety of different types of exercise. Provided you maintain quality, you can cheerfully double what you first thought of – but it's best to work up, with repeated praise for the workers.

Index

287